The Great Transformation of China

China's Economic Transformation, Innovation and Development

Series Editor
Fulin Chi
China Institute for Reform and Development
Haikou, Hainan, China

China is facing unprecedented challenges in its continued modernization process. This series brings together government insiders, academics, and policymakers in articulating specific social and political issues that China is trying to resolve, offering scholars around the world insights into what China's leadership see as the biggest challenges facing the nation and how best to resolve them. The series publishes monographs and edited volumes with contributions on a global basis dedicated to ground-breaking research on the Chinese modernization process.

More information about this series at
http://www.palgrave.com/gp/series/15346

Xiaowu Song · Shiguo Wu ·
Xin Xu

The Great Change in the Regional Economy of China under the New Normal

ZHEJIANG UNIVERSITY PRESS
浙江大学出版社

palgrave
macmillan

Xiaowu Song
State Council of the People's Republic of China
Beijing, China

Shiguo Wu
State Council of the People's Republic of China
Beijing, China

Xin Xu
State Council of the People's Republic of China
Beijing, China

ISSN 2509-6001 ISSN 2509-601X (electronic)
The Great Transformation of China
ISBN 978-981-32-9474-5 ISBN 978-981-32-9475-2 (eBook)
https://doi.org/10.1007/978-981-32-9475-2

The print edition is not for sale in Mainland of China. Customers from Mainland of China please order the print book from: Zhejiang University Press.

This Palgrave Macmillan imprint is published by the registered company Springer Nature Singapore Pte Ltd.
The registered company address is: 152 Beach Road, #21-01/04 Gateway East, Singapore 189721, Singapore

Series Editor's Foreword

2020: Historical Choices for Economic Transformation and Upgrading

A country of more than 1.3 billion people is in a "never-before situation as in the past millennium". Reform, transformation and innovation are the main melody and the main note of this era. In a new era of highly integrated growth, transformation and reform, the "great transformation" is the key to China's destiny. It is not only necessary to fully clean up the "toxic assets" left over from the traditional systems, but also imperative to accelerate the formation of a new development model which releases new driving forces for development.

China's "great transformation" in the 13th Five-Year Plan is historically decisive. Focusing on economic transformation, both social transformation and government transformation are in a crucial period of transition with difficulties and obstacles to overcome. The general judgment is that 2020 will be a threshold: it represents the hope of defusing short-term growth pressure, the key to transforming the economic development pattern, the critical juncture of achieving a moderately prosperous society in all respects and joining the ranks of high-income countries. If we make good plans and grasp the "medium term" of 2020, we will be able to lay a solid foundation for equitable and sustainable growth in the medium and long term. If we miss this important historical opportunity period, we will lose the initiative in "great transformation" and bring about many systemic economic risks.

The key to achieving a substantial breakthrough in economic transformation and upgrading during the 13th Five-Year Plan is to grasp and handle the "four threes". First, we must grasp three major trends: the trend of industrial transformation and upgrading from "Made in China" to "Made by China"; the trend of urbanization transformation and upgrading from scale urbanization to population urbanization; the trend of consumption structure from material consumption to service consumption. Secondly, we have to deal with three major challenges: First, under economic downward pressure, structural adjustment needs to be enhanced to achieve major breakthroughs in structural reforms; second, in response to a new round of global sci-tech revolution, we have to accelerate the improvement of innovation capabilities and achieve "curve overtaking"; the third challenge lies in "real changes" and "practical changes" in reforms. At present, the transition relies more on comprehensive breakthrough of reforms and its dependence on reforms is stronger. Without reforms in the institutional structure, the transformation will be difficult, and growth will also face tremendous pressure. Third, we should achieve three major goals: in the industry, accelerate the transition from manufacturing to service industry, forming a service-dominated industrial structure; in terms of growth momentum, a new economic growth pattern dominated by consumption should be in place, with consumption guiding investment and domestic needs being the main driving force of economy; the third is to open up a new pattern of service trade, and to achieve a multiplication of service trade. Lastly, we need to handle three major relationships: first is the short-term and medium/long-term relationship. Do a good job in the mid-2020 development by basing on the medium-term, resolving short-term problems and focusing on long-term issues; second is the relationship between speed and structure. While maintaining a growth rate of around 7%, we need to speed up structural adjustment; third is the relationship between policies and systems. Under economic downward pressure, the key lies in forming policy advantages in the institutional innovation.

The reform and opening up in the past 4 decades has left us with a lot of valuable wealth. The most important one is: the more complex the situation, the more volatile environmental changes, the more we need to maintain determination to reform and uphold unswervingly the direction of transformation. This requires great planning of the "big transformation" and major breakthroughs of reforms in the industrial structure, urban and rural structure, regional structure, ownership structure, opening up structure and administrative power structure. It is necessary to formulate forward-looking planning and make first moves for green and sustainable development as well as the "Internet Plus" trends.

Based on the judgments of the "13th Five-Year Plan" transformation and reforms, China Institute for Reform and Development and Zhejiang University Press jointly planned and published this series of "Great Power and Major Transformation—China's Economic Transformation and Innovative Development Series". The books focus on readability while providing strategic, forward-looking and academic views. We hope that this series will enlighten readers concerned about China's transformation and reforms and play a positive role in promoting the 13th Five-Year Plan transformation and reforms.

The authors of this series are mostly well-known experts and scholars in their fields. They spared their time from tight schedules and participated in the writing of the series. As the director of the Compilation Committee of this series, I would like to express my heartfelt thanks to the consultants, members of the Compilation Committee, the authors, leaders and editors at the publishing house who have made great efforts to publish this series.

This series spans many fields, with each book representing the author's own research conclusions and academic views. This series does not aim to pursue the consistency of views. We welcome readers to comment and make their suggestions!

Hainan, China
September 2015

Fulin Chi

Preface

Reviews and Prospects of China's Regional Development Strategies

Through the evolution of human history, many powers with vast territories and large populations have come into being. Every major country is faced with differences in natural environment, resource endowment, population density, economic development and ethnic distribution among different regions. How to balance development levels of different regions within a unified country, to improve regional layout and coordination, and to ensure that residents in different regions enjoy basic national treatment so as to increase the overall national cohesion constitutes an indispensable important strategy in the country governance. China faces much the same regional problems as other major countries. It is important to note that since the reform and opening up, compared with the highly centralized planned economic period, local governments have gained more autonomy in economic development. It can be said that the current regional problems are largely built on the relationship between the central government and local governments. When regional planning covers several local administrative divisions, regional policies highlight their regional characteristics more. In terms of implementing various regional planning, the central government plays a leading role, but more importantly, local governments need to materialize the planning. Therefore, when it comes to regional development strategies, the relationship between the central and local governments is inevitably involved.

China in the contemporary period is a large country with a civilization history of 5000 years, a population of 1.3 billion, 56 ethnic groups and an area of 9.6 million square kilometers. Since the establishment of unified prefectural and county systems in the Qin Dynasty (221 B.C. ~ 206 B.C.), the central and local governments have been contending over centralization and decentralization for more than 2000 years. In general, the period of centralization is longer than that of decentralization. The revolution of 1911 overthrew the decadent Qing Dynasty, and faced with warlordism, foreign wars and civil strife, the Republic of China failed to truly unify China, let alone tackle regional development issues.

New China founded in 1949 was faced with an extremely unbalanced regional development pattern. In 1948, more than 77% of the country's total industrial output was concentrated in the narrow strip along the east coast, which accounted for less than 12% of the country's land area, while the vast areas in the northwest and southwest, which accounted for 68% of the country's total, made up only 9% of the country's industrial output. This situation is the product of the colonial and semi-colonial economies. After the Opium War opened the closed door of the Qing Government in 1840, world powers mainly entered China from the sea. The southeast coastal areas established a modern foundation of foreign investment in industry and commerce earlier and stimulated a relatively independent or semi-dependent national industries and commerce. In order to change the distorted regional pattern formed in the colonial and semi-colonial period, the country generally implemented an inland-tilted regional development strategy from the founding of new China to the reform and opening up.

In the past 30 years after the founding of New China, the central government had insisted on implementing an inland-tilted regional development strategy. Although this was influenced by the Marxist–Leninist doctrine on balanced regional development, the more important reason is based on the severe assessment of the international situation at that time. Shortly after the founding of New China, the Korean War broke out, with a later succession of the Vietnam War, the self-defense war against India, and the Sino-Soviet Treasure Island incident. During this period, China also had to be alert to the Taiwan authorities' counterattacks against the mainland. In 1965, Minister of Foreign Affairs Marshal

Chen Yi cried loudly at a press conference: "If US imperialism is determined to impose a war of aggression on us, then we welcome them to come early and let the Indian reactionaries, US imperialists, and Japanese militarists also come with them". "I have waited for this day for so long, with my hair turning white!" Without knowing the international and domestic backgrounds of that era, it is difficult for people today to understand the regional strategic layout under the guidance of "preparing for war" thinking, to understand why so many companies "move into mountains and caves", which would increase production costs.

Most of the newly built industrial enterprises during the First and Second Five-Year Plan periods, especially the defense industrial enterprises, were laid out in the rear areas, as clearly stated in Chairman Mao Zedong's *On the Ten Major Relationships* published in 1956: "Coastal Industrial bases must be fully utilized, but in order to balance the layout of industrial development, we should vigorously develop the inland industries". Faced with severe international situations, the Central Committee of the Communist Party of China issued *Guidance on Strengthening Preparations for War* in 1965, and made strategic decisions to "gather strength, seize the time, and construct three-line areas". It should be noted that due to the planned economy at that time, the central government unified the redistribution of financial resources between regions, and the local governments only had limited management and control over the fiscal resources at their level. During this period, the national regional strategy was mainly realized through central infrastructure investment plans.

It can be seen that during the 30 years from the founding of New China to the end of the 1970s, the inland-tilted regional strategic layout had effectively promoted the industrialization and urbanization of inland areas, improving the pattern of extremely uneven regional development pattern left over from the history. Until now, the development of inland areas still depends on this foundation to a certain extent. However, due to the dominance of administrative forces, there were some non-negligible problems in the regional development of this period: First, the investment returns of some projects in the inland areas were not high. In 1978, the output value of fixed assets per hundred yuan in the "three-line" areas was only half compared with the coastal areas, with a profit rate of only 9.2%, while that figure in coastal areas was 23.4%. Second, since the national regional development strategy was tilted towards the inland, industrial bases in the coastal areas had not been fully utilized, thereby having a negative impact on the overall economic development. The third was due to the blind pursuit of complete local industrial systems regardless of resource constraints and actual feasibility—various projects of small, medium and large scales blossomed everywhere, resulting in an improper layout of some projects.

Shortly after the "Cultural Revolution", the Party Central Committee made a new analysis and assessment on the situations at home and abroad. In terms of international environment, Deng Xiaoping, the chief architect of the reform and opening up, believes that peace and development are the themes of the current era and world wars can be avoided. It is possible to strive for a peaceful environment for a long period of time. In terms of domestic situations, the Third Plenary Session of the Eleventh Central Committee of the Party decided to shift the focus of the whole party's work from class struggles to the socialist modernization drive centering on economic construction. Against this backdrop, China's regional development strategy has undergone a directional shift, from inland tilted to coastal areas tilted.

According to the strategic concepts of Comrade Deng Xiaoping's "Let some areas, some people get rich first, and gradually realize common prosperity" and "two overall situations", in 1979, the Party Central Committee and the State Council proposed a regional development strategy that actively supported the coastal areas to take the lead in development. The "Sixth Five-Year Plan" and "Seventh Five-Year Plan" clearly pointed out that it is necessary to actively utilize existing foundations in the coastal areas and give full play to their advantages to accelerate the development of eastern coastal areas as well as promote further development of the inland economy.

The regional strategy of this period was mainly implemented through central investment projects. "Issuing policies" had become an important regional development policy tool, mainly including: implementing special policies and flexible measures in Guangdong and Fujian provinces; establishing Special Economic Zones such as Shenzhen, Zhuhai, Shantou and Xiamen etc.; opening up 14 coastal cities including Dalian, Qinhuangdao and Tianjin etc.; opening up the Yangtze River Delta, the Pearl River Delta and the Xiamen-Zhangzhou-Quanzhou Delta as well as the Liaodong Peninsula, Shandong Peninsula, Shenyang and Nanjing as coastal economic open areas; setting up Pudong New Area and implementing preferential policies for special economic zones; and establishing 11 bonded areas such as Shanghai Waigaoqiao in the coastal areas.

These policies have greatly promoted the development of eastern coastal areas. By the mid-1990s, the southeastern coastal areas had not only absorbed nearly 90% of foreign capital, but also attracted talents from all over the country. At that time, the saying "Peacocks Fly Southeast" was popular in the western, northeastern and "three-line" areas, where skilled workers, technicians and managers trained for years moved to southeastern coastal areas. The development of coastal areas has led to a rapid increase in China's comprehensive strength, narrowing the gap with developed countries and making a great contribution to achieving the strategic goal of quadrupling GDP at the end of the twentieth century. At the same time, we should also face up to the fact that the development of the eastern region has outpaced central and western regions for 20 years, which led to increasingly uneven regional development. From 1978 to 2000, the average annual growth rate of regional GDP in the eastern, central, western, and northeastern regions was 12.01, 9.99, 9.74, and 8.58%, respectively, with the eastern region over 2 percentage points faster than others. A series of negative effects, such as the imbalance caused by widening regional gap in 20 years, have gradually become a major issue affecting the overall development of the national economy.

In response to emerging imbalances in regional development, the *Ninth Five-Year Plan for the National Economic and Social Development of the People's Republic of China National Economic and Outline of Perspective Objectives for 2010* first included coordinated regional development as one of the guiding principles for national economic and social development. It pointed out that it's necessary to "adhere to coordinate regional economic development and gradually narrow the gap among regions". Reviewing China's regional development strategies at this juncture, we can see clearly that after nearly 30 years of inland tilted and later 20 years of coastal areas tilted policy, the country has entered a stage of coordinated regional development.

From the end of the twentieth century to now, the Party Central Committee and the State Council have made quite remarkable efforts for coordinated regional development. Over the past decade, the central government has intensively introduced a series of major decisions to promote coordinated regional development: the Western Development Strategy was implemented in 1999, the revitalization strategy of old industrial bases in the northeast region etc. in 2003, and the strategy of promoting the rise of the central region in 2006. In 2010, China proposed the initiative of main functional areas, and enhanced support for special areas such as poverty-stricken areas, ethnic minority areas, old revolutionary bases, and resource-depleted areas at the same time. It also encouraged the eastern areas to take the lead in development. The implementation of these major policies has reversed the previous trend of widening the regional gap and contributed to an initial pattern of coordinated regional development.

In the decade of 2003–2013, the proportion of central and western regions in the national economy increased significantly. Remarkable achievements have been made in the Western Development Strategy, which focuses on infrastructure, ecological environment and special industries. The revitalization strategy of the old industrial bases in northeast China gives priority to supporting reforms of state-owned enterprises and other fields, and focuses on building bases for energy and raw materials, equipment manufacturing, national commodity grain production and national ecological barriers, thereby effectively promoting the transformation and development of old industrial bases. The rise of the central region supports the construction of comprehensive transportation hubs, and accelerates the construction of modern equipment manufacturing and high-tech industrial bases, energy and raw material bases, as well as grain production bases, thus invigorating the central plains. Under the guidance of coordinated regional development strategy, a large number of new regional economic growth poles, such as the middle reaches of the Yangtze River, Chengdu–Chongqing, central plains, middle-south part of Liaoning, Shandong Peninsula, West Coast of the Strait and Harbin–Changchun, have emerged, which are comparable to the Beijing-Tianjin-Hebei region, the Yangtze River Delta and the Pearl River Delta. At the same time, the eastern region as the most developed part in China has been constantly improving the quality and efficiency of economic development, adjusting industrial structures in line with the trend, and taking the lead in transforming the economic development mode. In addition, on the basis of differentiated policies of the four regional blocks, the state has also implemented special assistance policies for the difficult areas, and initially established a policy system to solve the specific difficult areas across administrative regions through typical areas and functional areas.

While commending progress in the regional coordination strategy since the twenty-first century, we must be clearly aware that there is still a long way to go before we truly achieve coordinated regional development. First, due to strong administrative divisions in sectoral regional policies, all regions hasten to make themselves "policy depressions" (places with preferential policies), resulting in prominent regional administrative barriers, which has hindered to some extent rational flows of production factors nationwide. Second, many places equate regional development with regional GDP or per capita GDP growth. They are keen to develop heavy chemical industry projects, which exacerbates overcapacity. Third, the gap in basic public service levels between regions has not been narrowed significantly, especially in terms of compulsory education, health care, and social security, etc. Fourth, differences in per capita GDP between regions remain not only prominent compared with major developed countries, but also with some developing countries. Fifth, compared with the provincial-level regions of 16 developed countries, China has witnessed a dumbbell-type distribution of GPR value, an indicator of a country's economy-population proportion, in extremely high and low regions, which accounts for large amount of labor flowing across provinces. In addition, it should be more clearly recognized that under the background of high-speed economic growth characterized by high investment, high consumption, high pollution and low labor costs, coordinated regional development is inevitably branded in such trend of times, which often evolved into interregional GDP competition. Therefore, coordinated regional development strategy also faces deep-seated problems in development model transformation.

By sorting out the evolutions of China's regional development strategies since 1949, especially after the reform and opening up, and the learning experience and lessons of coordinated development from foreign regions, we can adopt new ideas and new measures for coordinated regional development in the New Normal of Economy.

First, equalization of basic public services should be the main goal of coordinated regional development.

Decisions of the Central Committee of the Communist Party of China on Several Major Issues Concerning Comprehensively Deepening Reforms which was passed by the Third Plenary Session of the 18th CPC Central

Committee pointed out that it is necessary to give play to the decisive role of the market in resource allocation. Under the influence of market mechanisms, the resource elements will inevitably concentrate in areas with better development conditions and higher returns. It would be nearly impossible to complete the task of coordinated regional development if GDP or per capita GDP remains as the primary target for coordinated regional development. Due to differences in natural endowments and geographical locations, it is impossible to reach the same GDP or per capita GDP in different regions. For example, according to divisions of the main functional areas, it is difficult for areas prohibited from development to achieve an equivalent per capita GDP to those key development areas. In areas with relatively backward economic development, such as southern Xinjiang, Qinghai and Tibet, Qinba mountainous area, Wuling mountainous area, Yunnan-Guizhou-Guangxi desertification areas, southwestern ethnic poverty-stricken areas, western border poverty-stricken areas, and the "Three West" area, the per capita GDP is only equivalent to 1/3 or 1/4 of the national average at present. If per capita GDP is roughly the main indicator of coordinated regional development, then achieving this goal would be very difficult and quite distant. In the previous stage, China focused on its total GDP or per capita GDP indicator and due priority was not given to the equalization of public services, resulting in widening regional disparity after secondary distribution of household income. Moreover, the GDP competition between regions inevitably leads to the blind pursuit of heavy industrial projects in various areas, exacerbating overcapacity and ecological pollution.

Consideration should be given to the equalization of basic public services and the provision of basic public facilities as main indicators for measuring coordinated regional development. Regional development level can be considered as roughly coordinated when the livelihood indicators of education, medical care, social security, housing, etc. are roughly equal, the supply of water, gas, power and heating are generally balanced, and transportation facilities such as railway, highway, civil aviation as well as modern communication facilities are basically available. International experience also shows that governments' promotion of equalized basic public services and basic public facilities accessible to all is a common practice to narrow the household income gap between regions in the development process (see Chapter 5 of this book).

Second, establishing a unified market system should be the basic norm of coordinated regional development.

To promote coordinated regional development in the new era, we must integrate regional development with the overall national development, not only to solve problems in specific regions, but also to formulate regional development strategies based on holistic and long-term national goals. We should guard against excessive national-level regional planning, which may form various types of preferential policies regarding finance, taxation, land and foreign trade. This may as a result split the unified national socialist market economy system, leading to a privilege economy dominated by local governments and thereby adding to the difficulty of regional development coordination.

In accordance with the arrangement of the "Four-Pronged Comprehensive Strategy", regional coordination should pay more attention to the overall goal of comprehensively deepening reforms and building a moderately prosperous society, and strive to promote the formation of a unified national market and free flows of market factors, which would stimulate vitality, tap the full potential of various regions and promote a rational division of labor in various regions. Institutional mechanisms that hinder coordinated regional development should be removed to overcome various obstacles that restrict rational flows of production factors, especially the flow of labor. It is recommended to speed up the establishment of a unified national social security system for medical care, old-age support, unemployment, and correspondingly improve the level of overall planning, focusing on solving the problem of cross-regional transfer of basic social security projects and the continuation in different places; The eastern coastal areas, in particular, should strengthen social security services for migrant workers, enhance the responsibility of labor use places, and promote rational flows of labor elements across regions. In line with this, during the "Thirteenth Five-Year Plan" period, the reform of household registration system should be further strengthened, easing restrictions on population migration. On this basis, the establishment of citizens' right to freedom of migration should be promoted in an orderly manner. The right to freedom of migration for citizens in one country will greatly promote the equalization of public services, thereby further alleviating regional disparities and urban–rural disparities.

Third, reasonably defining the power and finances relationship between the central and local governments.

To list basic public services as the main indicator of coordinated regional development inevitably requires having a clear definition of the power and finances relationship between the central and local governments in basic public services. With regard to the current central and local financial relations, the division of responsibilities and powers across governments at all levels is unclear; there is an overlap of powers and responsibilities between the central and local governments, with overlarge responsibilities and over-small financial powers for local governments. In particular, although local governments are responsible for the provision of basic public services such as education, health, social security, public safety, and environmental protection, they do not have the corresponding financial powers. This has led to the phenomenon that economically developed regions have the financial resources to further improve basic public services in the region, while underdeveloped regions, despite receiving central transfer payments, lag far behind from keeping pace with the level of financial investment in basic public services of developed regions. In terms of the whole country, many basic public service projects, including compulsory education, public health and basic social security, still have the reverse transfer problem of expanding the previous gap between regions after redistribution.

The *Decisions of the Central Committee of the Communist Party of China on Several Major Issues Concerning Comprehensively Deepening Reforms* made at the Third Plenary Session of the 18th CPC Central Committee proposed that, "In terms of some social security, construction and maintenance of major cross-regional projects, we should get the relationship of powers and responsibilities right between the central and local governments, for they are common powers and responsibilities; Since regional public services function as local powers and responsibilities, the central and local governments shall share expenditure responsibilities according to the division of powers." "For cross-region public services with a huge impact on other regions, the central government can assume part of the expenditure responsibility for local affairs through transfer payments." In accordance with the spirits of decisions made at the Third Plenary Session of the 18th CPC Central Committee, and given that the equalization of basic public services is for the whole country, it is recommended that the central government assume more responsibility for expenditures in areas of basic public services such as education, health care and social security. First, the scope of basic public services should be clearly defined and adjusted accordingly with socio-economic development. Second, we need to clarify the standards for the equalization of basic public services throughout the country, with the central government balancing the input level of basic public services among regions and establishing a scientific evaluation system, so as to turn the tide of reverse transfer in which basic public service inputs enlarge the first distribution gap among regions in the "Thirteen-Five-year" period. After 5 to10 years of efforts, we should strive to initially achieve the equalization goal of major projects in basic public services nationwide. Third, the powers and responsibilities of providing basic public services should be clearly delineated at all levels of governments, so as to ensure clear and reasonable responsibilities. Fourth, we need to improve the fiscal and taxation system, rationally adjust the allocation of intergovernmental financial power and expand local sources of taxation. The financial transfer payment system should be improved in accordance with requirements of the equalization of basic public services. Fifth, developed regions are encouraged to absorb the population of underdeveloped regions and promote their integration into local communities, which would help them become stable migrants; the Central and local governments should base their development policies and goals of basic public services on the resident population rather than the household registration population; on policies such as fiscal transfers, the central government should provide appropriate incentives for areas that actively absorb migrants.

Fourth, reforming relevant taxation systems that hinder coordinated regional development.

Relevant data show that since 1994, compared with the per capita GDP gap, China's inter-provincial gap in per capita tax revenue has shown a significant trend of expansion. This indicates that the inter-provincial gap in per capita tax revenue is not entirely determined by differences in economic development. From the perspective of the taxation system, there are two major problems that affect coordinated regional development, which requires deepening reforms of relevant taxation systems.

The first is the unreasonable regional taxation caused by the deviation of tax land from tax sources. Specifically, tax revenues generated by one local government are not collected and enjoyed by this local government, but by another local government. For example, the business and income tax of the West-to-East Gas Pipeline Project and the value-added tax of power generation are levied by the local government which sells gas and electricity; the income tax formed by the national profits of the central enterprise group, especially the financial type of central enterprises, is collected by the headquarters location; the withholding system of personal income tax and the local sharing system allows the taxation of residents who receive income from different places to be collected by local governments that do not provide public services for the residents. According to statistics, at present, more than 90% of the total tax revenue has the problem of "deviation of tax lands from tax sources" in varying degrees. The problems arising from the design of this tax system have a great negative impact on the coordinated development of the region.

Since the headquarters of Central Enterprises are mostly located in developed regions, especially in large cities and megacities, the huge tax revenue generated by tax sources in backward areas, raw material origins and production bases of central enterprises has been collected by developed regions and central cities, widening the gap among regions. This itself also poses damage to the equal rights of different regions. Problems arising from the deviation of tax lands from tax sources were raised more than 10 years ago, but have not yet been reasonably resolved because of difficulties in breaking down vested interests. It is suggested that relevant departments should seriously study these problems and reform this tax system in the "Thirteenth Five-Year Plan" period, so that most tax sources with relatively backward economies can share local tax sources in an equitable way, which shall have great significance for coordinated regional development.

The second is the "resource curse dilemma" caused by the long-term lagging reform of resource taxes. With the development of science and technology, human's ability to develop resources has been remarkably enhanced. Many resource-producing countries in the world, such as oil-exporting countries, gain their wealth by resources. However, the vast majority of China's resource-rich regions are underdeveloped, with many resource-based cities and regions in tough situations due to exhausted resources or imminent exhaustion. This phenomenon is named by scholars in resource exhaustion as "the resource curse dilemma." This dilemma in China has a distinct regional feature. For a long time, the central and western regions mainly provide primary products such as raw materials, agricultural products, as well as upstream products such as minerals, forests, and electric power, while the eastern region mainly provides high value-added downstream products. Due to the inertia of administrative allocation of resources in the planned economy and imbalances between resource prices and the pricing mechanism of finished products, upstream products of some resource-producing areas in the central and western regions are imported into the east at low prices, while downstream products in the eastern coastal areas flow into the central, western and northeastern regions at high prices. Relatively low resource taxes and lack of reasonable sharing mechanism have led to a reverse operation of tax burdens between regions. Resource advantages of the central and western regions fail to be translated into local economic and financial advantages, which greatly restrict their economic development. From this perspective, it is safe to say that resource-producing areas in the central and western regions have contributed resource taxes to the prosperity of the eastern coastal areas.

In recent years, progress has been made in the reform of resource taxes. For example, Xinjiang has witnessed an increase of tens of billions of tax revenues every year after the reform of resource taxes. Having changed resource taxes for petroleum and coal from quantitative calculation to ad valorem, this year the State Council decided to apply this approach to rare earth, tungsten and molybdenum, determining reasonable tax rates in the principle of lessening corporate taxes. Some regions are also planning to include water resources in the scope of resource tax reform. Facts have proved that expanding the scope of resource taxation by selectively including some natural resources into the taxation scope and increasing the tax rates can slow down the reverse operation of prices and taxes in the eastern, central and western regions and raise the prices of resource-based products, thereby transferring tax burdens to the processing and use of resources. This will help the central and western regions to turn their resource advantages into economic and financial advantages. Of course, the reform of resource taxes will also guide enterprises to use natural resources in a rational and economical manner.

Fifth, implementing regional development strategies that integrate regions with axis belts.

The regional economic policies based on the "four major regions" (Western, Northeastern, Eastern and Central China) are proposed mainly on geographical locations and administrative divisions. It is worth noting that the four major regions have separated economic ties between each other to a certain extent, forming a comparison of various regions in terms of policies and resulting in a mismatch between development appeals and supporting conditions. At the same time, relevant data for the past decade have shown that for the western and northeastern regions with vast territories and differences in natural conditions, historical foundations and economic development, the division of four major regions is still large on the spatial scale, covering up development issues of some provinces. Due to expanding differences within various regions, targeted approaches of regional policies have been weakened.

In the new era, we must give full play to important axis belts that run from east to west and connect the north to the south, and enhance the leading and promoting role of axis belts in regional development coordination. We can consider great rivers like the Yangtze River, the Pearl River, the Yellow River and important transportation routes such as Beijing–Guangzhou, Beijing–Harbin, Beijing–Shanghai and Lanzhou–Lianyungang, promoting the concentration and diffusion of production factors and optimizing population, industries and urban layouts in regions, thereby gradually forming an economic development axis. Meanwhile, we should give full play to the core role of primary axis belts, driving surrounding areas to form secondary and composite development belts, such as fully utilizing the role of the Yangtze River Economic Belt to form extended secondary belts like the Hanjiang Economic Belt, the Xiangjiang Economic Belt, and the Ganjiang River Economic Belt, which would be a main axis belt in the development of eastern, central and western regions. Relying on the extension of first-class Beijing-Guangzhou belt to the east and west, a main composite development belt running from north to south will be in place, about 300 km wide and 2000 km long.

While developing axis belts, we need to further specify the four major regions and gradually cultivate eight economic regions including the northeast, southwest, northwest, Beijing-Tianjin-Hebei (including Shandong), Pan-Yangtze River Delta, Pan-Pearl River Delta, the middle reaches of the Yangtze River, and west coast of the Taiwan Straits by building on existing city clusters and economic zones. We should combine axis belts and regions with a focus on both coordination of axis belts on balanced regional development and internal concentration of production factors within regions, thereby forming a new pattern of grid and multi-support regional development.

Sixth, implementing regional development strategies featuring organic integration between international and domestic regions.

Since the 1990s, economic globalization and regional economic grouping have become two major trends in world economic development. According to incomplete statistics, about 80% of the countries in the world currently participate in regional cooperation organizations at different levels. Major regional groups and organizations that have been established or is being established in the world include the European Union, North American Free Trade Area (NAFTA), Asia-Pacific Economic Cooperation (APEC), Association of Southeast Asian Nations (ASEAN), the China-ASEAN Free Trade Area, Commonwealth of Independent States (CIS), the Caribbean Community, the Andean Group, and so on. Regional economic integration has become an important strategy and means for many countries to cope with globalization and integrate into the world economy. At present, China has participated in substantive international cooperation and sub-regional cooperation, including: APEC, Shanghai Cooperation Organization, China-ASEAN Free Trade Area, China-Switzerland Free Trade Agreement, Bangkok Agreement, Lancang-Mekong International Sub-Regional Cooperation, China and Central Asia sub-regional cooperation, and Tumen River sub-regional cooperation. However, on the whole, the depth and breadth of China's participation in international regional cooperation and sub-regional cooperation are insufficient. It is high time we should strengthen international regional cooperation and sub-regional cooperation further and promote the development of various regions in the country by the "Belt and Road" Initiative. Promoting reforms, cooperation and development through opening up to the outside world marks a new trend for China's regional development in the future. Of course, we must see that there are great differences between international cooperation and domestic regional development coordination. Taking the "Belt and Road" as an example, we should not only handle economic cooperation between the countries to achieve win-win and all-win results, but also consider factors such as geopolitics, religions, internal political stability and terrorism in the cooperative countries. Territorial disputes are also difficult to evade. At the same time, it should be clear that cautious and active implementation of the "Belt and Road Initiative" corresponds to current international and domestic situations. If we can handle relevant issues properly, we can benefit and avoid disadvantages, thereby creating a new way for regional development featuring organic integration between international and domestic regions.

It is highly recommended to support the southwestern region through the Pearl River-Xijiang Economic Belt and make full use of the China-ASEAN platform under the Belt and Road Initiative, so as to deepen cooperation between the Pearl River Delta and the Beibu Gulf Region. Guangdong and Guangxi can be built into core zones of China's cooperation towards Southeast Asia, while Yunnan and Sichuan can develop into "bridgeheads" for an opening to South Asia. We support the northwestern region to strengthen cooperation with Central Asian countries, build core areas of Xinjiang's Silk Road, and closely integrate its development with opening to the west. The northeastern region is encouraged to enhance cooperation with Russia, Mongolia, Japan, South Korea and the DPRK to build Heilongjiang, Jilin, Liaoning and Inner Mongolia into important hubs opening up to Northeast Asia, thereby promoting domestic regional cooperation and development via international regional cooperation.

It is foreseeable that with equalization of basic public services between regions as the main goal and the construction of a unified socialist market economy as the basic norm, and by reasonably defining the power and finances relationship between the central and local governments, and deepening reforms of relevant taxation systems that hinder coordinated regional development, we would be able to witness integration between major regions and axial belts, between international and domestic regions and form three new support belts of the Belt and Road Initiative, the Yangtze River Economic Belt and coordinated development of Beijing-Tianjin-Hebei on the basis of respective advantages in the four major regions. This will remarkably enrich China's regional development strategies and form a new pattern of China's regional prosperity.

Beijing, China

Xiaowu Song
Shiguo Wu
Xin Xu

Contents

List of Figures

List of Tables

Chapter 5

CHAPTER 1

An Overview of China's Regional Development and Overall Pattern

China is a large country with a vast territory. Regional policies constitute an important part of the country's macro-regulation policies. The regional development strategies after the founding of New China can be divided into three stages. After the founding of the PRC and before the reform and opening up, the state generally implemented a regional development strategy tilted toward the inland. From the reform and opening up to the end of the twentieth century, China's regional development strategy was featured by prioritized development of coastal areas. In the following decade, the central government issued a series of major decisions to promote coordinated development among regions: Western Development Strategy implemented in 1999, the revitalization strategy of old industrial bases in the northeast region in 2003, and the strategy of promoting the rise of the central region in 2006. In 2010, China proposed to promote the initiative of main functional areas and enhance support for special areas such as poverty-stricken areas, ethnic minority areas, old revolutionary bases, and resource-depleted areas at the same time. It also encourages the eastern areas to take the lead in development. The implementation of these major policies has contributed to an initial pattern of coordinated regional development.

X. Song et al., *The Great Change in the Regional Economy of China under the New Normal*, The Great Transformation of China,
https://doi.org/10.1007/978-981-32-9475-2_1

1 The Evolution of China's Regional Development Strategies Since the Founding of New China

1.1 Development Stage Before the Reform and Opening Up

After the founding of the PRC and before the reform and opening up, China generally implemented a regional development strategy tilted to the inland areas. This period can be subdivided into two parts, namely the First and Second Five-Year Plan period and "the three-line construction" period. It should be noted that due to the planned economy at that time, the central government was mainly in charge of the redistribution of financial resources between regions, with limited power of management and control over fiscal resources in local governments. During this period, the national regional strategy was mainly realized via central infrastructure investment plans.

During the "First Five-Year Plan" period, the state initiated economic construction with "156" key projects aided by the Soviet Union as the core, and more than 900 large and medium-sized projects above the designated size as a focus, involving 17 provinces, autonomous regions and municipalities in the inland regions (see Table 1). The *First Five-Year Plan for the Development of the National Economy of the People's Republic of China* clearly points out that "Properly distribute industrial productivity in all regions of the country, so that industries are close to raw materials, fuel-producing areas and consumption areas, and suitable for consolidating national defense to gradually improve the economic level of backward areas". Under the guidance of this idea, from 1953 to 1959, a total of 921 large and medium-sized construction projects with a quota above (with an investment of more than 10 million yuan) were arranged, including the "156" key projects aided by the Soviet Union (150 actual constructions). Among these projects there were 20 metallurgical industrial enterprises, 7 chemical industrial enterprises, 24 mechanical industrial enterprises, 52 energy industrial enterprises, 3 light industrial enterprises and pharmaceutical processing enterprises, 44 military industrial enterprises, with four-fifth located in the central, western and northeastern regions, and 68% of 921 projects in the inland.[1]

[1] Liu Junlin: "On Mao Zedong's Exploration of China's Industrialization Road", *Journal of the Graduates of Sun Yat-Sen University* (*Social Sciences*), No. 3, 2000.

Table 1 Provinces involved with "156" key construction projects during the "First Five-Year Plan" period

Province/Region/Municipality	*Municipal layout of "156" key construction projects*
Heilongjiang Province	Harbin City, Hegang City, Jixi City, Shuangyashan City, Qiqihar City, Jiamusi City
Jilin Province	Changchun City, Jilin City, Liaoyuan City
Liaoning Province	Shenyang City, Dalian City, Anshan City, Fushun City, Benxi City, Fuxin City, Huludao City
Shaanxi Province	Xi'an City, Baoji City, Tongchuan City
Gansu Province	Lanzhou City, Baiyin City
Hebei Province	Shijiazhuang City, Chengde City
Yunnan Province	Gejiu City
Inner Mongolia Autonomous Region	Baotou City
Sichuan Province	Chengdu City
Beijing Municipality	Beijing Municipality
Henan Province	Zhengzhou City, Luoyang City, Jiaozuo City, Pingdingshan City
Hubei Province	Wuhan City
Hunan Province	Zhuzhou City, Xiangtan City
Shanxi Province	Taiyuan City, Datong City, Houma City
Anhui Province	Huainan City
Chongqing Municipality	Chongqing Municipality
Xinjiang Uygur Autonomous Region	Urumqi City
Jiangxi Province	Nanchang City, Ganzhou City

Source Dong Zhikai, Wu Jiang: *The Cornerstone of New China's Industries: Research on "156" Construction Projects*, Guangdong Economic Publishing House, 2004

Among the total investment in infrastructure construction nationwide, the coastal and inland regions accounted for 36.9 and 46.8%, respectively.[2] During the "Second Five-Year Plan" period, the focus of state investment remained in the inland areas of the central and western regions. After two Five-Year Plans, the economic landscape of the central and western inland parts has been remarkably changed, with major changes in the national productivity distribution as well.

[2]Zheng Zhiguo: "The Historical Evolution and Institutional Changes of China's Regional Economic Policies", Master's Thesis of Chongqing Technology and Business University, 2006.

[Column 1-1]
"156" major projects during the "First Five-Year Plan"
Notes: Among the "156" key projects issued in the first Five-Year Plan of 1955, the Gannan Power Station was changed to Chengdu Power Station and Department of Aviation, while the Shaanxi 422 Factory was divided into two projects. Therefore, indeed there were 154 projects, among which No. 2 automobile manufacturing plant and No. 2 tractor factory failed due to unsettled sites, and Shanxi Pan'an No. 1 shaft, Shanxi Datong Baituyao shaft were not built due to geological problems. Actually, only 150 projects have been officially constructed.

1. Coal (25 projects): Fuxin Thermal Power Station, Hegang Dongshan No. 1 shaft, Hegang Xing'antai No. 10 shaft, Liaoyuan Central shaft, Fuxin Safety Shaft,
Fuxin Xinqiu No. 1 Shaft,
Fuxin Haizhou Opencast Mine,
Xing'antai Coal Washing Plant,
Chengzihe Coal Washing Plant,
Chengzihe No. 9 Vertical Shaft,
Shanxi Lu'an Coal Washing Plant,
Jiaozuo Zhongma Village Vertical Shaft,
Xing'antai No. 2 Vertical Shaft,
Datong E'maokou Vertical Shaft,
Huainan Xiejiaji Central Coal Washing Plant,
Xinghua Wangou Vertical Shaft,
Fengfeng Central Coal Washing Plant,
Fushun West Opencast Mine,
Fushun Longfeng Mine,
Fushun Laohutai Mine,
Fushun Shengli Mine,
Shuangyashan Coal Washing Plant,
Tongchuan Wangshiao Shaft,
Fengfeng Tongshun No. 3 Shaft,
Pingdingshan No. 2 Shaft,
Fushun East Opencast Mine.

2. Oil (2 projects): Lanzhou Refinery, Fushun No. 2 Oil Plant.

3. Power (25 projects):
Fuxin Thermal Power Station,
Fushun Power Station,
Chongqing Power Station,

Fengman Hydropower Station,
Dalian Thermal Power Station,
Taiyuan No. 1 Thermal Power Station,
Xi'an Thermal Power Station,
Zhengzhou No. 2 Thermal Power Station,
Fulaerji Thermal Power Station,
Urumqi Thermal Power Station,
Jilin Thermal Power Station,
Taiyuan No. 2 Thermal Power Station,
Shijiazhuang Thermal Power Station,
Huxian Thermal Power Station,
Lanzhou Thermal Power Station,
Qingshan Thermal Power Station,
Gejiu Power Station,
Baotou Sidao Shahe Thermal Power Station,
Baotou Ningjiahao Thermal Power Station,
Jiamusi paper mill Thermal Power Station,
Zhuzhou Thermal Power Station,
Chengdu Thermal Power Station,
Luoyang Thermal Power Station,
Sanmenxia Water Control Project,
Beijing Thermal Power Station.

4. Iron and steel (7 projects):
Anshan Iron and Steel Company,
Benxi Steel Company,
Fulaerite Steel Works,
Jilin Ferroalloy Company,
Wuhan Iron and Steel Company,
Baotou Iron and Steel Company,
Rehe Vanadium Iron Ore.

5. Nonferrous metals (13 projects):
Fushun Aluminum Factory,
Harbin Aluminum Factory,
Jilin Cable Factory,
Zhuzhou Cemented Carbide Factory,
Yangjiazhangzi Molybdenum Mine,
Yunnan Tin Industry Corporation,
Jiangxi Dajishan Tungsten Mine,
Jiangxi Xihuashan Tungsten Mine,
Jiangxi Guimeishan Tungsten Mine,

Baiyin Nonferrous Metals Corporation,
Luoyang Nonferrous Metals Processing Factory,
Dongchuan Mining Bureau,
Huize Lead-Zinc Mine.

6. Chemical industry (7 projects):
Jilin Dyestuff Factory,
Jilin Ammonia Fertilizer Plant,
Jilin Calcium Carbide Plant,
Taiyuan Chemical Plant,
Lanzhou Synthetic Rubber Factory,
Taiyuan Nitrogen Fertilizer Plant,
Lanzhou Nitrogen Fertilizer Plant.

7. Machinery (24 projects):
Harbin Boiler Factory,
Changchun No. 1 Automobile Factory,
Shenyang No. 1 Machine Tool Plant,
Harbin Measuring and Cutting Tool Factory,
Shenyang Pneumatic Tools Factory,
Shenyang Cable Factory,
Harbin Instrument Factory,
Harbin Steam Turbine Works,
Shenyang No. 2 Machine Tool Plant,
Wuhan Heavy Machine Tool Plant,
Luoyang Tractor Factory,
Luoyang Ball Bearing Factory,
Lanzhou Petroleum Machinery Factory,
Xi'an High Voltage Electric Porcelain Factory,
Xi'an Switching Rectifier Factory,
Xi'an Insulation Material Factory,
Xi'an Power Capacitor Factory,
Luoyang Mining Machinery Factory,
Harbin Electric Machinery Factory steam turbine generator workshop,
Fulaer Heavy Machinery Plant,
Harbin Carbon Brush Factory,
Harbin Ball Bearing Factory,
Xiangtan Marine Motor Factory,
Lanzhou Refinery Chemical Machinery Factory.

8. Light industry (1 project): Jiamusi Paper Mill.

9. Pharmacy (2 projects):
North China Pharmaceutical Factory,
Taiyuan Pharmaceutical Factory.

10. Military (44 projects) (omitted).

Source Dong Zhikai, Wu Jiang: *The Cornerstone of New China's Industries: Research on "156" Construction Projects*, Guangdong Economic Publishing House, 2004, pp. 336–345.

The "three-line construction" started in September 1964 and large-scale construction basically ended in 1980, with a focus on Yunnan, Guizhou and Sichuan Provinces in the southwestern region, Shaanxi, Gansu, Ningxia and Qinghai in the northwestern region, as well as the "three western areas" (western Hunan, Hubei and Henan Province). The "three-line region" defined by the state at that time included provinces of Sichuan, Guizhou, Yunnan, Shaanxi, Gansu, Qinghai, Ningxia, and parts of Henan, Hubei, Hunan, Shanxi, Guangxi, Guangdong, namely all or part of 13 provinces or autonomous regions in total (see Table 2). During the Third Five-Year Plan period, inland infrastructure investment accounted for 64.7% of the country's total, of which "three-line region" accounted for 52.7%.[3] From 1964 to 1980, the "three-line construction" accumulated investment of 205.2 billion yuan, with more than 70% of industrial investment. Over 1100 large and medium-sized industrial and mining enterprises, scientific research institutes and colleges and universities have been built, with a gathering of more than 500,000 well-trained scientific and technological talents and hundreds of thousands of most advanced technical equipment at that time. This is the period in which the state offers the strongest development assistance to the central and western regions, enabling rapid economic development in those regions. An industrial system based on transportation, electronics, chemicals, steel and other industries with a focus on national defense industry has been basically established.[4]

[3]Lu Dadao et al.: *Theory and Practice of Regional Development in China*, Science Press, 2003, p. 113.

[4]Zheng Zhiguo: *The Historical Evolution and Institutional Changes of China's Regional Economic Policies*, Master's Dissertation of Chongqing Technology and Business University, 2006.

Table 2 Major cities involved in the "three-line" key construction projects

Province/Region/Municipality	*Industrial cities distributed with key construction projects*
Sichuan Province	Chengdu City, Panzhihua City, Deyang City, Zigong City, Leshan City, Mianyang City, Luzhou City, Guangyuan City
Guizhou Province	Guiyang City, Liupanshui City, Zunyi City, Anshun City
Yunnan Province	Kunming City, Qujing City
Shaanxi Province	Xi'an City, Baoji City, Hanzhong City, Tongchuan City
Gansu Province	Jinchang City, Lanzhou City, Tianshui City
Qinghai Province	Xining City
Ningxia Hui Autonomous Region	Yinchuan City
Henan Province	Luoyang City, Pingdingshan City, Nanyang City
Hubei Province	Xiangyang City, Yichang City, Shiyan City
Shanxi Province	Taiyuan City, Houma City
Chongqing Municipality	Chongqing Municipality

Source Gathered according to national economic plans in the third, fourth and fifth Five-Year Plan periods

[Column 1-2]
Key projects during the "three-line construction" period
Transportation construction: Newly built railways such as Sichuan–Guizhou Railway, Guiyang–Kunming Railway, Chengdu–Kunming Railway, Hunan–Guizhou Railway, Xiangfan–Chongqing Railway, Yangpingguan–Ankang Railway, Jiaozuo–Liuzhou Railway, Zhiliu Railway, Taiyuan–Jiaozuo Railway, and Qinghai–Tibet Railway (Xige Section) etc.

Coal industry construction: Large coal bases of Liupanshui in Guizhou, Weibei in Shaanxi and Shitanjing in Ningxia were built. Large and medium-sized mining areas such as Pingdingshan, Jiaozuo, Hebi, Yima and Xinmi were built in the western Henan area.

Petroleum industry construction: Henan Oilfield, Changqing Oilfield, Jianghan Oilfield, South Sichuan Natural Gas Field and Beizhongba Natural Gas Field in West Sichuan were built. Eight oil and natural gas production bases such as Zhongyuan, Nanyang, Jianghan, Sichuan, Qinghai, Yumen, Changqing and Yanchang were formed.

Construction of iron and steel industry: Newly established projects include Panzhihua Iron and Steel Company, Guizhou Shuicheng Steel Plant, Sichuan Jiangyou Great Wall Steel Plant, Xining Steel Plant, Xining Special

Steel Plant, Xi'an Metal Products Factory, etc. Continued construction, renovation and expansion of Wuhan Iron and Steel Company, Daye Iron and Steel Company, Taiyuan Iron and Steel Company, Xiangtan Iron and Steel Company, Chengdu Seamless Steel Tube Plant, Chongqing Special Steel Plant, Guiyang Iron and Steel Plant, Shaanxi Iron and Steel Plant.

Nonferrous metal industry construction: In the aluminum industry, new alumina plants include Guizhou Aluminum Plant and Zhengzhou Aluminum Plant. Guizhou, Lanzhou, Qingtongxia and Liancheng aluminum smelters were newly built. Aluminum processing works in the northwest and southwest (Chongqing) were established. In the copper industry, new copper smelters such as Baiyin, Daye and Yunnan, as well as two copper processing plants in the northwest and Luoyang have been built. In the lead and zinc industry, Baiyin and Zhuzhou smelters have been set up.

Automobile manufacturing industry: Three key enterprises including No. 2 Automobile Manufacturing Plant, Shaanxi Automobile Manufacturing Plant and Sichuan Automobile Manufacturing Plant.

Machinery manufacturing industry: In terms of heavy machinery manufacturing industry, key project of Deyang No. 2 Heavy Machinery Factory was implemented. In terms of electric appliance manufacturing, Deyang Dongfang Power Plant Complete Equipment Company was prioritized. And Guiyang Abrasives Production Base marked the focus in the machine tool manufacturing industry.

Source Gathered according to national economic plans in the Third, Fourth and Fifth Five-Year Plan periods.

In general, from the founding of the PRC to the end of the 1970s, due to the tilt of national regional strategic layout toward inland areas, the industrialization and urbanization of the hinterland were remarkably promoted, and the pattern of extremely uneven economic development among regions before 1949 has improved. Up to now, the development of inland areas still depends on this foundation. However, due to the predominance of administrative forces, there are some problems that cannot be ignored in the regional development strategy of this period: First, investment returns of some projects in the inland areas are not high. In 1978, the realized output value of fixed assets per hundred *yuan* in the "three-line" region was only half of that in the coastal areas, with a profit rate of only 9.2 and 23.4% in the coastal areas. Second, since the national regional development strategies were tilted toward the inland, industrial bases in the coastal areas had not been fully utilized, thereby having a negative impact on the overall economic development. The third is due to the blind pursuit of complete local industrial systems regardless of resource constraints and actual feasibility, various projects of small, medium and large scales blossomed everywhere, resulting in an improper layout of some projects.

1.2 *The Development Stage from the Reform and Opening up to the End of the Twentieth Century*

The Third Plenary Session of the Eleventh Central Committee of the CPC made a significant decision to shift the focus of the Party's work to the socialist modernization drive centered on economic construction. In 1979, based on Deng Xiaoping's strategic thinking of "letting some regions and some people become rich first and gradually realizing common prosperity" and "Two Overall Situations", the Central Committee of the Party and the State Council put forward the guideline of "strengthening advantages and avoiding shortcomings" and established the regional development strategy which actively supports the coastal regions to take the lead in development. The Sixth Five-Year Plan clearly pointed out that it is necessary to actively use the existing foundations of the coastal regions and give full play to their advantages in order to drive the economic growth of the inland. The Seventh Five-Year Plan further proposed to accelerate the development of the eastern coastal regions.

[Column 1-3]
Deng Xiaoping's strategic thinking of "Two Overall Situations"
In terms of economic policies, I (Deng Xiaoping) believe that some regions, some enterprises, and some workers and farmers should be allowed to earn more and get well off first because of their hard work and diligence. After they get well off, their examples will definitely create substantial demonstration effect, which helps to affect their neighbors and motivate people from other regions or other sections of society to learn from them. In this way, the entire national economy will continue to develop in a wave-like manner, so that people of all ethnic groups in China can become richer soon.

The coastal regions must speed up the pace of opening up, so that this vast tract of land with a population of 200 million can develop rapidly, driving better development of the inland. This is a matter concerning the big picture. Therefore, the inland must take the overall situation into account. Conversely, when the coastal regions have developed to a certain extent, they should exert more efforts to promote the development of the inland. This is also a kind of big picture. At that time, the coastal regions have to realize the overall situation and conform to it as well.

Source Excerpted from *Emancipate the Mind, Seek Truth from Facts and Unite as One in Looking to the Future* (a speech by Deng Xiaoping on December 13, 1978) on page 9 and *The Central Leadership Must Have Authority* (a speech by Deng Xiaoping on September 12, 1988) on page 507 of *Selected Works of the 30th Anniversary of Reform and Opening up (I)* compiled by the Party Literature Research Center of the CPC Central Committee and published by Central Party Literature Press in 2008.

The regional strategy in this period (1979–1992) was based on the layout of central investment projects, and "Give policy support" has become an important regional policy tool, which mainly included the following six aspects.

1.2.1 Implement Special Policies and Flexible Measures in Guangdong and Fujian Provinces

In July 1979, the central government decided to implement special policies and flexible measures in Guangdong and Fujian provinces. That is to say, the finance and foreign exchanges of these two provinces were subject to quotas; supplies and commerce were properly regulated by the market under the guidance of national plans; and local authorities in terms of external activities such as planning, prices, and wages were expanded.

1.2.2 Establish Special Economic Zones

In August 1980, the central government officially approved the establishment of the Shenzhen Special Economic Zone, and successively established the Zhuhai, Shantou and Xiamen Special Economic Zones. In April 1983, the central government decided to speed up the development and construction of Hainan and implemented a policy similar to the special economic zone. In April 1988, the Seventh National People's Congress decided at its First Session to set up Hainan Special Economic Zone and approved the establishment of Hainan Province.

[Column 1-4]

Decisions on the establishment of special economic zones

On July 19, 1981, the *Notice of the Central Committee of the CPC and the State Council on the Approval of the Minutes of the Working Meetings of Guangdong and Fujian Provinces and Special Economic Zones* pointed out that Guangdong and Fujian are the southern gates of China as well as the main hometown of overseas Chinese. What's more, they enjoy great strategic importance and many favorable conditions for their economic development; If these two provinces can open up a new situation and accumulate experience in economic adjustment, system reform, expansion of foreign economic and technological exchanges, and construction of special economic zones, it will be of substantial significance not only for the economic prosperity of these two provinces, but for the development of the national economy as well. Besides, it will also be politically conducive to reassuring citizens in Hong Kong and Macao as well as to striving for Taiwan's return to the motherland.

On the use of foreign capital to construct special economic zones under socialist circumstances: On the basis of self-reliance, opening up and actively expanding economic cooperation and exchanges with other countries are a major policy of the Party. At present, China's productive forces are still relatively backward, and there is a shortage of construction funds. Under the conditions that the people's democratic dictatorship is increasingly consolidated and the socialist economy is dominant, it is necessary to take various forms to utilize overseas Chinese capital and foreign capital, to accelerate the development of socialized large-scale production, to improve technical and management skills, and to promote socialist modernization drive. Piloting special economic zones is an important part in the implementation of special policies for these two provinces and a special way to implement opening-up policies and to absorb foreign capital. Some people have doubts about it: Will the special economic zone become a concession? Is it a colony? The meeting believes that these worries are groundless. A special economic zone is not a special political zone. The full exercise of China's national sovereignty within the special economic zone is fundamentally different from the concessions and colonies which resulted from unequal treaties. The experience of many other countries in the world has proved that the special economic zone is a rather successful means to expand export trade, make use of foreign capital, introduce foreign technologies, and develop the economy. For China, the special economic zone is a school where we can learn how to compete with foreign capital, how to act in accordance with economic laws, and learn modern economic management. It is also a base for training and cultivating talents for these two provinces and even for the whole country.

Source Excerpted from page 114 to 119 of *Literature on China's Special Economic Zone* compiled by Research Center of China's Special Economic Zone, Shenzhen University, published by Social Sciences Academic Press in 2010.

1.2.3 Open Up Coastal Cities

In April 1984, in order to speed up the pace of opening up, the State Council decided to further open up 14 coastal cities including Dalian, Qinhuangdao, Tianjin, etc. The main policies included easing limits of local management authority, expanding local power to enhance external economic activities, and so on and so forth in opening up.

[Column 1-5]

Open up 14 national economic and technological development zones

In 1984, *Minutes of the Coastal Cities Symposium* approved by the Central Committee of the CPC and the State Council pointed out: Some of these cities (referred to as Tianjin, Shanghai, Dalian, Qinhuangdao, Yantai, Qingdao, Lianyungang, Nantong, Ningbo, Wenzhou, Fuzhou, Guangzhou, Zhanjiang and Beihai) can designate an area with definite boundaries to set up new economic and technological development zones. The economic and technological development zones should vigorously introduce advanced technologies that are urgently needed in China, and concentrate on establishing Chinese-foreign equity joint ventures, Chinese-foreign contractual joint ventures, foreign-funded enterprises and Chinese-foreign cooperative scientific research institutions, developing cooperative production, cooperative research and design, developing new technologies and high-end products, increasing export proceeds, providing new materials and key components to the inland, and disseminating new process, new technology and scientific management experience. Besides, some economic and technological development zones should also develop into bases for international entreport trade. Within the economic and technological development zones, limits of authority for examining and approving the use of foreign capital in projects can be further relaxed, generally in accordance with the provisions for the special economic zones. The government shall implement necessary regulatory measures for economic and technological development zones, and the economic and technological development zones shall provide necessary regulatory conditions for the government to supervise in the planning and construction process.

Source Excerpted from page 325 to 326 of *Selected Works of the 30th Anniversary of Reform and Opening Up (I)* compiled by Party Literature Research Center of the CPC Central Committee and published by Central Party Literature Press in 2008.

1.2.4 Open Up the Coastal Economic Open Zones

In February 1985, the Central Committee and the State Council decided to open up 59 cities and counties in the Yangtze River Delta, the Pearl River Delta, and the Xiamen-Zhangzhou-Quanzhou Triangle in southern Fujian Province into coastal economic open zones. In March 1988, the State Council further expanded the scope of the coastal open economic zones and opened 140 cities and counties in the Liaodong Peninsula, Shandong Peninsula, Shenyang, Nanjing, and other places.

[Column 1-6]
List of cities and counties in coastal economic open zones

Jiangsu Province: Suzhou and Changshu, Wu County, Shazhou County, Taicang County, Kunshan County, Zhangjiagang District of Wujiang County (all six are under Suzhou's jurisdiction); Wuxi and Wuxi County, Jiangyin County, Yixing County (all three are under Wuxi's jurisdiction); Changzhou and Wujin County, Jintan County, and Shuyang County (all three are under Changzhou's jurisdiction).

Zhejiang Province: Jiaxing and Jiashan County, Tongxiang County, Haining County (all three are under Jiaxing's jurisdiction); Huzhou and Deqing County (under Huzhou's jurisdiction).

Guangdong Province: Foshan and Zhongshan, Nanhai County, Shunde County, Gaoming County (all four are under Foshan's jurisdiction); Jiangmen and Kaiping County, Xinhui County, Taishan County, Heshan County, Enping County (all five are under Jiangmen's jurisdiction); Panyu County and Zengcheng County of Guangzhou; Bao'an County of Shenzhen; Doumen County of Zhuhai; Dongguan County of Huiyang District.

Fujian Province: Tong'an County of Xiamen; Zhangzhou, Longhai County, Zhangpu County and Dongshan County of Longxi District; Quanzhou, Hui'an County, Nan'an County, Jinjiang County, Anxi County and Yongchun County of Jinjiang District.

Shanghai: Shanghai County, Jiading County, Baoshan County, Chuansha County, Nanhui County, Fengxian County, Songjiang County, Jinshan County, Qingpu County and Chongming County.

Liaoning Province: Dandong, Dalian, Yingkou, Panjin, Jinzhou, Shenyang, Anshan, Liaoyang and some other counties and districts.

1.2.5 Establish Pudong New Area

In June 1990, the Central Committee of the CPC and the State Council officially approved the development and opening of the Pudong New Area in Shanghai and agreed to adopt some preferential policies of special economic zones in the Pudong New Area.

[Column 1-7]

The development and opening of Pudong New Area

On June 2, 1990, the State Council issued *Reply on the Development and Opening of Pudong* and decided to develop and open the Pudong New Area. The reply pointed out that the development and opening up of Pudong is a major deployment that will help to deepen reforms and to further opening up. It is also a major event that has a bearing on the overall situation. Shanghai has a lot of advantages such as good political and economic foundations, a group of high-quality technology and management talents, an outstanding team of industrial workers, superior geographical environment, convenient transportation conditions and extensive contacts with overseas countries. If we can make full use of these advantages and develop and open Pudong in a planned, step-by-step, active and steady way, it will undoubtedly have a significant impact on the political stability and economic development of Shanghai and the whole country.

Source Extracted from *Reply from the State Council on the Development and Opening up of Pudong*, 1990.

1.2.6 Establish a Free Trade Zone in the Coastal Areas

In June 1990, the State Council approved the establishment of China's first free trade zone, Shanghai Waigaoqiao Free Trade Zone. In 1991, the State Council approved the establishment of Tianjin Port Free Trade Zone, Shenzhen Futian Free Trade Zone and Shatoujiao Free Trade Zone, and subsequently established 11 free trade zones such as Shenzhen Yantian Port Free Trade Zone, Dalian Free Trade Zone and Zhangjiagang Free Trade Zone.

These six policies have substantially promoted the development of the eastern coastal regions. During the period of time from the Sixth Five-Year Plan to the Eighth Five-Year Plan, capital construction investment in the coastal areas exceeded half of the national total. From 1978 to 1995, coastal areas accounted for 84.7% of the total foreign investment in China. The GDP of the eastern coastal provinces grew at an average annual rate of 11.7%, 1.8 percentage points higher than the national average and 2.1 percentage points higher than the central and western regions.[5] A coastal open area extending from the south to the north along the coastline was gradually formed.

Generally speaking, the coastal areas have taken the lead during this period, which accelerated the process of China's reform and opening up, made China's economic strength rise rapidly, narrowed its gap with developed countries, and made great contribution to achieving the strategic goal of quadrupling the GDP of 1980 by the end of the twentieth century and helping the people reach a well-off standard of living.

However, the development speed of the eastern region continues to grow faster than that of the central and western regions, and the gap between the development speeds of the eastern region and the central and western regions has gradually widened, leading to an increasingly prominent problem of regional development imbalance. From 1978 to 2000, the average annual growth rate of regional GDP in the eastern, central, western, and northeastern regions was 12.01, 9.99, 9.74, and 8.58%, respectively. The growth rate of eastern region was more than 2 percentage points higher than that of other regions. During the Eighth Five-Year Plan period, the growth rate in the eastern region was 5 percentage points higher than that of other regions. In 1978, the absolute gap of GDP per capita between the eastern region and the central and western regions was 153.6 yuan and 212.9 yuan, respectively, and expanded to 700.1 yuan and 885.9 yuan respectively in 1990, and further expanded to 4790.2 yuan and 6162.0 yuan, respectively in 2000. In the early 1990s, the relative gap between the eastern and central and western regions was not only expanding year by year, but by over 2 percentage points per year. Particularly, from 1990 to 1994, the relative gap coefficient between the eastern and central regions rose rapidly from 35.6 to 46.7%. From 1990 to 1999, the relative gap coefficient between the eastern and western regions increased from 45.1 to 58.7% rapidly. In general, from 1990 to 2000, the relative gap coefficient between the eastern and central and western regions increased by 8.9 percentage points and 12.1 percentage points, respectively (see Table 3). The widening gap among regions has gradually become a problem that affects the overall development of the national economy.

[5] Lu Dadao et al.: *Theory and Practice of Regional Development in China*, Science Press, 2003, p. 118.

Table 3 Gap of GDP per capita between the eastern region and the central and western regions from 1978 to 2000

Year	*Absolute gap (yuan)*		*Relative gap coefficient (%)*	
	Between the eastern and central regions	*Between the eastern and western regions*	*Between the eastern and central regions*	*Between the eastern and western regions*
2000	4790.2	6162.0	44.5	57.2
1999	4643.1	5930.6	46.0	58.7
1998	4233.6	5430.8	44.6	57.3
1997	3892.9	5033.8	44.0	56.9
1996	3520.5	4510.9	44.3	56.8
1995	3086.8	3835.5	45.5	56.6
1994	2532.7	3032.8	46.7	55.9
1993	1874.6	2194.7	45.9	53.8
1992	1320.5	1514.7	43.5	49.9
1991	977.2	1133.5	40.0	46.4
1990	700.1	885.9	35.6	45.1
1989	685.7	897.1	36.8	48.1
1978	153.6	212.9	33.1	45.9

Source Extracted from page 122 of *Theory and Practice of Regional Development in China* written by Lu Dadao et al. and published by Science Press in 2003

1.3 The Implementation Stage of Coordinated Regional Development Since the Twenty-First Century

In September 1997, *Report to the Fifteenth National Congress of the CPC* pointed out, to "gradually narrow the development gaps between regions by various efforts", "accelerate the reasonable layout and coordinated development of regional economy". The *"9th Five-Year" Plan for the National Economic and Social Development of the People's Republic of China and Outline of Perspective Objectives for 2010* determined the coordinated development between regions as one of guidelines for national economic and social development for the first time, pointing out, to "keep coordinated development of regional economy, and gradually narrow the development gaps between regions". To accelerate the economic development of the central and western regions, the country launched a series of important policies, which, respectively, were: *Western Development Strategy* in 1999; *Revitalization Strategy of Old Industrial Bases in Northeast China* in 2003; *The Strategy of Promoting the Rise of*

Central China in 2006; in 2010, the country launched measures and policies to promote the formation of main functional area, meanwhile devoting greater efforts in supporting impoverished areas, areas inhabited by ethnic minorities, old revolutionary base areas, border areas, resource-exhausted areas and other special areas. "The 11th Five-Year Plan" comprehensively elaborated on accelerating coordinated development between regions, explicitly disclosing that the country would accelerate the development in western China, revitalization of old industrial bases in northeast China, rising of central China, and encourage eastern China to take the lead in developing, which demonstrated that China has entered a new stage of overall implementation of Reginal Coordinated Development Strategy.[6]

[Column 1-8]
Deployment of regional development in the "11th Five-Year" Plan
1. Promoting Western Development.
The western region should accelerate reform and opening up and to strengthen self-development ability through national support, its own endeavor and regional cooperation. It should insist on relying on trunk transportation lines and central cities and implement key development. It should strengthen infrastructure construction, construct new routes for departure, for cross-region railway and for the West-East Coal Transportation Project, complete the western section of "Five Vertical and Seven Horizontal Trunk National Highways" and eight provincial highways, construct electricity base and the West-East Electricity Transmission Project. It should consolidate and build upon the progress made in the Grain for Green Project, continue carrying forward ecological projects such as Return Farmland to Forests Project, Natural Forest Protection Project, etc., strengthen vegetation protection, put greater efforts in combating desertification and stony desertification, and strengthen water pollution prevention in key areas. It should strengthen protection and construction of ecological maintenance of the Tibetan Plateau. It should support resource advantage to be transformed into industry advantage, strive to develop featured industries, strengthen the exploitation and processing of clean energy and advantageous mineral resource, and support the development of advanced manufacturing industry, high technology industry and other advantageous industries. It should strengthen and improve public services, give priority to development of compulsory education and

[6]The Forth Session of the Tenth National People's Congress: *Outline of the 11th Five-Year Plan for the National Economic and Social Development of the People's Republic of China*, approved on March 14, 2006.

vocational education, improve health care in rural areas, and explore talent resource and technology innovation. It should construct and improve facilities at the border crossings, strengthen economic and technological cooperation with adjacent countries, and develop border trade. It should put the Western Development Strategy into effect and further intensify it, strengthen budget support and fiscal transfer, push forward establishing stable capital channel for Western development in the long term.

2. Revitalization of Old Industrial Bases including Northeast China.
The northeast China region should speed up industrial restructuring and the reform, reorganization and transformation of state-owned enterprises, achieve prosperity in Reform and Opening-Up. It should develop modern agriculture, strengthen the construction of grain production bases, promote large-scale, standardized, mechanized and industrialized management of agriculture, and increase commodity rate and added value. It should construct bases of advanced equipment, quality steel, petroleum chemicals, automobile, shipping and intensive processing of agricultural and sideline products, and develop high technology industry. It should establish a compensation system of resources development and an aid system of the declined industry, do a good job of managing the pilot areas of economic transformation in resource-exhausted cities such as Fuxin, Daqing, Yichun, Liaoyuan, etc., and do a good job of transforming shantytowns and administering coal mining subsidence areas. It should strengthen infrastructure construction such as railway in the eastern part of northeast China and trans-provincial highways, speed up the construction of market system, accelerate regional economic integration. It should expand economic and technological cooperation with adjacent countries. It should strengthen comprehensive administration of soil erosion in black land and desertification of the west in northeast China. The northeast China region should also support the revitalization of old industrial bases in other regions.

3. Promoting the Rise of Central China.
The central China region should build on its existing foundation, enhance industrial level, push forward industrialization and urbanization, and make great use of its geographical advantage of linking the east and west and industrial advantage. It should strengthen the construction of modern agriculture, particularly the major grain producing areas, put greater efforts in constructing agricultural infrastructure, strengthen the production capacity of bulk agricultural products like the grain, enhance the processing, transformation and added value of agricultural products. It should support Shanxi, Henan and Anhui provinces to strengthen the construction of large-scale coal bases, develop power stations near coal mines, and

realize joint management of coal and electricity. It should accelerate the structural adjustment of advantageous industries such as steel, chemical engineering, nonferrous metals and building materials and form qualified bases for raw materials. It should support the development of equipment manufacturing industries such as mining machinery, automobile, agricultural machinery, haulage motor, and electric transmission and transformation equipment, as well as high technology industries such as software, photoelectron, new materials, and biological engineering. It should establish an integrated traffic and transport system, with a focus on the construction of main line railway, highway, inland port, and regional airport. The region should also strengthen the construction of infrastructure such as logistics centers and perfect the market system.

4. Encouraging Eastern China to take the lead in development.

Eastern China should take the lead to improve the capability of independent innovation, to complete the optimization and upgrade of economic structure and transformation of growth pattern, to perfect the socialist market economy system, and to help the central and western China to develop in leading development and reform. It should accelerate the formation of a series of proprietary intellectual property, key technology and famous brands, and enhance industrial quality and competitiveness. It should give priority to the development of advanced manufacturing industry, high technology industry and service industry. It should boost the upgrade of processing trade, actively take the transfer of high technology industry and modern service industry, improve the export-oriented economy and increase international competitiveness. It should strengthen the protection of farmland and develop modern agriculture. It should enhance the utilization efficiency of resources, in particular land and energy, strengthen the protection for ecological environment, and enhance the capacity of sustainable development. Special economic zones and Pudong New Area of Shanghai should continue to play their roles and push forward the development and opening up of Tianjin Binhai New Area, support economic development of the west coast of the Taiwan Straits and other areas where Taiwan businessman are relatively concentrated, as well as drive regional economic development.

5. Encouraging the Development of Old Revolutionary Base Areas, Areas Inhabited by Ethnic Minorities and Border Areas.

The country should devote greater efforts in fiscal transfer payment and investment, and encourage faster development of old revolutionary base areas, areas inhabited by ethnic minorities and border areas. It should protect natural ecology and improve infrastructure. It should develop early childhood education, popularize compulsory education at a faster pace, effectively manage the ethnic classes of secondary schools in central cities, and intensify the establishment of ethnic universities and higher education in minority areas. It should establish folk traditional cultural community for ethnic minorities, support the publishing causes of ethnic minorities, and establish bilingual teaching demonstration areas. It should strengthen the construction of minority talents and stabilize the talent teams of areas inhabited by ethnic minorities. It should support the development of ethnic characteristic industries, special needed commodities for ethnic minorities, ethnic pharmaceutical industry and other advantageous industries. It should give priority to resolving the poverty issue of extremely impoverished ethnic minorities, support the economic and social development of minorities with less population, and push forward the Program to Revitalize Border Areas and Enrich Residents' Lives. It should insist on policies that support the development of Tibet, Xinjiang, and the Xinjiang Production and Construction Corps.

Source Extracted from the *11th Five-Year Plan for the National Economic and Social Development of the People's Republic of China* approved by the 4th Session of the 10th National People's Congress on March 14, 2006.

2 Overall Pattern of China's Regional Development Since the Twenty-First Century

2.1 The Western Development Strategy

Western China consists of 12 provinces, regions and cities (Chongqing City, Sichuan Province, Guizhou Province, Yunnan Province, Tibet Autonomous Region, Shaanxi Province, Gansu Province, the Ningxia Hui Autonomous Region, Qinghai Province, the Xinjiang Uygur Autonomous Region, the Inner Mongolia Autonomous Region, and the Guangxi Zhuang Autonomous Region), covering about 6.85 million square kilometers and taking up 71.5% of China's territory; the population is about 3.7 hundred million, making up 27% of all China's population; ethnic minorities take up 70% of the total population; the length of land boundary takes up 82% of totality, bordering on 14 countries and districts. Western China boasts abundant energy resources, has important ecologic significance but with a relatively backward economic and social development. In June 1999, the Party Central Committee proposed that "we must accelerate the development of central and western regions in good time, especially the western development". In September 1999, the Fourth Plenary Session of the Fifteenth Central Committee of the

Communist Party of China officially proposed that "the country plans to implement the Western Development Strategy".

To implement the Western Development Strategy, in October 2000, the State Council issued *Notice of the State Council on Implementing Several Policies and Measures for the Western Development Strategy*, making strategic goals for western development and relevant implementation of policies. In September 2001, the General Office of the State Council forwarded *Notice of the Opinions of the State Council Western Development Office on Implementing Policies and Measures for the Western Development Strategy*, and proposed 70 opinions on the implementation of policies and measures. After this, the State Council and relevant departments successively issued a series of supporting policies and documents on further developing the western region. According to incomplete statistics, since the implementation of the Western Development Strategy, the country has successively issued 215 policy documents focused on Western development (among them, 27 were issued by the central government and the State Council, 108 by relevant ministries and 80 supporting policy documents by provincial governments), which laid solid policy foundation for the implementation of the Western Development Strategy.

The first is fiscal policy: from 2000 onwards, the rate of construction capital from the central budget on the western region would be increased, and a part of budget would come from the central government, which would go to transfer payment in areas inhabited by ethnic minorities; special fund for local governments from the central government would be inclined to the western region; subsidy for Grain for Green would be authorized; for villages and towns that suffered fiscal difficulty caused by rural tax and fee reform, proper subsidy would be authorized.

The second is tax policy: corporate tax rate for domestic and foreign-owned enterprises entering the western region would be lowered or freed; corporate tax for new enterprises of transportation, electricity, hydraulic engineering, postal service, radio and television would be reduced or freed; tax on agricultural specialty products would be freed; tax on highway construction conversion of farmland would be freed; imported equipment for own good would be freed from tariffs and import added-value tax.

The third is investment policy: great infrastructure construction projects newly scheduled by the country would be invested by central fiscal construction capital, etc.; the central government would raise special capital to support focus projects of western development and give priority to infrastructure construction projects in the western region; foreign-invested agriculture in the western region would benefit from various favorable policies of encouraging industries.

The fourth is credit financing: properly extend the length of maturity for infrastructure construction; expand the scope of loans pledged by usufruct or right to charge of infrastructure projects; expand credit investment in infrastructure construction in the western region; increase credit investment in agriculture and ecological construction; support the development of advantageous industries in western regions, such as electricity, natural gas, tourism and reasonable exploitation of biological resources; as for major projects with larger loan amount, it could be settled by direct-loan from commercial bank headquarters and the loan would not be considered in loan-to-deposit ratio of local branches or the range of limit authorization.

In addition to the supporting policies mentioned above, the country has also offered policy support to the western region in terms of education, social undertaking, and foreign economic relations and trade.

[Column 1-9]
Outline of *Several Opinions of the State Council on Further Promoting the Development of the Western Region*

In November 2004, the State Council issued *Several Opinions of the State Council on Further Promoting the Development of the Western Region*, pointing out that the Sixteenth National Congress of the Communist Party of China and the Third Plenary Session of the Sixteenth Central Committee made it clear that promoting the development of the western region, effectively playing the comprehensive advantages of the central region, supporting the acceleration of reform and development in the central and western regions, revitalizing old industrial bases including the northeast region, and encouraging eastern regions with advantages to take the lead in basically realizing modernization and promoting the coordinated development of the regional economy are major measures for building a moderately prosperous society in an all-round way and improving the socialist market economic system.

It is of vital importance to coordinate regional development and accelerate the development of the western region. Without a moderately prosperous society in the western region, there would be no national well-being. Without the modernization of the western region, it cannot be said that the modernization of the country has been achieved. Therefore, we must further improve our understanding of the major strategic significance of the development of the western region, conscientiously study and grasp the regularity of the development in the western region, put the implementation of the development of the western region as a major task on the important agenda, continuously improve and strengthen leadership over the development of the western region, and fully mobilize the polarity of all parties and create a new situation in the development of the western region.

1. We will promote ecological construction and environmental protection, achieve ecological improvement and increase farmers' income.
2. We will continue to speed up the construction of key infrastructure projects and lay a solid foundation for the accelerated development of the western region.
3. We will further strengthen the construction of agriculture and rural infrastructure, and accelerate the improvement of farmers' production and living conditions.
4. We will vigorously adjust the industrial structure and develop advantageous industries with characteristics.
5. We will promote the development of key areas and accelerate the cultivation of regional economic growth poles.
6. We will vigorously strengthen social undertakings such as science and technology, education, health and culture, and promote coordinated economic and social development.
7. We will deepen the reform of the economic system and create a favorable environment for the development of the western region.
8. We will broaden the funding channels to provide financial support for the development of the western region.
9. We will strengthen the construction of the talent team in the western region and provide a strong talent guarantee for the development of the western region.

Source Adapted from *Several Opinions of the State Council on Further Promoting the Development of the Western Region*, March 11, 2004.

In 2010, on the occasion of the tenth anniversary of the implementation of the strategy for the development of the western region, the CPC Central Committee and the State Council issued *Several Opinions of the Central Committee of the Communist Party of China and the State Council on Further Implementing the Western Development Strategy*. They organized a conference on the development of the western region and made comprehensive deployment: clarifying the key tasks in eight aspects such as strengthening infrastructure and ecological environment construction, and granting preferential policies in ten aspects such as finance, taxation and investment, including the policy of levying an enterprise income tax of 15% for industries encouraged to develop in the western region.

Source The website of the Leading Group for the Construction of the Ningxia Inland Open Economy Experimental Zone: http://www.nxsyq.com.

The main policies include:

1. Fiscal policy. We will increase the central government's balanced transfer payments to the western region, gradually reduce the local standard fiscal revenue and expenditure gap in the region, and promote the equalization of basic public services among areas. The central government will use special transfer payments for energy conservation, environmental protection, new energy, education, talents, medical care, social security, poverty alleviation and development, with the focus on the western region. We will raise funds through various means and increase the central government's financial support for the development of the western region. The central government will increase the subsidy for infrastructure construction projects in the state-level economic and technological development zones, high-tech industrial development zones and border economic cooperation zones in the western region.

2. Tax policy. Enterprise income tax will be levied at the rate of 15% on the industrial enterprises that are encouraged by the state and located in the western region. Enterprises engaged in the state's key support of public infrastructure projects investment income, as well as in line with the conditions of environmental protection, energy-saving and water-saving projects income, can enjoy the preferential enterprise income tax of "three exemptions and three halved". We will promote the resource tax reform, and change the resource tax on coal, crude oil, natural gas, etc. from metering to ad valorem, and appropriately increase the tax on other resources and the local fiscal revenue of the resource. Local governments at all levels must be inclined to the grassroots government of resource-producing areas in the allocation of resource taxes. For self-use equipment imported within the total amount of investment for projects of domestic-funded, foreign-funded and advantageous industries in the western region, customs duties shall be exempted within the scope of policies and regulations.

3. Investment policy. We will increase the central government's financial investment in favor of livelihood projects, infrastructure and ecological environment in the western region. We will increase the proportion of special construction funds invested by relevant state departments in the western region, and raise the investment subsidy standards and capital injection ratio for construction projects such as roads, railways, civil aviation and water conservancy. The central government will arrange public welfare construction projects, cancel supporting funds at the county level or below in the western region (including counties) and at the prefecture level in contiguous cities with special difficulties, clarify the responsibilities of local governments, and strengthen project supervision and inspection. We will increase the support for technological transformation and industrial restructuring of enterprises in existing investments to support the development of advantageous industries in the west. The central budget investment arrangement funds will support the preliminary work of key projects for the development of the western region. Concessional loans from international financial organizations and foreign governments will continue to support the western region.

4. Financial policy. We will further increase credit support for the western region. We will strengthen the effective convergence of fiscal and financial policies, encourage policy-oriented financial institutions to increase financial services to the western region, and explore the use of policy-based financial means to support the development of the western region. We will deepen the reform of rural credit cooperatives and foster new rural financial institutions such as rural mutual funds. We will promptly formulate and implement measures such as subsidies for newly established rural financial institutions in remote areas, and gradually eliminate the blank townships of basic financial services. We will implement and improve policies on tax incentives for agricultural loans, targeted fee subsidies, and incremental incentives, and further improve the policy of mainly using newly absorbed deposits by banking financial institutions within the county for local loans. Local governments at all levels are encouraged to support financing guarantee institutions to engage in small and medium-sized enterprise (SME) guarantee business through capital injection and implementation of tax reduction and exemption policies. We will support the listing of eligible enterprises and the refinancing of listed companies in the western region. We will support venture capital enterprises and develop equity investment funds. We will study and explore effective ways to transfer shares of non-listed

companies in the western region, and regulate the development of property rights trading market.

5. Industrial policy. Differentiated industrial policies will be implemented, lists of encouraged industries will be formulated, and the development of characteristic advantageous industries in the western region will be encouraged. All energy and resource development and utilization projects that are qualified to be processed and converted in the western region will be supported in their layout and construction and will be given priority for examination and approval. We will support private capital to enter industries such as oil and gas exploration, development, storage and transportation in the form of cooperation and shareholding. We will expand the scope of the list of foreign-invested advantageous industries in the western region. We will increase the investment of the Central Geological Exploration Fund and the Land and Resources Survey and Evaluation Fund in the western region, and encourage and guide the investment of diversified funds. Foreign investment will be encouraged to participate in the development and application of new technologies for improving mine tailings utilization rate and mine ecological environment restoration and management.

6. Land policy. We will further improve the approval system for construction land, simplify procedures, and ensure the construction of key projects for the development of the western region. The implementation of the differentiated land policy and arrangement of the annual land use planning indicators will be moderately inclined to the western region, and the land use index for unused land such as barren hills, sandy land and the Gobi Desert in the western region will be increased. We will steadily carry out pilot projects to link rural land consolidation with the increase or decrease of urban and rural construction land. The minimum standard for industrial land transfer fees can be implemented according to 10–50% of the *National Minimum Standard for Industrial Land Transfer*, and the benchmark land price for construction land in development parks (districts) in the western region can be appropriately reduced.

7. Price policy. Special freight rates for new and branch railway lines can be approved according to the actual situation, the principle of repayment of loan principal and interest and compensation of reasonable operating costs, and the level of local economic development and the affordability of users. We will accelerate the reform of resource product prices, improve the system of paid use of resources, and establish and improve production factors and resource price formation mechanisms

that reflect the relationship between market supply and demand, resource scarcity and environmental damage. We will support people in resource areas to use high quality and affordable gas and electricity. We will promote the use of water resources, rationally determine the price of urban water supply, and gradually implement stepped water prices. We will improve the preferential utilization price of reclaimed water, encourage the reuse of it, and the central government will support the investment in the construction of reclaimed water reuse facilities. We will scientifically formulate water resource fee collection standards and gradually bring the price of sewage treatment fees to a reasonable level. We will actively promote pricing mechanisms such as bidding for power generation companies, direct trading of power users and power generation companies. Close attention will be paid to improve the pricing policy for renewable energy power generation.

8. Ecological compensation policy. According to the principle of "who develops, who protects, who benefits, who compensates", we will gradually establish and improve the ecological compensation mechanism in the fields of forests, grasslands, wetlands, watersheds and mineral resources development. We will explore and promote the internalization of resource and environmental costs. The compensation standards for ecological benefits of national public welfare forests will be improved. Grassland ecological compensation will be carried out in accordance with the measures of reducing the number of overloaded livestock and verifying the forbidden grazing area. Close attention will be paid to researching and carrying out the ecological compensation for wetlands. Taking full account of the importance of ecological protection in the upper reaches of the major rivers, the central government will increase the balance transfer payments to key ecological functional areas such as the upper reaches. The establishment of an ecological environment compensation mechanism between the upstream and downstream ecological protection and ecological benefit areas in the same basin will be encouraged. We will continue to increase the intensity of funds for the compensation of ecological benefits of soil and water conservation. We will continue to improve the water consumption control and water rights trading system, and carry out water rights trading pilot projects in Gansu, Ningxia and Guizhou. We will establish a resource-based enterprise sustainable development reserve system. Resource-based enterprises shall extract special funds for environmental protection and ecological restoration according to regulations, and be granted pre-tax deduction. The government of

the place where the mineral resources are located will use the reserves drawn by enterprises in a coordinated way and according to a certain proportion, which will be specially used for comprehensive environmental management and solving social problems brought about by resource development. We will accelerate the development and publication of guidance on ecological compensation policy measures and ecological compensation regulations.

9. Talent policy. We will improve the wage policy for personnel in government agencies and institutions and gradually raise the wage level. We will further increase the policy inclinations for the rural and remote areas, especially the grassroots, and implement the dynamic adjustment mechanism for subsidies in the remote areas. We will study and improve the preferential policies for retaining talents and attracting all kinds of talents to work at the grassroots level in the western region, and give policy inclinations in terms of job promotion, job title evaluation, children's enrollment, and medical services.

10. Aid policy. We will further strengthen and promote counterpart support for Tibet and Xinjiang, establish a comprehensive counterpart support mechanism that combines economic support, cadre support, talent support, and technology support and improve support methods. Counterpart support and assistance will be carried out in Qinghai and other minority areas and concentrated contiguous areas with special difficulties. We will continue to implement targeted poverty alleviation and counterpart support by the central and state organs, enterprises and institutions. We will establish and improve the military and land coordination mechanism, and give full play to the advantages and positive role of the people's army in participating in and supporting the development of the western region. We will widely mobilize all sectors of society to support and participate in the development of the western region. Various forms of public welfare activities and charitable donations are encouraged.

2.2 Revitalization Strategy of Old Industrial Bases Including Northeast China

2.2.1 Revitalization Strategy of Old Industrial Bases Including Northeast China

In the early days of the founding of New China, in order to speed up the process of national industrialization, the state concentrated its efforts to construct a number of heavy industry and resource mining and processing enterprises in the northeast and central and western regions, forming a group of old industrial cities and resource-based cities. These old industrial bases have accumulated a large number of strategic industries and key enterprises that are related to the lifeline of the national economy. They have made historic and significant contributions to the construction of an independent and complete national economic system to promote China's industrialization and urbanization. After the reform and opening up, due to the contradiction between the long-term accumulation of the planned economic system and the internal mechanism of the market economy, the gap between the old industrial base and the developed coastal areas has been widening.

During the "Sixth Five-Year Plan" to the "Seventh Five-Year Plan" periods, the state began to carry out the adjustment and renovation of the super-large and large old industrial bases in Shanghai, Tianjin, Shenyang and Dalian. In 1984, the state designated six cities, namely Shanghai, Tianjin, Wuhan, Chongqing, Shenyang, and Harbin, as key urban renewal cities for old industrial bases, and established an old industrial base adjustment and transformation fund. During the same period, the adjustment and transformation of the old industrial bases in the central and western regions built during the "three-line construction" period were initiated. During the "Eighth Five-Year Plan" period, the state provided 20.2 billion yuan of state-specific loans to the key urban transformation centers of the six old industrial bases, and the special loans for the old industrial bases were 13.4 billion yuan. The support of these reform policies and supporting funds have achieved varying degrees of effectiveness. In particular, old industrial bases such as Shanghai and Wuhan, which reformed and opened up earlier, have undergone transformation and have shown vigorous vitality.

[Column 1-10]
The "Seventh Five-Year Plan" and the "Tenth Five-Year Plan" for National Economic and Social Development

Deployment of the adjustment and transformation of old industrial bases

For accelerating the pace of technological transformation of existing enterprises, we will focus on the transformation of old industrial cities and old industrial bases in Shanghai, Tianjin, Shenyang and Dalian. At the same time, we will actively use various foreign capital and overseas Chinese funds to introduce advanced and applicable technologies and necessary key equipment.

For accelerating the adjustment and transformation of the "three-line construction", and for enterprises with reasonable layout, clear product direction and good economic returns, we will further improve their technical level and operation and management. For enterprises with basic success of construction that have not fully utilized their capabilities due to the constraints of energy, transportation, information and other conditions, we will strengthen technological transformation, and supplement production capacity. For a small number of enterprises that cannot be maintained, have issues with their plant sites and have no clear directions for their products, we will make necessary adjustments through means such as shutting down, stopping, merging, transferring and moving.

Source Extracted from the *Seventh Five-Year Plan for the National Economic and Social Development of the People's Republic of China*, March 25, 1986.

We will support and promote the transformation and structural adjustment of old industrial bases in the Northeast and other places. We will give full play to its strong foundation and talent pooling advantages, combine the adjustment of the state-owned economy layout, optimize the industrial structure, enterprise organizational structure and regional layout, form new advantageous industries and enterprises, and turn advantageous areas into new equipment manufacturing bases. Mines with depleted resources will be closed in an orderly manner, the development of connecting industries and alternative industries in cities and large mining areas that focus on resource exploitation will be carried out, and new models for mine development will be developed.

We will introduce foreign capital to invest more in the central and western regions, especially the transformation of old industrial bases in the central and western regions, infrastructure construction, ecological construction and environmental protection, mineral and tourism resources development, and advantageous industries.

Source Extracted from *Outline of the Tenth Five-Year Plan for the National Economic and Social Development of the People's Republic of China*, March 15, 2001.

During the "Ninth Five-Year Plan" period, while continuing to adjust the industrial structure with the focus of the six old industrial cities, the development of the old industrial bases in Northeast China has been highly valued by the Party Central Committee. In September 1997, the 15th National Congress of the Communist Party of China proposed to create a new situation of reform and development of state-owned enterprises, and further emphasized to "speed up the transformation of old industrial bases". In September 1999, the issued *Decision of the CPC Central Committee on Several Major Issues About State-Owned Enterprise Reform and Development* stipulated the adjustment of the state-owned economic layout of the old industrial bases, pointing out that it is necessary to "make overall planning, adopt effective policy measures, and accelerate the adjustment of the old industrial bases and the layout of the state-owned economy in the central and western regions". These documents mark that the revitalization strategy of the old industrial base has become a very important issue to be solved in the overall situation of China's economic and social development in the twenty-first century.

In November 2002, the report of the 16th National Congress of the Communist Party of China explicitly stated in the party's document for the first time to "support northeast China and other old industrial bases to accelerate the adjustment and reform", thereby adjusting the national strategic level to transform and upgrade the old industrial bases. In October 2003, the CPC Central Committee and the State Council issued *Several Opinions of the Central Committee of the Communist Party of China and the State Council on the Implementation of Revitalization Strategy of Old Industrial Bases Including Northeast China*, thus officially launching the strategy of revitalizing northeast China and other old industrial bases. The *Opinions* also clearly stated that the old industrial bases will be transformed and developed into a new industrial base with advanced technology, reasonable structure, perfect functions, obvious characteristics, flexible mechanism and strong competitiveness, which will gradually become a new important growth region of China's economy. This meant that the revitalization policy of China's old industrial bases has already upgraded from the adjustment of enterprises and industries in the past to the regional revitalization strategy.

[Column 1-11]
Outline of *Several Opinions of the Central Committee of the Communist Party of China and the State Council on the Implementation of Revitalization Strategy of the Old Industrial Bases Including Northeast China*

In October 2003, the CPC Central Committee and the State Council issued *Several Opinions of the Central Committee of the Communist Party of China and the State Council on the Implementation of Revitalization*

Strategy of the Old Industrial Bases Including Northeast China, which pointed out that it is an important mission put forward by the Sixteenth CPC National Congress and also a great strategic decision made by the Party Central Committee to support and speed up the adjusting and restructuring of the northeast and other old industrial bases, contributing to the overall building of a well-off society. All departments and localities shall make concerted efforts, make steady headway and ensure the strategy to be implemented smoothly as the Special Economic Zones in Coastal Areas, the Pudong New Area and the Western Development Strategy.

1. It is of great strategic significance to speed up the revitalization of the northeast and other old industrial bases.
2. The guidelines and principles of revitalizing the northeast and other old industrial bases.
3. Speed up the institutional and mechanism innovation.
4. Advance the adjusting and restructuring of the industry comprehensively.
5. Develop modern agriculture vigorously.
6. Develop the tertiary industry actively.
7. Promote the economic transformation of resource-based cities.
8. Strengthen the construction of fundamental facilities.
9. Further expand the opening up to both domestic and foreign investors.
10. Speed up the development of technology, education and culture industries.
11. Formulate and perfect relevant policies and measures.
12. Strengthen the government leadership.

Source *Several Opinions of the Central Committee of the Communist Party of China and the State Council on the Implementation of Revitalization Strategy of the Old Industrial Bases Including Northeast China*, October 2003.

In 2009, when the international financial crisis was sweeping the world, the State Council issued *Several Opinions of the Central Committee of the Communist Party of China and the State Council on the Further Implementation of Revitalization Strategy of the Old Industrial Bases Including Northeast China*, which came up with 28 measures from 9 aspects to promote the all-round revitalization of the northeast and other old industrial bases. In 2014, the State Council issued another document—*Opinions of the State Council on Major Policy Measures for*

Supporting the Revival of Northeast China in the Near Future, which put forward 35 policies to accelerate the revitalization of northeast China. During this period, the government formulated and implemented a series of policies to revitalize the northeast old industrial bases, including policies about fundamental facilities and treasury bonds investment, fiscal and tax policies, financial policies, policies about state-owned-enterprises reform, social security, qualified technical personnel, subsidence area controlling and other aspects. The relevant ministries also introduced a number of supporting policies and measures to revitalize the northeast old industrial bases.

First is fiscal policies. In 2004, Heilongjiang Province and Jilin Province, the first two pilots, were exempt from agriculture tax. Then the Rural Tax-fee Reform was practiced in the three northeast provinces with a series of policies such as transfer payment, direct grain subsidy and subsidy for growing superior crop varieties; in 2014, a new bonus was given to major grain producing areas according to the amount of food commodities. Meanwhile, more fund and subsidies were also given to projects building terminal arterial highways and projects of alpine areas in Northeast China.

Second is tax policies. For mining enterprises which are in the period of exploitation depletion and low-abundance oilfield development projects, the resource tax standard shall be lowered within a range of not more than 30%; for industrial restructuring projects in the Northeast, interest subsidies shall be provided, and the scope of value-added tax (VAT) deduction for old industrial bases shall be expanded—the VAT included in the newly purchased machinery and equipment was allowed to be deducted, for the equipment manufacturing, petrochemical, metallurgy, shipbuilding, automobile, agricultural product processing, military and high-tech product manufacturers; the historical tax owed by the enterprises of the old industrial bases in Northeast China before December 31, 1997 were all exempted; tax reform measures in line with the tax policy direction were first practiced in Northeast China.

Third is investment policies. The subsidy standards for the three northeastern provinces shall be the same as that for the western region, when arranging central budgetary investments in infrastructure, ecological construction, environmental protection, poverty alleviation and development, and social undertakings; central budgetary investment shall provide necessary support for major equipment research and design of old industrial bases in Northeast China such as providing funding for urban heating, water supply and other pipe network facilities renovation, infrastructure construction, water conservancy construction, rural road construction, and coal mining subsidence area management; special projects shall be established for adjustment and transformation and restructuring of key industries in Northeast and other old industrial bases by offering national debt fund to these adjusting and transforming enterprises; special projects of high-tech industrial development for the revitalization of the old industrial bases in Northeast China shall be established and supported.

Fourth is policies to deepen the reform. After *Guiding Opinions on the Pilot Work of the Large-scale Collective Reform of the Factory in Northeast China* was issued, Northeast China took the lead in launching the pilot reform of the collective reform of the factory. The Northeast region was allowed to use the equity transfer income of state-owned enterprises and state-owned capital operating income to pay for the necessary reform costs; the policy closure and bankruptcy of state-owned enterprises in Northeast China shall be encouraged; the central government shall free the enterprises directly under the central government from performing social functions, and provide certain financial subsidies; the pilot reform of private economy development in the northeast region shall be supported, and Liaoning Province shall carry out the pilot reform to streamline the administration and delegate power in the investment field; collaborative innovation reform trial shall be conducted among enterprises, educational institutions, research institutes and users in the northeast region.

Fifth is livelihood policies. The northeast region shall be the pilot to complete the transformation of resource-exhausted cities; the social security pilot will be extended from Liaoning to Heilongjiang and Jilin, and financial subsidies would be given to integrate and guarantee the social security of the three provinces; more favorable employment and re-employment policy would be implemented to the northeast region, focusing on the re-employment of laid-off and unemployed people in resource-exhausted cities, independent mining areas, the military, and the coal, metallurgical and forestry industries; the scale of bond issuance shall be expanded in the shantytown renovation project in Northeast China, the National Development Bank shall provide the projects with capital bridge loans (soft loan recovery and refinancing) for shantytown renovation with the same standard as that in the western region.

[Column 1-12]
Documents on the Revitalization of Northeast China
I. Programmatic and comprehensive documents to promote revitalization

- *Several Opinions of the Central Committee of the Communist Party of China and the State Council on the Implementation of Revitalization Strategy of the Old Industrial Bases Including Northeast China (2003)*
- *Opinions of the General Office of the State Council on Implementing the Promotion of Further Opening-up of the Old Industrial Bases in Northeast China (2005)*
- *Several Opinions of the State Council on Accelerating the Revitalization of the Equipment Manufacturing Industry (2006)*
- *Several Opinions of the State Council on Promoting the Sustainable Development of Resource-dependent Cities (2007)*
- *Several Opinions of the State Council on Further Implementing the Strategy of Revitalizing the Old Industrial Bases Including Northeast China (2009)*
- *Official Reply of the State Council on the Revitalization Plan of the Northeast Region (2007)*
- *Official Reply of the State Council on the 12th Five-Year Plan for the Revitalization of Northeast China (2012)*
- *Official Reply of the State Council on the Adjustment and Reconstruction Plan (2013–2022) of the National Old Industrial Bases (2013)*
- *Notice of the State Council on Issuing the Sustainable Development Plan (2013–2020) of Resource-dependent Cities Nationwide (2013)*
- *Opinions of the State Council on Major Policy Measures for Supporting the Revival of Northeast China in the Near Future (2014).*

II. Documents on deepening the reform of systems and mechanisms to solve the problems left over from the history of old industrial bases
1. To free enterprises from performing social functions

- *Notice of the General Office of the State Council on Relevant Issues Concerning the Pilot Work of the Separation of Social Functions of Central Enterprises (2004)*
- *Notice of the General Office of the State Council on Relevant Issues Concerning the Pilot Work of the Separation of Social Functions of the Second Batch of Central Enterprises (2005)*
- *Official Reply of the State Council on Guiding Opinions on the Agreement of the Pilot Work of the Large-scale Collective Reform of the Factory in Northeast China (2005)*

2. Policy-mandated closures or bankruptcies of state-owned enterprises (SOEs)

- *Notice of the General Office of the State Council on Forwarding the Guiding Opinions of the State-owned Assets Supervisory and Administration Commission (SASAC) on Accelerating the Adjustment and Restructure of Central Enterprises in Northeast China (2004)*

3. To lighten the burden on enterprises

- *Notice of the Ministry of Finance and the State Administration of Taxation on Issuing the Provisions on Expanding the Scope of Value-Added Tax Deduction in the Northeast Region (2004)*
- *Urgent Notice of the Ministry of Finance and the State Administration of Taxation on Further Implementing the Policy of Expanding the VAT Deduction Scope in Northeast China (2004)*
- *Notice of the Ministry of Finance and the State Administration of Taxation on the Exemption of the Historically Unpaid Taxes of Enterprises in the Northeast Old Industrial Base (2006)*
- *Notice of the Ministry of Finance and the State Administration of Taxation on Implementing the Enterprise Income Tax Preferential Policies for Revitalizing the Northeast Old Industrial Base (2004)*
- *Notice of the Ministry of Finance and the State Administration of Taxation on Adjusting the Amount of the Resource Taxes of Some Mine Oilfield Enterprises in the Northeast Old Industrial Base (2004)*

III. On the Adjusting and Upgrading of the Industrial Structure

- *Notice of the Ministry of Science and Technology on Issuing the Science and Technology Action Plan for Revitalizing the Northeast Old Industrial Base (2004)*
- *Notice of the National Development and Reform Commission and the Office for the Promotion of the Northeast of the State Council on Issuing the Guiding Opinions on Developing High-Tech Industries to Promote the Revitalization of Old Industrial Bases in Northeast China (2005)*
- *Notice of the Ministry of Land and Resources and Office for the Promotion of the Northeast of the State Council on Issuing Policy and Measures on Mineral Resources of Old Industrial Bases in Northeast China (2005)*
- *Notice of the National Development and Reform Commission and the National Tourism Administration on Issuing the Plan of Tourism Development in Northeast China (2010)*

- *Notice of the General Office of the State Council Forwarding the Guiding Opinions of the Ministry of Agriculture of the Ministry of Development and Reform on Accelerating the Transformation of Agricultural Development Mode in Northeast China to Build Modern Agriculture (2010)*
- *Notice of the National Development and Reform Commission on Issuing the Development Plan of Logistics Industry in Northeast China (2011)*

IV. On Guaranteeing and Improving People's Livelihood

- *Reply of the State Council on Approval of the Pilot Implementation Plan for Urban Social Security System in Liaoning Province (2001)*
- *Notice of the General Office of the Central Committee of the Communist Party of China on Issuing the Implementation Opinions of the Central Committee on Revitalizing the Old Industrial Bases in Northeast China and Strengthening the Construction of Talent Teams in Northeast China (2004)*
- *Opinions of the Ministry of Construction on Opinions of the Central Committee of the Communist Party of China and the State Council on Implementing the Strategy for Revitalizing Old Industrial Bases including Northeast China (2004)*
- *Notice of the Ministry of Construction on Issuing the Guiding Opinions on Promoting the Renovation of the Shanty Towns in Northeast China (2005)*
- *Notice of the Ministry of Human Resources and Social Security, the Ministry of Education, the Ministry of Finance and the National Development and Reform Commission on Issuing the Guiding Opinions on Promoting the Reform and Innovation of Vocational Education in the Northeast Region (2011)*

Source Extracted from *Compilation of Policy Documents for Revitalizing Old Industrial Bases in Liaoning Province (2003–2012)*, pp. 1–5.

2.2.2 The Implementation Scope of the Revitalization Strategy of Northeast China and Other Old Industrial Bases

It is written in *Several Opinions of the Central Committee of the Communist Party of China and the State Council on the Implementation of Revitalization Strategy of the Old Industrial Bases Including Northeast China* that, "Revitalizing the old industrial base is a very arduous task. It is necessary to make overall plans and implement them step by step. The current focus is to do a good job in the adjustment and transformation of the old industrial bases in Northeast China. The old industrial cities in the central region should give full play to their own advantages and accelerate development. When conditions are ripe, appropriate support will be given in accordance with the relevant policies of the old industrial bases in Northeast China. Those in the western region should make full use of the western development policy to achieve revitalization. Those in the eastern region should make full use of the policy environment of opening up to the outside world and continue to give full play to the advantages of local economic strength". The old industrial bases in Northeast China are the major targets of old industrial base revitalization.

The old industrial bases in Northeast China, with a total population of about 120 million people, has a total area of 1.453 million Square kilometers, including the three northeastern provinces (Liaoning Province, Jilin Province, Heilongjiang Province) and the Five Leagues and Cities in the eastern part of Inner Mongolia Autonomous Region (Hulunbuir City, Xing'an League, Tongliao City, Chifeng City and Xilin Gol League, referred to as Mengdong Area). Northeastern region is a key heavy industrial base of New China—during the "First Five-Year Plan" period, 58 of the "156" items, namely more than 1/3, were targeted to the Northeast; during the "Second Five-year Plan" period, the state continued to invest and concentrated on building strategic industries and key enterprises based on energy, raw materials, equipment manufacturing and national defense in the northeast, and has made significant contributions to the formation of an independent and complete industrial system and national economic system, and to Reform and Opening up as well as the construction of modernization. Until now, the old industrial bases in Northeast China have gathered a large number of key enterprises in China, and continue to play a supporting role in major technical equipment and defense-related science and technology industries. In August 2007, the State Council officially approved the *Northeast Region Revitalization Plan*, which proposed to accelerate the Reform and Opening-up, speed up structural adjustment and upgrading, focus on improving independent innovation capabilities, promote industrial structure optimization and upgrading, accelerate regional cooperation, economic transition of resource-exhausted cities, the construction of resource-conserving and environment-friendly society, and the development of various social undertakings such as education, health, culture and sports. After 10–15 years of hard work, the Northeast region will be built into a major economic development region with a relatively complete system and mechanism, a relatively rational industrial structure, a harmonious society and a comprehensively prosperous economy. By then, cities and towns will develop compatibility with each other, so will different regions, and resource-based cities will develop soundly. The revitalization of the Northeast Region will be achieved comprehensively because different bases will be settled here including an internationally competitive equipment manufacturing base, a national new raw material and energy security base, a national important commodity grain and husbandry production base, an important national technology research, development and innovation base, and an important national ecological security zone.

In addition to the northeastern region, there are also some old industrial bases in the mid-west region and the eastern region. With the significant progress in the adjustment and transformation of the old industrial bases in Northeast China, and drawing on the experience of revitalizing the Northeast, the adjustment and transformation of old industrial bases in other regions has gradually been put on the agenda. In January 2007, the General Office of the State Council issued the *Notice of the General Office of the State Council on the Entitled Cities in Central China to Refer to Policies of Revitalizing Old Industrial Bases including Northeastern China and the Western Development Strategy*, which says to implement the measures for the 26 old industrial cities in the six central provinces according to part of the policy of the old industrial bases in Northeast China.

In 2013, the State Council approved the *National Old Industrial Base Adjustment and Reconstruction Plan (2013–2022)*, which for the first time clarified 120 old industrial cities across the country, and called for the overall adjustment of the old industrial bases in the country. The old industrial bases in Northeast China and the old industrial cities across the country together constitute the implementation scope of the revitalization strategy of the old industrial bases including Northeast China (see Table 4).

2.3 The Strategy of the Rise of Central China

Central China includes Shanxi, Anhui, Jiangxi, Henan, Hubei and Hunan provinces, covering an area of 1.028 million square kilometers, accounting for 10.7% of China's total land area. At the end of 2010, the total population was about 360 million, accounting for nearly 27% of the whole country. It is located in the heartland of China with a large population and rich natural, cultural and tourism resources, boasting a solid

Table 4 The scope of the national old industrial bases

Prefectural cities (95 in total)
Hebei Province (6): Zhangjiakou, Tangshan, Baoding, Xingtai, Handan, Chengde
Shanxi Province (5): Datong, Yangquan, Changzhi, Jinzhong, Linfen
Inner Mongolia Autonomous Region (2): Baotou, Chifeng
Liaoning Province (11): Anshan, Fushun, Benxi, Jinzhou, Yingkou, Fuxin, Liaoyang, Tieling, Chaoyang, Panjin, Huludao
Jilin Province (6): Jilin, Siping, Liaoyuan, Tonghua, Baishan, Baicheng
Heilongjiang Province (6): Qiqihar, Mudanjiang, Jiamusi, Daqing, Jixi, Yichun
Jiangsu Province (3): Xuzhou, Changzhou, Zhenjiang
Anhui Province (6): Huaibei, Handan, Huainan, Wuhu, Maanshan, Anqing
Jiangxi Province (3): Jiujiang, Jingdezhen, Pingxiang
Shandong Province (2): Zibo, Zaozhuang
Henan Province (8): Kaifeng, Luoyang, Pingdingshan, Anyang, Hebi, Xinxiang, Jiaozuo, Nanyang
Hubei Province (6): Huangshi, Fuyang, Jingzhou, Yichang, Shiyan, Jingmen
Hunan Province (6): Zhuzhou, Xiangtan, Hengyang, Yueyang, Shaoyang, Loudi
Guangdong Province (2): Shaoguan, Maoming
Guangxi Zhuang Autonomous Region (2): Liuzhou, Guilin
Sichuan Province (8): Zigong, Panzhihua, Luzhou, Deyang, Mianyang, Neijiang, Leshan, Yibin
Guizhou Province (3): Zunyi, Anshun, Liupanshui
Shaanxi Province (4): Baoji, Xianyang, Tongchuan, Hanzhong
Gansu Province (4): Tianshui, Jiayuguan, Jinchang, Baiyin
Ningxia Hui Autonomous Region (1): Shizuishan
Xinjiang Uygur Autonomous Region (1): Karamay
Municipal jurisdictions, cities with separate plans, and municipal districts of provincial capitals (25 in total)
Shijingshan District of Beijing, Tanggu District of Tianjin, Minhang District of Shanghai, Dadukou District of Chongqing, Chang'an District of Shijiazhuang City, Wanbailin District of Taiyuan City, Dadong District of Shenyang City, Wafangdian City of Dalian, Kuancheng District of Changchun City, Harbin Xiangfang District, Nanjing Yuandachang District, Hefei Yaohai District, Nanchang Qingyunpu District, Jinan Licheng District, Zhengzhou Zhongyuan District, Wuhan Qiaokou District, Changsha Kaifu District, Chengdu Qingbaijiang District, Guiyang City Xiaohe District, Wuhua District of Kunming City, Baqiao District of Xi'an City, Qilihe District of Lanzhou City, Chengzhong District of Xining City, Xixia District of Yinchuan City, Toutunhe District of Urumqi City

Source Extracted from *Notice of the National Development and Reform Commission on Issuing the National Old Industrial Base Adjustment and Reconstruction Plan (2013–2022)*, April 2013

foundation of science and education and convenient access to water, land and air transportation. Its geographical advantages enable the region to link other parts of China. It is an important base in China of agricultural products, energy, raw materials and equipment manufacturing, with obvious advantages in agricultural production, especially in grain production, and a complete range of industries, a good ecological environment and a strong bearing capacity.[7]

In January 2004, the Central Economic Work Conference made it clear for the first time to promote the rise of Central China; in April 2006, the Central Committee of the Communist Party of China and the State Council issued *Several Opinions of the Central Committee of the Communist Party of China on Promoting the Rise of the Central Region* which proposed to build the central region into a national important base of grain production, energy and raw materials, modern equipment manufacturing and high-tech industries, and a comprehensive transportation hub (the "Three Bases and One Hub"); in May of the same year, the General Office of the State Council issued *Notice of the General Office of the State Council on Implementing Policies and Measures of the CPC Central Committee and the State Council on Promoting the Rise of Central China*, putting forward 56 policy measures towards speeding up the construction of the national important grain production base, energy raw materials base and modern equipment manufacturing and high-tech industry base, improving status of the transport hub, promoting the development of urban agglomerations and counties, opening wider to both home and foreign countries, accelerating system and mechanism innovation, advancing the development of social programs, and strengthening resource conservation and ecological and environmental protection.

After that, in September 2009, the State Council passed the *Plan for Promoting the Rise of Central China*, and in 2012, the State Council issued *Several Opinions of the State Council on Vigorously Implementing the Strategy of Promoting the Rise of Central China*, both of which made the policy "Promote the Rise of Central China" clear.

[Column 1-13]

Outline of *Approval of the State Council on the Plan for Promoting the Rise of Central China* (the "Plan")

In China, the central region is an important base for grain production, energy production, modern equipment manufacturing and high-tech industries and a comprehensive transportation hub, which plays an

[7] Fan Hengshan: *Study on Major Policies on Promoting the Rise of Central China*, People's Publishing House, 2011, p. 1.

important role in the national economic and social development. The next five to ten years will be a crucial period for the central region to give full play to its advantages, achieve breakthroughs and accelerate its rise. The formulation and implementation of the *Plan* will help it counter the international financial crisis, tap the development potential of the central region, bring into full play its comparative advantages, accelerate its development and strengthen its support for national development.

The government should focus on reform and opening up, innovate institutions and mechanisms, transform the pattern of development, and enhance the overall strength and competitiveness of the economy; focus on independent innovation, adjust and optimize the economic structure, actively transfer industries, and vigorously promote a new type of industrialization; focus on optimizing the spatial layout, foster growth poles in urban agglomerations, strengthen counties and central towns, and actively yet prudently promote urbanization; focus on strengthening the foundation of agriculture, improve rural landscapes, accelerate agricultural modernization, and promote integrated development between urban and rural areas; and focus on developing a circular economy, conserve resources and energy, protect the ecological environment, and promote regional sustainable development; focus on improving people's well-being, increase employment, promote social harmony, leverage the advantages of linking the east with the west and developing industries, and achieve comprehensive, coordinated and sustainable economic and social development in the central region.

Source *Approval of the State Council on the Plan for Promoting the Rise of Central China*, October 26, 2009.

The first is to be sure that the 26 old industrial base cities in the central region are covered by policies of the Northeastern China Revitalization Strategy in aspects of deepening the reform of state-owned enterprises, accelerating technological progress, strengthening the construction of enterprise-focused technological innovation systems, promoting industrial restructuring, and improving the social security system (see Table 5). In addition, it needs to ensure that the 243 underdeveloped counties (cities, districts) in the central region refer to policies of the "Western Development Strategy" in improving rural production and living conditions, increasing fiscal transfer payments, enhancing basic public services, accelerating poverty alleviation and development, developing characteristic industries, and promoting commerce and trade (see Table 6).

Table 5 Cities in the six provinces of Central China which refer to policies of the "Northeastern China Revitalization Strategy"

Province	*Cities (26)*
Shanxi Province	Taiyuan, Datong, Yangquan, Changzhi
Anhui Province	Hefei, Ma'anshan, Bengbu, Wuhu, Huainan
Jiangxi Province	Nanchang, Pingxiang, Jingdezhen, Jiujiang
Henan Province	Zhengzhou, Luoyang, Jiaozuo, Pingdingshan, Kaifeng
Hubei Province	Wuhan, Huangshi, Xiangyang, Shiyan
Hunan Province	Changsha, Zhuzhou, Xiangtan, Hengyang

Source Extracted from *Notice of the General Office of the State Council on the Entitled Cities in Central China to Refer to Policies of Revitalizing Old Industrial Bases including Northeastern China and the Western Development Strategy*, 2007

Table 6 Counties (cities, districts) in the six provinces of Central China which refer to the policies of the "Western Development Strategy"

Province	*243 counties (cities, districts)*
Shanxi Province	50 in total: Yangqu County, Loufan County, Yanggao County, Tianzhen County, Guangling County, Lingqiu County, Hunyuan County, Datong County, Pingshun County, Huguan County, Wuxiang County, Qin County, Qinyuan County, Lingchuan County, Yushe County, Zuoquan County, Heshun County, Xiyang County, Wanrong County, Wenxi County, Xinjiang County, Lishi District, Yuanqu County, Xia County, Pinglu County, Wutai County, Dai County, Fanshi County, Ningwu County, Jingle County, Xinfu District, Hequ County, Baode County, Pianguan County, Pinglu District, Yuanping City, Gu County, Fushan City, Xiangning County, Fenxi County, Wenshui County, Jiaocheng County, Xing County, Lin County, Liulin County, Shilou County, Lan County, Fangshan County, Zhongyang County and Jiaokou County
Anhui Province	30 in total: Changfeng County, Huaiyuan County, Zongyang County, Qianshan County, Taihu County, Susong County, Wangjiang County, Yuexi County, Dingyuan County, Linquan County, Taihe County, Funan County, Yingshang County, Jieshou City, Dangshan County, Xiao County, Lingbi County, Si County, Wuwei County, Shou County, Huoqiu County, Shucheng County, Jinzhai County, Huoshan County, Yu'an District, Guoyang County, Lixin County, Shitai County, Langxi County and Jing County
Jiangxi Province	41 in total: Leping City, Lianhua County, Xiushui County, De'an County, Duchang County, Gan County, Shangyou County, Anyuan County, Ningdu County, Yudu County, Xingguo County, Huichang County, Xunwu County, Shicheng County, Ruijin City, Ji'an County, Jishui County, Xiajiang County, Xingan County, Yongfeng County, Taihe County, Suichuan County, Wan'an County, Anfu County, Yongxin County, Jinggangshan City, Wanzai County, Tonggu County, Lichuan County, Nanfeng County, Le'an County, Yihuang County, Zixi County, Guangchang County, Shangrao County, Hengfeng County, Yiyang County, Yugan County, Poyang County, Wannian County, Dexing City

Province	*243 counties (cities, districts)*
Henan Province	54 in total: Qi County, Tongxu County, Lankao County, Luanchuan County, Songxian County, Ruyang County, Yiyang County, Luoning County, Ye County, Lushan County, Jia County, Hua County, Neihuang County, Linzhou City, Yuanyang County, Fengqiu County, Nanle County, Fan County, Taiqian County, Puyang County, Wuyang County, Lushi County, Nanzhao County, Xichuan County, Sheqi County, Tongbai County, Minquan County, Sui County, Ningling County, Zhecheng County, Yucheng County, Xiayi County, Yongcheng City, Luoshan County, Guangshan County, Xin County, Shangcheng County, Gushi County, Huaibin County, Xi County, Fugou County, Shangshui County, Shenqiu County, Dancheng County, Huaiyang County, Taikang County, Luyi County, Shangcai County, Pingyu County, Zhengyang County, Queshan County, Biyang County, Runan County, Xincai County
Hubei Province	28 in total: Yangxin County, Yun County, Yunxi County, Zhushan County, Zhuxi County, Fang County, Danjiangkou City, Yuan'an County, Xingshan County, Zigui County, Changyang Tujia Autonomous County, Wufeng Tujia Autonomous County, Dangyang City, Nanzhang County, Baokang County, Xiaochang County, Dawu County, Jianli County, Honghu City, Tuanfeng County, Hong'an County, Luotian County, Yingshan County, Xishui County, Qichun County, Macheng City, Chongyang County, Tongshan County
Hunan Province	40 in total: Chaling County, Yanling County, Shaoshan City, Hengshan County, Qidong County, Leiyang City, Xinshao County, Shaoyang County, Longhui County, Suining County, Xinning County, Chengbu Miao Autonomous County, Pingjiang County, Li County, Jinshi City, Cili County, Sangzhi County, Nan County, Anhua County, Yuanjiang City, Yongxing County, Rucheng County, Guidong County, Anren County, Qiyang County, Jiangyong County, Ningyuan County, Lanshan County, Xintian County, Jianghua Yao Autonomous County, Yuanling County, Huitong County, Mayang Miao Autonomous County, Xinhuang Dong Autonomous County, Zhijiang Dong Autonomous County, Jingzhou Miao and Dong Autonomous County, Tongdao Dong Autonomous County, Shuangfeng County, Xinhua County, Lengshuijiang City

The second is to promote the construction of the "Three Bases and One Hub" and support the implementation of a large number of major projects in Central China. The focus is to be put on strengthening the production capacity of the main grain producing areas, the construction of energy and raw material bases, the development of competitive emerging manufacturing industries, and the construction of comprehensive transportation systems including railways, highways, trunk roads, shipping, and civil aviation.

The third is to strengthen fiscal and taxation policy support, which includes introducing transfer payment policies targeted at the central region, and increasing support in the adjustment of funding subsidies. The central government has increased the general and special transfer payments to the six central provinces.

The fourth is to carry out a comprehensive reform experiment for the construction of a resource-conserving and environment-friendly society (referred to as "Two-oriented Society") in the Wuhan Urban Circle and the Changsha-Zhuzhou-Xiangtan Urban Agglomeration, and another comprehensive reform experiment on resource-based economic transformation in Shanxi Province.

The fifth is to formulate guidance for promoting the development of urban agglomerations in the central region, to support the development of Wuhan Urban Circle, Urban Agglomerations in Central China, Changsha-Zhuzhou-Xiangtan Urban Agglomeration, Urban Agglomeration surrounding the Poyang Lake and the Taiyuan Urban Circle, and to back up the construction of China's first industrial shift demonstration area of the urban belt along Anhui-Yangtze River.

2.4 Development of Key Economic Zones in Eastern China

With the strongest comprehensive strengths, the eastern coastal areas are the main concentrated areas of China's industry, economy and population. Promoting the transformation and development of the eastern coastal areas is the work that the state has always attached great importance to. In recent years, the state has issued a series of policy documents and plans for key areas in the eastern region to support its accelerated transformation.

2.4.1 Yangtze River Delta

The Yangtze River Delta region includes Shanghai (Municipality), and Jiangsu and Zhejiang provinces with a regional area of 210,700 square kilometers and a permanent resident population of 157.77 million. This region has superior location conditions, excellent natural endowment, strong economic foundation, relatively comprehensive mechanisms, complete urban systems and developed science and education culture, and is one of the regions with the best development foundation, institutional environment and overall competitiveness in China. The region occupies a very important strategic position in the overall modernization. In 2013, the total GDP of the Yangtze River Delta reached 10 trillion yuan, accounting for 17.2% of the country. Regarding Jiangsu, Zhejiang and Shanghai as a single economy, the total GDP in 2014 has ranked in the top ten in the world. It is estimated that by 2015, the per capita GDP of the Yangtze River Delta will reach 82,000 yuan (100,000 yuan in the core areas), the service industry share will reach 48% (50% in the core areas), and the urbanization level will reach 67% (about 70% in the core areas). In 2008, the State Council issued *Guiding Opinions of the State Council on Further Promoting the Reform, Opening Up and Socio-Economic Development of the Yangtze River Delta* which clarified the policy measures to support the development of the Yangtze River Delta.

[Column 1-14]
Outline of *Guiding Opinions of the State Council on Further Promoting the Reform, Opening Up and Socio-Economic Development of the Yangtze River Delta*

With the strongest comprehensive strength in China, the Yangtze River Delta region enjoys an important strategic position in driving socialist modernization.

Further promoting the reform, opening up and socio-economic development of the Yangtze River Delta region can help promote regional economic integration, independent innovation capability and overall economic quality; can help exert its demonstration role in the central and western regions, thus promoting the coordinated development among all of China's regions; can help improve our open economy, international competitiveness and anti-risk capability; can help promote institutional innovation and build a more vibrant, efficient and more open system.

We should further emancipate our minds, advance with the times, deepen reform and open our door wider. We should focus on promoting the strategic adjustment of our economic structure, enhancing independent innovation capability, promoting the coordinated development among urban and rural areas and regions, promoting resource conservation and environmental protection, and boosting social harmony and spiritual civilization.

We aim to achieve the scientific, harmonious, initiative and integrated development of the Yangtze River Delta region and build it into an important international gateway in the Asia-Pacific region, an important global advanced manufacturing base and a world-class city cluster with relatively strong international competitiveness. Therefore, the region will contribute more to the building of a moderately prosperous society in all aspects and modernization drive.

Source Extracted from *Guiding Opinions of the State Council on Further Promoting the Reform, Opening Up and Socio-economic Development of the Yangtze River Delta*, September 2008.

In 2010, *Approval from the State Council on the Regional Planning of the Yangtze River Delta* further clarified that the Yangtze River Delta includes Shanghai Municipality, and Jiangsu and Zhejiang provinces, with 16 cities as the core area, i.e. Nanjing, Suzhou, Wuxi, Changzhou, Zhenjiang, Yangzhou, Taizhou and Nantong of Jiangsu Province, Hangzhou, Ningbo, Huzhou, Jiaxing, Shaoxing, Zhoushan and Taizhou of Zhejiang Province, and Shanghai. The overall layout framework of "one core and nine belts" in the Yangtze River Delta region was clearly put forward and the development directions of "one core" and "nine belts" were separately defined. To be specific, Shanghai, as the core, should give full play to its role as an international economic, financial, trading and shipping center, make use of the overall regional advantages and enhance the international competitiveness; Shanghai-Nanjing and Shanghai-Hangzhou-Ningbo Development Belt should build itself into a high-tech industrial belt, a belt intensive with modern service industries and a belt clustered with urban areas of a relatively high international level that serves the Yangtze River Delta region and even the whole country; as for the Development Belt along the Yangtze River, it should develop itself into an urban agglomeration belt and a basic industrial development belt with distinctive features, reasonable layout and good ecology, thus growing into a core part of the Yangtze River industrial belt; for the Development Belt along the Hangzhou Bay, we should build a modern manufacturing-intensive belt and an urban agglomeration belt featured by clear division of labor, reasonable layout and coordinated function so as to promote the all-round development of the southern part of the Yangtze River Delta; for the Development Belt along the sea, we should foster emerging port industries and marine economic development belt that are in harmony with ecological protection and with the ability to drive the economic development of northern Jiangsu and southwestern Zhejiang; for the Development Belt along Ningbo, Huzhou and Hangzhou of Zhejiang Province, we should develop a new development belt with gathered ecological industries and well-organized urban development, thus driving the development of the central and western regions; as for the Development Belt surrounding the Taihu Lake, we should develop it into China's important tourism and leisure belt, regional exhibition center and research and development base; for the Development Belt along the East Longhai Railway, we should foster a resource-processing industrial base so as to develop northern Jiangsu and drive the economic development of regions along Longhai Railway and Lanxin Railway; for the Development Belt along the Grand Canal, we should build an ecological industrial corridor with distinct canal culture; for the Development Belt along Wenzhou, Lishui, Jinhua and Quzhou of Zhejiang Province, we should grow it into a belt connecting the Yangtze River Delta region and the Western Taiwan Straits Economic Zone. At the same time, the *Regional Planning of the Yangtze River Delta* also clarifies specific requirements for strengthening interaction and cooperation and promoting coordinated development among the surrounding areas of the Yangtze River Delta region, especially the Pan-Yangtze River Delta region.

China has also clarified the development direction, targets, tasks and specific measures of the eight key areas in the Yangtze River Delta region. In terms of urban development and urban–rural integration, the government proposed that we should remain committed to a new urbanization path. We should take Shanghai as the core and improve the functions of regional central cities such as Nanjing and Hangzhou, enhance the strength of other important cities, encourage the development of small and medium-sized cities and towns, regulate the population layout of cities and towns, and promote urban and rural integration. By doing so, we can establish a complete urban system and a world-class city cluster with strong international competitiveness. In terms of industrial development and layout, the government put forward that we should give priority to the modern service industry, perfect advanced manufacturing industries such as electronic information, equipment manufacturing, steel and petrochemical industries, move faster to develop emerging industries such as biomedicine, new materials, new energy and civil aviation and aerospace, and consolidate and upgrade traditional industries such as agriculture, textiles and clothing. We aim to foster a batch of world-class enterprises and brands with international competitiveness, upgrade the industrial structure, and build the Yangtze River Delta region into an important global modern service industry center and advanced manufacturing base. In terms of independent innovation and innovative regional development, the government put forward that we should take key areas and core technological innovations as breakthroughs, strengthen the position of enterprises as innovators, improve regional science and technology innovation platforms, create a policy environment conducive to independent innovation, and enhance independent innovation capability. Therefore, we can form an internationally competitive regional innovation system with complementary advantages, resource sharing, and mutual benefit and take the lead in building an innovative region in China.

In terms of infrastructure construction and layout, we will focus on the construction of eight major transportation corridors, i.e. Shanghai-Nanjing line, Shanghai-Hangzhou line, the line along the Yangtze River, the line along the coast, Ningbo-Huzhou-Hangzhou line, Hangzhou-Ningbo line, East Longhai Railway and southwestern Zhejiang line. We will also strengthen the construction of national and regional comprehensive transportation hubs to efficiently connect all means of transportation. Meanwhile, the government has come up with projects to build infrastructure such as coal, oil and gas, electric power and new energy and deployed the construction of water infrastructure and information infrastructure. In terms of resource utilization and the protection of ecological environment, our focus is to use land more economically and intensively, strengthen environmental protection and ecological construction, and comprehensively improve regional sustainability. Particular emphasis was given to the implementation of the most stringent farmland protection system so as to use construction land more efficiently, safeguard ecological land and optimize land resource allocation. We should also strengthen the protection of drinking water sources, strengthen the prevention and treatment of water pollution and air pollution, and carry out comprehensive environmental improvement in rural areas. Therefore, a "three vertical and two horizontal" ecological network can be established, with land bridge and the Yangtze River as two horizontal axes, the line along China's coast, Beijing–Harbin Railway, Beijing–Guangzhou Railway and Baotou–Kunming Railway as three vertical axes. In terms of social undertakings and public services, the government stressed that we should focus on improving people's livelihood, highlight key areas, break through weak links and focus on developing education, health, culture and other social undertakings. Also, we should accelerate the improvement of the employment system and social security system and strengthen the services and management of migrant population. Our aim is to take the lead in establishing a social security system covering urban and rural areas and promote the equalization of basic public services. In terms of institutional reform and innovation, the government proposed that we should let Shanghai's Pudong New Area play an exemplary role in comprehensive supporting reforms, promote reforms in key areas and links, re-create new institutional advantages at a new higher starting point and take the lead in establishing and improving the socialist market economy system. We should focus on the reform of the administrative management system and state-owned enterprises, develop the non-public economy, accelerate the development of market system, carry out major reform experiments and strengthen the construction of a legal environment, thus forming an institutional mechanism that is conducive to scientific and harmonious development. In terms of opening up and cooperation with the outside world, it is proposed that we should make full use of both domestic and international markets and resources, participate in international cooperation and competition in a wider, broader range and at a higher level so as to achieve a new leap in the open economy and develop the Yangtze River Delta region into an important gateway serving the Asia-Pacific region and beyond; we should also accelerate the change in the development mode of foreign trade, improve the quality of foreign investment utilization, implement the "Going Global" strategy of enterprises to make our economy more open; At the same time, we should strengthen the cooperation in the Pan-Yangtze River Delta region, regional cooperation with the Yangtze River Basin as the priority, the cooperation with Hong Kong, Macao and Taiwan and international cooperation.[8]

In the development of the Yangtze River Delta region, Shanghai is the core while Shanghai Pudong New Area is the pioneer. In June 2005, the executive meeting of the State Council approved the comprehensive supporting pilot reform in Shanghai Pudong New Area and clarified the overall requirements, i.e. taking the lead in establishing a socialist

[8]Fan Hengshan: *The Action Plan to Take the Lead in Achieving Modernization—On Regional Planning in the Yangtze River Delta Region, China Economic Herald*, 5th Edition, July 20, 2010.

market economy system, and focusing on transforming government functions, economic operating mode and urban–rural dual economic and social structure. In the past decade, Pudong New Area has followed the requirement of "what Pudong New Area can break through can also be popularized in Shanghai and be referred to by other parts of China" and successively implemented three three-year action plans in the area and practiced over 200 reform tasks. As a result, Pudong New Area has gained some progress and breakthroughs from something that was first tried and tested in key areas and key links, while Pudong's ability to drive the Yangtze River Delta region has also been enhanced.

[Column 1-15]
The reform exploration of Pudong New Area
First, taking the lead in upgrading from a special area supervised by customs into a free trade zone and establishing China's first free trade pilot zone. Focusing on the cross-border capital operation needs of the headquarter enterprises, Pudong is the first area to explore a series of breakthroughs such as cross-border lending, centralized foreign exchange management, and centralized foreign exchange collection and payment. For the convenience of port entry and exit, the customs of the area took the lead in piloting reforms of classified and paperless customs clearance and promoted the "three-in-one" declaration form of customs, border inspection and inspection and quarantine. Aiming to improve the development environment of the headquarter economy, in 2012, the State Administration of Industry and Commerce launched 18 policy measures to support Shanghai's socio-economic development, including delegating registration and jurisdiction right, and encouraging debt-for-equity swap.

Second, making finance play a larger role in boosting the real economy. In 2006, China Financial Futures Exchange was registered and established in Pudong. In 2010, the National Interbank Market Loan Transfer Trading System was launched in Pudong. In 2012, the Shanghai Equity Custody Trading Center settled in Pudong. In 2010, one of China's first consumer finance companies and Shanghai's first consumer finance company, Bank of China Consumer Finance, Co., Ltd., was listed in Pudong, Shanghai. In 2012, Pudong took the lead in conducting commercial factoring pilots. At the same time, equity investment, venture capital, hedge funds, financial leasing, financing guarantees, and microfinance companies and other emerging financial business forms as well as financial institutions have been gathering at a faster speed, initially establishing an equity investment system covering technology companies at different stages and a bond financing system conforming to the characteristics of technology companies.

Third, encouraging innovation and entrepreneurship. In 2011, Pudong launched "Ten Articles to Encourage Innovation in Zhangjiang", which provided incentives to innovative and entrepreneurial talents through equity incentives, guiding entrepreneurship and investment with state-owned capital, and making entry and exit more convenient. For example, the pilot of equity incentives combined the commercialization of scientific and technological fruits with profit distribution of enterprises, thus enhancing the creativity and motivation of technology and management personnel. A series of measures have been launched to reduce the cost of living for talents. Talent apartments, rent subsidies, double-limited houses (specially supplied houses whose construction sites, buying group, prices and transactions are all limited by the government), incubators, entrepreneurial workshops and other channels have been utilized to lower the housing cost and entrepreneurship threshold of innovative and entrepreneurship talents, especially young talents.

Fourth, breaking the bottleneck of the industrialization of high tech. For example, for the problem that the entry inspection and quarantine mode failed to meet the needs of biomedical R&D enterprises, since 2008, the quality inspection department has launched pilot inspection and quarantine of imported biological materials in Zhangjiang, promoting reforms in six aspects including shortening the examination and approval time, reducing the scope of examination and approval, reducing application materials, and allowing verification in batches. For another example, as for the problem that the heavy tax burden of integrated circuit (IC) design companies in entrusted processing, since 2008, a new model of bonded supervision for integrated circuit has been actively explored. For the IC design enterprise in Zhangjiang Hi-Tech Park, "the self-designed products with independent intellectual property brands that are exported after entrusted processing are regarded as self-produced products that enjoy tax exemption, deduction and reimbursement". In 2011, the entire process of processing from chip design to manufacturing, packaging and testing became bonded. At the same time, in consideration of the demand for industrial parks such as Zhangjiang and Jinqiao to upgrade from manufacturing economy to innovation economy and develop mixed business formats, Pudong New Area piloted the reform of the "secondary exploitation" of land, used the inventory of industrial land to build R&D buildings and increased the plot ratio as planned.

Fifth, deepening the reform of administrative management system. The area explored to establish an administrative system with "Big Department System", "Big Management Committee" and "Big Cities and Towns". Pudong's district government has established 19 departments, which are equivalent to 2/3 of other districts and counties; the number of people in administrative establishment among 10,000 people is 3.8, which is less than half of Shanghai's average. The "Big Management Committee" system was implemented in the development zone. At present, a management pattern of "4 + 3" has been formed in the development zone. Fully authorized by the municipal and district governments, we have basically achieved that the matters of development zone are treated by its own government. The "Big Town" system was explored. The new Chuansha New Town and Zhuqiao Town were established and were given greater management right so as to enhance their ability to coordinate resources and develop independently. We established a new town in Nanhui in Lingang area and carried out the practice of having "two names but one government" with the Lingang Administrative Committee. Thus, we were able to maximize the overall development of Linggang area and promote the integration of industries and the city. After six rounds of reform of the administrative examination and approval system, a comprehensive approval service mechanism for construction projects was established, which separated management and approval and realized "one-stop acceptance, one-door management, one-door settlement" in the administrative service center.

Sixth, vigorously promoting urban and rural coordination. We have promoted the integration of education and management, and strengthened the investment and development of education. As a result, we have unified the funding standards, hardware allocation and information platform for basic education, and provided equal training and development opportunities for teachers. We have promoted the integration of medical and health services and their management system, and uniformly managed human resources, capital and property at the district level in all the community health service centers, thus promoting the synchronous development of medical and health undertakings in urban and rural areas.

Seventh, optimizing the development environment of social organizations. We have worked to establish an ecological chain of social organizations that has foundations at the upstream, supportive hub-type social organizations at the midstream and operational non-profit organizations at the downstream. We have also broadened the living and developing space of social organizations, explored and optimized an effective mechanism for the establishment and development of social organizations, and promoted reforms to simplify the registration procedure of social organizations, the registration management system of industry associations, and the supply model of public services.

Source Extracted from the Evaluation Report of the Shanghai Pudong New Area Comprehensive Supporting Reform Pilot by the Evaluation Team of Renmin University of China, 2013.

2.4.2 Pearl River Delta Region

The Pearl River Delta covers an area of about 56,000 square kilometers. Located in the south-central part of Guangdong Province and the lower reaches of the Pearl River Basin, it is adjacent to Hong Kong and Macao and faces Southeast Asia across the sea. With convenient sea and land transportation, the Pearl River Delta region is known as "China's Southern Gateway". Over more than 30 years of reform and opening up, by taking advantage of its geographical vicinity with Hong Kong and Macao, the region took the lead to establish an export-oriented economic system and become a region with the highest marketization level, the most complete market system and the highest portion of export in its economy throughout China and an important window for China's opening up, which laid a solid foundation for building a world-class manufacturing base here, and became an engine for China's economic and social development.

In 2008, the State Council's reply on the *Outline of the Plan for Reform and Development of the Pearl River Delta (2008–2020)* pointed out that the Pearl River Delta is a region "with the cities of Guangzhou, Shenzhen, Zhuhai, Foshan, Jiangmen, Dongguan, Zhongshan, Huizhou and Zhaoqing as its core and reaches out to the Pan-Pearl River Delta Region". The *Outline* specified to further play the region's leading and exemplary role for the whole country and build an experimental region for exploring the patterns of scientific development, a pilot region for deepening reforms, an important international gateway for expanding the opening-up program, a world-class base for the advanced manufacturing and modern service industries and a major economic center nationwide. Related contents of close cooperation with Hong Kong and Macao should also be included. In 2013, the GDP of the nine prefecture-level cities in the Pearl River Delta region was 4789.7 billion yuan, accounting for 8.4% of the economic aggregate of the Chinese mainland, only second to the Yangtze River Delta metropolitan economic circle and Beijing-Tianjin-Hebei metropolitan economic circle. In 2013, its per capita GDP was 84,563 yuan (over 12,000 US dollars), which has reached the level of moderately developed countries.

[Column 1-16]

Outline of the State Council's reply on the *Outline of the Plan for the Reform and Development of the Pearl River Delta (2008–2020)*

As the pioneer of the reform and opening up and an important economic hub of China, the Pearl River Delta has played a remarkable leading role and had an important strategic status in the overall effort of China to pursue economic and social development and carry on the reform and opening up.

By further emancipating the mind, deepening reform and opening up, stepping up the transformation of economic development pattern as well as improving the comprehensive economic strength, independent innovation capacity and international competitiveness, the region should be built into an experimental region for exploring the patterns of scientific development, a pilot region for further reforms, an important international gateway for expanding the opening-up program, a world-class base for the advanced manufacturing and modern service industries and a major economic center nationwide. The region should continue to take the lead in reform and opening up, and in achieving scientific, harmonious development and modernization, thus further playing its leading and exemplary role in promoting economic development in the Pearl River Delta and Pan-Pearl River Delta Region and closer cooperation between Guangdong, Hong Kong and Macao, maintaining long-term prosperity and stability in Hong Kong and Macao and participating in regional cooperation in the Asia-Pacific region and global economic competition.

Source Extracted from the State Council's Reply on the *Outline of the Plan for the Reform and Development of the Pearl River Delta (2008–2020)*, December 2008.

According to the functional positioning of the Pearl River Delta, the state defined that the spatial deployment of development in the Delta will be optimized. With Guangzhou and Shenzhen as centers and the eastern and western banks of the Pearl River as essential parts, the Pearl River Delta will push forward its regional economic integration, and help its surrounding areas to develop faster. This will bring a new pattern of coordinated development that enables optimal configuration of resource factors and the full play of local advantages. Guangzhou will fully make use of its advantages as a provincial capital, strengthen its role in conglomerating high-end elements, technological innovation, cultural leadership, and comprehensive service, further optimize its functional zoning and industrial layout, and develop itself into the core of the one-hour ride metropolitan area of the Pearl River Delta. Shenzhen will continue to play its role as the window of special economic zones, an experimental field, and a demonstration area, strengthen its functions in research and development and high-end services, solidify its status as a national economic center and a national-level innovative city, and grow into an international city. The eastern bank of the Pearl River mouth, with Shenzhen as the core and Dongguan and Huizhou as major nodes, will optimize the structure of its population, improve the efficiency of land use, raise the levels of comprehensive urban services, facilitate the conglomeration of productive factors and intensive development, strengthen the capabilities of independent innovation and forge a world-class base of the electronics and information industries. The western bank of the Pearl River mouth, with Zhuhai as the center and Foshan, Jiangmen, Zhongshan, and Zhaoqing as the main nodes, will enhance its capabilities of agglomerating population and industries, play a stronger function of assembling productive factors and serving production, optimize its urban system and industrial distribution, and develop a number of internationally competitive industry clusters. The construction of the petrochemical, steel and iron, shipbuilding, and energy production bases in eastern and western Guangdong will be accelerated to form a coastal belt of heavy and chemical industries, and the north of Guangdong will be developed into an accessory base for the advanced manufacturing industries in the Pearl River Delta.

While promoting the overall development of the Pearl River Delta, the state also encouraged a closer cooperation with Hong Kong and Macao, advanced the convergence of major infrastructure, strengthened industrial cooperation, built a quality life circle, and carried out cooperation in education, medical care, social security, culture, emergency management and intellectual property protection. Guangdong has planned the Pan-Pearl River Delta regional cooperation, including the provinces of Guangdong, Guangxi, Hainan, Yunnan, Guizhou, Sichuan, Hunan, Jiangxi and Fujian, as well as the special administrative regions of Hong Kong and Macao ("9 + 2" for short), which has become a new attempt in China's regional cooperation and development.

Shenzhen plays a crucial role in the innovative development of the Pearl River Delta. In recent years, Shenzhen has deepened its reform on the basis of special economic zone development. Substantive steps have been taken in the reform of the administrative management system. It has conducted a series of reform in the large department system, the classification of civil servants, employment system, the administrative examination and approval system, public institutions, and the establishment of new functional areas. Reform in the economic field has been carried out in an orderly way. Qianhai's system and mechanism innovation, commercial registration system reform, and land management system reform have attracted much attention nationwide. Solid progress in social reform has been made by actively innovating systems and mechanisms for social development, deepening reform of social organization and management system, and improving reform in housing, medical care and education. Efforts have been made to improve the cultural system, ecological sector and democracy. All these have provided strong support for the transformation and development of the Pearl River Delta.

[Column 1-17]
Shenzhen's reform exploration
First, build Qianhai Shenzhen-Hong Kong Modern Service Industry Cooperation Zone into "a Special Zone among Special Zones". At the national level, an inter-ministerial joint meeting system for Qianhai construction has been established. In Guangdong, the provincial government has been pushed to delegate a number of provincial economic management authorities. In Shenzhen, "One Regulation and Two Methods" (*Regulations on Qianhai Shenzhen-Hong Kong Modern Service Industry Cooperation Zone*, *Tentative Method for the Administration of Qianhai Shenzhen-Hong Kong Modern Service Industry Cooperation Zone*, and *Tentative Method for the Administration of Qianhaiwan Free Trade Port Area*) were officially issued, a new flexible and efficient operation pattern of centralized management was established and 69 administrative functions, including land planning and investment project management, were authorized to Qianhai. The *Tentative Method for the Administration of Qianhai Cross-Border RMB Loans* has been approved and issued by People's Bank of China at the end of 2012. In addition, institutions including Shenzhen Petrochemical Exchange, Shenzhen Qianhai Financial Assets Exchange, Shenzhen Culture Assets and Equity Exchange, China Emissions Exchange (Shenzhen), Shenzhen Agricultural Products Exchange, Qianhai Equity Exchange, and Shenzhen Insurance Settlement Center have all been settled in Qianhai, achieving the concentrated development of factor trading market. On the basis of Shenzhen-Hong Kong high-level joint meeting and functional working group system, four working groups, including the financial policy group and legal environment group, were jointly established with Hong Kong government departments for policy support. Under the inter-ministerial joint meeting system, a regular communication mechanism has been established with Hong Kong. The establishment of a high-level advisory committee jointly attended by

Shenzhen and Hong Kong members, with nearly 50% of the members from Hong Kong, has formed a regular operation mechanism of high-level and multidisciplinary think tanks.

Second, implement the reform of commercial registration system and activate the market environment. The State Administration of Industry and Commerce issued *Opinions of the State Administration for Industry and Commerce on Supporting Guangdong to Accelerate its Transformation and Upgrading and Building a Happy Guangdong*, clearly supporting Guangdong to carry out pilot reform of commercial registration system in the Shenzhen Special Economic Zone and Hengqin New Area of Zhuhai Special Economic Zone. At present, *Several Regulations on Commercial Registration in the Shenzhen Special Economic Zone*, which was China's first commercial registration law to separate the qualification of business subject from the qualification of business operation, has been officially implemented. The first new business license has also been issued at the same time. The reform of the commercial registration system has greatly lowered the threshold for business registration and the application cost for enterprises, further improving the business environment.

Third, implement the civil servants classification management and appointment system and improve the employment system. In 2010, Shenzhen implemented the reform of the classified management of civil servants in administrative organs. The appointment system was, in an incremental-reform way, implemented for civil servants appointed by the administrative organs after January 1, 2010. In August 2012, *Opinions of Shenzhen Municipal People's Government on Further Deepening the Reform of Classified Management of Civil Servants* was issued to further deepen the reform. The reform of civil servant management system has enhanced the scientific civil servant management, clarified the professional development channel of civil servant, invigorated the employment mechanism of administrative organs, and optimized the human resource allocation and administrative operation mechanism.

Fourth, cultivate social organizations and reform their management system. We have deepened the reform of the registration system and separated government administration from commune management. Taking "the direction must be positive, the step must be steady" as the instruction, the reform of the registration system was promoted step by step and the scope of direct registration was expanded. At present, eight types of social organizations, including industrial and commercial economy, public charity, social welfare, social services, culture and entertainment, science and technology, sports and ecological environment, can be registered in the civil affairs department directly. A dual-track system of social organization registration in the community will be promoted by accelerating the rapid development of community social organizations, and it will play an important role in enhancing community construction, community services and community harmony. Focusing on the innovation of public service system and mechanism and combining with the reform of administrative management system, the Shenzhen government has vigorously cultivated and supported social organizations and transferred part of its social management functions to social organizations, gradually transforming its role from "paddler" to "helmsman". The transfer and delegation of government functions will be accelerated. The boundary between government and social organizations will be clarified and the transfer of government functions and public services will be defined, which is a prerequisite for social organizations to carry on government functions. Since 2009, in combination with the reform of large department system, social organizations have taken over some government work items cut from bureaus, committees and offices. In 2010, *Implementation Plans of Shenzhen City on Promoting the Transfer and Delegation of Government Functions and Work Items* was issued. At present, Shenzhen is preparing the catalogue of government's transferred functions, of services government functional departments purchase from nongovernmental sectors and of social organizations for government's transferred functions, making government function transfer institutionalized and normalized.

Fifth, explore to solve the problem of the reform of land management system in highly urbanized areas. The *Overall Plan on the Reform of Land Management System in Shenzhen City*, which has won the joint approval of the Ministry of Land and Resources and Guangdong provincial government, pointed out the direction for the development and land management system reform, clarified the content of reform and authorized Shenzhen to plan based on land usage, independently formulate land use planning for functional areas and examine and approve construction land. The government has also improved the system of state-owned land property rights, the development of land marketization, the ability to regulate and control land scientifically as well as the legal environment for land management, and has made innovations in the stock land recycling mechanism.

Source Extracted from the evaluation report of the National Information Center Evaluation Team on the Shenzhen Comprehensive Reform Experimental Zone, 2013.

2.4.3 Development of Other Key Economic Areas in the Eastern Region

Tianjin Binhai New Area

Located on the east coast of Tianjin, Tianjin Binhai New Area covers an area of 2270 square kilometers with a coastline of 153 kilometers and a permanent population of 2.6352 million people. Situated at the intersection of the economic belt surrounding the Bohai Sea and Beijing-Tianjin-Hebei metropolis circle, 120 kilometers away from Beijing, it has a spacious hinterland which reaches out to 12 provinces and cities in Northwest China, North China and Northeast China. It has a comprehensive port with the world's top five cargo handling capacity. The port connects more than 400 harbors worldwide, making it an important gateway for landlocked countries in Central Asia. The Area also has the largest air cargo airport in North China that connects over 30 world-renowned cities at home and abroad, making it an important transportation hub.

In 2005, the Eleventh Five-Year Plan put forward requirements for accelerating the development and opening up of Tianjin and the development of Tianjin Binhai New Area. In 2006, the State Council approved Tianjin Binhai New Area as a comprehensive reform pilot area. In November 2009, the State Council formally approved the administrative system reform plan of Binhai New Area and canceled Tanggu District, Hangu District and Dagang District of Tianjin, whose administrative region is now under Binhai New Area. According to the State Council, the functional positioning of Binhai New Area is that it should rely on the Beijing-Tianjin-Hebei Region, serve the Bohai Sea zone, reach out to "the Three Norths" and face Northeast Asia, striving to become a gateway for North China to open up to the outside world, a high-level modern manufacturing and R&D commercialization base, a northern international shipping center and logistics center, and gradually become a new habitable ecological district with prosperous economy, harmonious society and beautiful environment.

According to the approval of the State Council, Binhai New Area will be developed into an overall layout of "one city, two ports and nine zones". "One city" refers to the core urban area of Binhai New Area, "two ports" the southern and the northern port area, and "nine zones" the nine industrial functional zones. Each functional zone concentrates on 3–4 leading industries and strives to form industrial plates of "port in the east, high-tech in the west, heavy chemical industry in the south, tourism in the north and services in the middle". The modern port logistics industry in the east will focus on international transit, international distribution, international procurement, international entrepot trade and export processing to build the first free port in Chinese mainland. The advanced manufacturing sector in the west will highlight strategic emerging industries such as biomedicine, new energy and new materials to build a hi-tech industries center and a leading independent innovation area. The heavy chemical and heavy equipment sector in the south will stress on the development of the petrochemical, modern metallurgy, shipbuilding, offshore engineering equipment and high-speed locomotives industries to build a world-class heavy chemical industry and heavy equipment manufacturing base. The northern leisure tourism sector will emphasize on the coastal tourism, headquarters economy, business exhibition, service outsourcing, cultural creativity and high-tech ecological industries. The financial services sector in the middle will develop modern service industries such as modern finance, modern commerce and high-end commerce and build the largest financial service area in the world.

Since 2008, Tianjin has seized the strategic opportunity for the development and opening up of Binhai New Area, implemented the linkage development strategy of "Binhai New Area takes the lead, the central city improves comprehensively and each district and county accelerate its development", improved the reform working mechanism of "department cooperation and linkage between superior and subordinate", carried out reform in finance, foreign affairs, science and technology, land and administration, broken the constraints of traditional systems, accelerated the transformation of development pattern and upgraded industrial structure, thus gradually forming the leading role and regional service function of Binhai New Area.

[Column 1-18]
Exploration on the reform of Binhai New Area in Tianjin

First, we have innovated the financial service system. We have initially established a diversified financial service system based on traditional finance such as banking, insurance, trust and securities and backed by modern finance such as financial leasing, consumer finance, monetary economy and foreign currency exchange. We have taken the lead in developing new business such as commercial factoring and guaranteed housing fund supporting bills, and have set up the first Internet Securities Fund in China. We have deepened foreign exchange reform and innovation, and have actively carried out pilot projects such as using RMB as the settlement currency in cross-border trade and conducting the willingness settlement of foreign exchange capital of foreign-funded enterprises. We have developed Techfin by initially establishing a financing model combining financial allocation, loan discount and equity investment, and building a comprehensive service system supported by financing supermarkets, franchised institutions and innovative financial products. We have developed shipping finance by supporting banks to set up shipping financial centers and supporting financial leasing companies specializing in the import and export leasing of planes, ships and other products, and we have taken the lead in developing single-plane or single-ship leasing Special Purpose Vehicles (SPVs) and bonded leasing business in China.

Second, we have further strengthened development and opening up. We have established China (Tianjin) Pilot Free Trade Zone and formulated the *Pilot Plan for Innovation of International Ship Registration System in Dongjiang Free Trade Port Zone of Tianjin*, in which we advocated ship registration, adequate manning, and financial lease of ships to play their roles in pioneering new approaches, and accordingly started pilot projects of international ship registration system and international shipping tax policy. Drawing lessons from international practices, we have explored ways to facilitate the flow of goods, talents, capital and investment. We actively explored innovations in the management system of the Special Control Areas Administration of Customs by implementing innovative measures such as centralized declaration and batch clearance, basically realizing the linkage of the northern and southern regions and 24-hour clearance. The construction of the public information platform of ports and the electronization of all ports have been carried out comprehensively, realizing the informationized management of customs clearance; Tianjin Customs District of P.R. China has carried out the "territorial declaration and port inspection" mode of clearance; the Tianjin Inspection and Quarantine Bureau has innovated its system, improved the on-site inspection module of the "three centralized" system of centralized examination, centralized inspection and centralized transfer, realizing the remote registration of inspection results, real-time release, automatic document preparation and all-weather self-printing; we have also further improved the system of "one employment and separate declaration", fully implemented electronic instruction release, and promoted the pass-through release mode, paperless inspection report, electronic supervision and self-service visa.

Third, we have improved our capacity for independent innovation. We have strengthened joint construction and cooperation with Beijing, especially the Zhongguancun Science Park, and worked hard to promote industry-university-research cooperation. We have completed more than 500 projects linking the achievements of universities and research institutes with enterprises, and successfully promoted the transformation and upgrading of more than 3800 traditional enterprises, by removing institutional obstacles affecting entrepreneurship among teachers and students, transfer of state-owned scientific and technological achievements, and equity incentives.

Fourth, we have innovated the land system. In combination with the fact that there were many projects in the initial stage of Binhai New Area construction and the land demand was large, the flexible land use method of "appropriate concentration in the early stage and corresponding adjustment and reduction in the later stage" have been implemented. Within the total supply of the construction land, the annual land use plan index has been set and the land has been pooled for use according to the project allocation. In the pilot reform of small demonstration towns, the original homestead replaced by the government has been consolidated and reclaimed, so as to provide land for farmers' residential areas with state-owned land. Land for construction purposes other than rural housing has been sold by means of bidding, auction and listing in a market-oriented manner to ensure that cultivated land is not reduced.

Fifth, we have steadily advanced the reform of the administrative system. After abolishing the working committee and management committee of Binhai New Area, and the administrative system of Tanggu, Hangu and Dagang districts, the unified administrative framework of Binhai New Area has been established. We have explored the large department system and established the working mechanism of "affairs of the new district shall be handled in the new district", initially forming a unified administrative examination and approval service system of the whole district. We have set up two administrative licensing service centers at the municipal and district levels, forming a three-level administrative service system. We have built four platforms, which are administrative examination and approval, factor allocation, social services, and efficiency supervision, integrating approval and serving into the first platform for centralized handling, realizing "one-stop" services and real-time electronic supervision.

Sixth, we have steadily advanced the reform of state-owned enterprises and the restructuring of the state-owned economy. We have strengthened and improved the supervision of state-owned assets, improved the corporate governance structure, and formulated seven rules and regulations including the reporting of the board of directors of municipal enterprises and external directors, thus realizing the centralized and unified supervision of state-owned assets under municipal management. We focused state capital on five fields, including strategic emerging industries, high-end service industries, modern manufacturing, national economy and people's livelihood, and urban infrastructure construction and public utilities.

Source Extracted from the *Evaluation Report of the Evaluation Group of Institute of Finance and Banking, Chinese Academy of Social Sciences on the Binhai New Area in Tianjin Comprehensive Reform Pilot Zone*, 2013.

Shandong Peninsula Economic Zone

The Shandong Peninsula Economic Zone covers eight cities with districts including Jinan, Qingdao, Yantai, Zibo, Weifang, Weihai, Dongying and Rizhao, and 22 county-level cities. The sea area is 159,500 square kilometers and the land area is 64,000 square kilometers. In 2011, the State Council approved the *Blue Economic Zone Development Plan of Shandong Peninsula* and defined the overall development framework of "one core, two poles, three belts and three groups". The core area takes Qingdao as the leader, Yantai, Weifang, Weihai and other coastal cities as the backbone, and the Jiaodong Peninsula high-end marine industrial agglomeration area as the core area to build an important national marine high-tech industrial base and a high-end marine industrial agglomeration area with an international advanced level. The high-efficiency eco-marine industrial zone in the Yellow River Delta and the offshore industrial zone in southern Shandong are the important growth poles. The zonal areas such as coastal exploration protection zone, offshore exploration protection zone and high sea exploration protection zone are taken as strategic areas for marine economic development.

[Column 1-19]
Qingdao West Coast New Area

On September 30, 2012, the State Council approved the revocation of Huangdao District and Jiaonan City at the county level and the establishment of a new Huangdao District in Qingdao City. On June 3, 2014, the State Council approved the establishment of the state-level Qingdao West Coast New Area relying on Huangdao District. The Qingdao West Coast New Area has a land area of 2096 square kilometers, a sea area of 5000 square kilometers and a coastline of 282 kilometers. In 2013, the GDP of the region reached 226.6 billion yuan, accounting for 28.3% of Qingdao

City; the GDP of scale industry reached 513.48 billion yuan, accounting for 31.9% of Qingdao City; and the investment in fixed assets reached 122.62 billion yuan, accounting for 24.4% of Qingdao City. According to the approval of the State Council, the mission and requirements of Qingdao West Coast New Area can be summarized as "one theme, two missions and five orientations".

"One theme" is to build the strategic fulcrum of a powerful marine country with the theme of marine economic development.

The "two missions" are to give full play to the two roles of the new zone, which are to play a demonstration role in exploring a new path for the scientific development of national marine economy, and to play a positive role in promoting the economic transformation and development of the eastern coastal areas and in building a powerful marine country.

"Five orientations", namely, building "four districts and one base". We should adhere to scientific and technological guidance, innovative development, give full play to and enlarge the advantages of Qingdao's marine scientific research and industrial base, speed up the construction of marine scientific and technological innovation system and major innovation platform, promote the industrialization of marine scientific and technological achievements, and build independent innovation pilot areas of marine science and technology. We should build deep-sea development and protection bases relying on ports and national ship manufacturing and marine engineering bases, as well as national ship export bases. Through the construction of Guzhenkou Military Port and Aircraft Carrier Base, we will build an internationally renowned naval city and an innovative demonstration zone of civil–military integration. Relying on the bonded port area, Sino-Germany Ecopark, China-Japan-South Korea Innovation Industrial Park and other parks, we will build a demonstration platform for China's participation in global marine development and cooperation and a pilot zone for international cooperation in marine economy. We will establish an integrated land-sea development mechanism and build a pilot zone for marine economic cooperation.

Source Extracted from the State Oceanic Administration, National Development and Reform Commission and National Cultural Heritage Administration's *Exploration of Coastal Territorial Areas in 2014.*

Western Taiwan Straits Economic Zone

The Western Taiwan Straits Economic Zone is to the west of Taiwan, bordering the Yangtze River Delta in the north and the Pearl River Delta in the south. It is an important part of China's coastal economic zone and has unique advantages in contacts with Taiwan. In May 2009, the State Council issued *Several Opinions of the State Council on Supporting Fujian Province in Accelerating the Construction of the Western Taiwan Straits Economic Zone*. In 2011, *Development Plan of the Western Taiwan Straits Economic Zone* was released, specifying the scope which includes Fujian Province, cities of Wenzhou, Quzhou, Lishui in Zhejiang Province, Shantou, Meizhou, Chaozhou, and Jieyang in Guangdong Province, as well as Shangrao, Yingtan, Fuzhou, and Ganzhou in Jiangxi Province, the land area covering about 270,000 square kilometers. It calls for the construction of the Western Taiwan Straits Economic Zone as a pilot area for people's exchanges and cooperation between the two sides, serving the surrounding areas to develop new comprehensive channels for opening up, an important base for advanced manufacturing industry in the eastern coastal areas, and an important natural and cultural tourism center in China. It is expected to become a zone combining scientific development, reform and opening up, civilized harmony and beautiful ecology. The network development pattern of "one line, five axes and nine areas" in the Western Taiwan Straits Economic Zone was defined. "One line" refers to accelerating the construction of coastal development line. We have actively promoted a leading development of the coastal front line on the Western Taiwan Straits, forming bridgeheads connecting the Yangtze River Delta and the Pearl River Delta on the north and south flanks. We have vigorously developed advanced manufacturing and modern service industries to promote the concentrated development of port-vicinity industries and high-tech industries in accordance with the requirements of the national main functional areas planning. "Five axis" refers to the radiation from coastal areas to inland areas, which takes Fuzhou, Xiamen, Quanzhou, Wenzhou and Shantou as the leading places and relies on railways and expressways to form a new pattern of point-to-area and linkage development, with emphasis on the construction of Fuzhou-Ningde-Nanping-Yingtan-Shangrao Development Axis, Xiamen-Zhangzhou-Longyan-Ganzhou Development Axis, Quanzhou-Putian-Sanming-Fuzhou Development Axis, and Wenzhou-Lishui-Quzhou-Shangrao Development Axis as well as Shantou-Chaozhou-Jieyang-Meizhou-Longyan-Ganzhou Development Axis. "Nine areas" refers to the development of nine centralized development zones into industry clusters and dense belts of cities, including Xiamen Bay Development Zone with Xiamen as the leader and an further interior city Zhangzhou, Minjiangkou Estuary

Development Zone with Fuzhou as the core and Luoyuan Bay and Jiangyin Port Area as two wings, Meizhouwan Bay Development Zone with Putian as the core, Quanzhou Bay Development Zone with Quanzhou as the core, Sandu'ao-centered Development Zone, Wenzhou Coastal Development Zone, Eastern Guangdong Coastal Development Zone with Shantou as the leader, Chaozhou and Jieyang as two wings, and Fujian-Guangdong-Jiangxi Interactive Development Zone with Longyan, Sanming, Ganzhou and Meizhou as the center, as well as Fujian-Zhejiang-Jiangxi Interactive Development Zone with Nanping, Yingtan, Fuzhou, Shangrao, Quzhou and Lishui as the center.

[Column 1-20]
Exploration of Xiamen's construction of an important economic center on the Western Taiwan Straits

First, we have built advanced manufacturing and emerging industrial bases across the Taiwan Strait. With resources of both sides of the Taiwan Strait, and in accordance with the goal and requirement of promoting free investment, we focused on strengthening the in-depth industrial cooperation between the two sides. By broadening channels of and innovated modes of cooperation, we sped up the construction of carrier parks and started the construction of Xiamen Science and Technology Innovation Park.

Second, we have promoted cross-strait scientific and technological cooperation. With the release of *Measures of Xiamen Municipal People's Government to Encourage the Establishment of Scientific and Technological Research and Development Institutions in Xiamen*, more than 10 research and development (R&D) platforms such as "Cross-Strait Joint Research and Development Center of LED Photoelectric Integrated Technology" have been built. "Special funds for scientific and technological cooperation with Taiwan" were raised for base construction, talent introduction and matching of state-level Taiwan-related projects. Taiwan and domestic enterprises shall receive equal treatment when applying for support of scientific and technological projects in Xiamen. We have embraced the innovation of cloud computing applications. China Telecom and Taiwan's Chunghwa Telecom took Xiamen as a pilot and carried out "Healthy Cloud" cooperation in telemedicine, telecare, health inquiry and other aspects.

Third, we have strengthened cross-strait trade association exchanges. We promoted the establishment of cooperative relations with Taiwan counterparts in industrial design, mold, water heating, kitchen and bath, printing and other industry associations. Xiamen Industrial Design Association signed a memorandum of cooperation with Taiwan Design Center.

Fourth, we have strengthened cross-strait trade cooperation. We promoted the construction of headquarters of cross-strait trade centers, set up a platform for commodity exhibition and trading, business conference services and comprehensive trade services, and further promoted the construction of markets such as Dadeng Island Xiamen China-Taiwan small goods trading market, Taiwan Fruit Distribution Hub, Taiwan Book Distribution Hub, Taiwan Wine Distribution Hub and Taiwan Rice Distribution Hub. With the opening of the first public yacht bonded warehouse in the mainland, Tongyi Wharf in Xiamen has been approved as a pilot port for small-scale trade with Taiwan under more open management measures.

Fifth, we have deepened cross-strait financial service cooperation. We promoted cross-strait currency exchange and trade settlement pilot projects. 26 counterpart banks, amounting to 52 banks in Xiamen and Taiwan signed cross-border RMB agency clearing agreement. The head office of the Agricultural Bank of China has set up a Cross-Strait RMB Clearing Center in Xiamen. People's Bank of China authorized its Xiamen Central Branch to carry out the management of RMB underlying fund quota of Taiwan RMB clearing banks and participating banks and the monitoring and analysis of Taiwan RMB market. China Securities Regulatory Commission approved Xiamen to set up the first cross-strait joint venture securities investment fund management company in Xiamen, and supported Xiamen to set up in mainland China the first cross-strait joint venture securities full-licensed company with 51% Taiwan capital.

Sixth, we have expanded cross-strait cultural exchanges and cooperation. With the southern Fujian culture as a link, we adhered to the principle of promoting both private and market operation, innovated ways of exchanges and cooperation, and upgraded the quality of cross-strait cultural exchanges and cooperation. On the basis of "small three links" and "big three links", we opened up air rights, optimized air routes, expanded air lines and increased flights, thus optimizing cross-strait direct flight transport system. We have built a parcel exchange center and a maritime express logistics center with Taiwan. We have also built important transfer hubs and distribution centers for direct cross-strait exchanges.

Source Extracted from the *Evaluation Report of the Evaluation Group of the Institute of International Strategies, CPC Central Party School on Comprehensive Reform Pilot Zone of Xiamen for Deepening Cross-Strait Exchanges and Cooperation*, 2013.

2.5 Regional Development of Special Types

While supporting the development of the four major regions, China has furthered its support to the economic development of the poor and old border areas, to strengthen infrastructure construction, to improve ecological protection and restoration, to advance the level of public services, and to effectively improve the production and living conditions of the region.

2.5.1 Supporting the Development of Poor Areas

China is the most populous developing country in the world. With so many poor people in rural areas, it is very difficult to solve poverty. Since the establishment of the People's Republic of China, the state has always regarded poverty alleviation as an important goal of national development. Since the mid-1980s, the state has started to carry out rural poverty alleviation and development in an organized, planned and large-scale manner. It has successively formulated and implemented poverty alleviation plans such as the *Seven-Year Priority Poverty Alleviation Program* (1994–2000) (to solve the problem of food and clothing for 80 million people in 7 years), the *Outline of China's Rural Poverty Alleviation and Development Program* (2001–2010), and the *Outline of China's Rural Poverty Alleviation and Development Program* (2011–2020), making poverty alleviation a consensus and action of the whole society.

Since 1986, the state has identified three county-level support units for poverty alleviation and development. In 1994, with the implementation of the *Seven-Year Priority Poverty Alleviation Program (1994–2000)*, the number of poverty-stricken counties at the national level increased to 592. The *Seven-Year Priority Poverty Alleviation Program (1994–2000)* clearly put forward the need to concentrate human, material and financial resources, mobilize all sectors of society, and strive to basically solve the problem of food and clothing for the rural poor by the end of 2000. The *Seven-Year Priority Poverty Alleviation Program (1994–2000)* has also defined a number of specific objectives, including: the per capita income of the vast majority of poor households to reach more than 500 yuan (fixed price in 1990), the basic farmland with stable and high yields to be built in the areas where conditions permit, the average household to have one mu of forest or orchard or one mu of cash crops, and the transfer of one labor of each household to non-agricultural industries in the local or developed areas. Other objectives include that every household to live on one breeding industry or have a domestic sideline industry, and every household in grazing area to have a fenced grassland or an enclosed pasture. Poor towns were expected to basically solve the drinking water difficulties of people and livestock and to build local market. The main commodity producing areas should build highways, electricity should be available for poor rural areas, and basic primary education should be in the reach of all people.

In 2001, the *Outline of China's Rural Poverty Alleviation and Development Program (2001–2010)* was unveiled, abolishing all the state-level poverty-stricken counties in developed coastal areas and increasing the number of poverty-stricken counties in the central and western regions, but the total number remained stable at 592. At the same time, the state-level poverty-stricken counties have been renamed as the key counties in the national poverty alleviation and development work. Tibet, as a concentrated poverty-stricken area, was in a prioritized position.

In 2011, the central government unveiled the *Outline of China's Rural Poverty Alleviation and Development Program (2011–2020)*. It clearly pointed out that by 2020, poverty alleviation targets should not worry about food and clothing, and their right of compulsory education, basic medical care and housing should be guaranteed. The net income of farmers at per capita of 2300 yuan would be a new standard for national poverty alleviation. It was proposed that by 2020, the construction of farmland infrastructure in poverty-stricken areas would be significantly improved, the characteristic pillar industry system would be preliminarily constructed, the security level of rural drinking water and the popularization rate of tap water would be further improved, and the problem of electricity for the those without the power would be solved in an all-round way. The qualified construction of village-to-village asphalt (cement) roads would be completed, the hardening of roads in villages would be promoted so that regular buses can be available for every village; the service level of rural highway and the ability of disaster prevention and resilience should improve markedly, and the living conditions of the people would improve significantly. The basic popularization of preschool education would be realized, quality of compulsory education would be improved, and high school education would be further popularized. The public health and basic medical services will be more equal for the people in poor areas. The radio and television household communication will be realized in an all-round way, broadband access will be basically achieved in villages and rural public cultural service will be improved. We will basically achieve the specific objectives of libraries and cultural centers in key counties of poverty alleviation and development (hereinafter referred to as key counties), comprehensive cultural stations in towns and townships, and cultural activity rooms in administrative villages. The construction of clean and honest government culture in rural areas will be promoted through public cultural construction, and an increase of forest coverage by 3.5 percentage points over the end of 2010 will be realized.

[Column 1-21]
Major policies of poverty alleviation

China has integrated poverty alleviation into the overall development plan of national economic and social development, and has formulated and implemented policies and measures that support development in rural poverty-stricken areas.

First, China has successively abolished the animal husbandry tax, live pig slaughter tax, agricultural and forestry specialty tax, and in particular agriculture tax which has been existing in China for more than 2600 years and now fixed in the form of law. Direct subsidy for grain producers, subsidy for growing superior crop varieties, subsidy for purchasing agricultural machinery and tools, as well as general subsidy for purchasing agricultural supplies have been implemented comprehensively. A rural social security system has been gradually set up and improved, while rural infrastructure such as drinking water, electricity, roads and biogas has been built and dilapidated housing in rural areas have been renovated. The collective forest right institutional reform has also been conducted, thereby enabling farmers to have the contractual management rights of forest land and proprietorial rights of forests and woods. In addition, various preferential policies have been implemented and the forestry economy and forest-based tourism have been developed to increase farmers' income.

Second, China has continuously increased policy support to strengthen agriculture, benefit farmers, enrich rural areas and alleviate poverty. Investment into the "three rurals" (agriculture, rural areas and farmers) by the central government has increased from 214.42 billion yuan in 2003 to 857.97 billion yuan in 2010, with an average annual increase of 21.9%. The coverage of public finance in rural areas has notably increased. Poverty-stricken areas have also taken the lead in carrying out policies that strengthen agriculture, benefit farmers and enrich rural areas. Among these areas, key counties of national poverty alleviation have taken the lead in implementing exemption of agricultural tax; the "two exemptions and one allowance" policy of rural compulsory education (exemptions of textbook and miscellaneous fees for students undertaking rural education from poverty-stricken households and living allowance for school-residing students); as well as reducing the number of public welfare infrastructure projects newly planned by the country or removing supporting policies of the county level or below. In the arrangement of the minimum subsistence allowance for rural areas, new rural cooperative medical insurance and new rural social pension insurance, the central government has given great support to the central-western regions of China. In 2010, 46.154 million people benefited from the new rural cooperative medical insurance supported by the Civil Administration Apartment, with a total funding of 1.4 billion yuan and a per capita funding of 30.3 yuan.

Third, China has implemented hydraulic projects, converted cultivated land into forests, and carried out resource development projects under the Western Development Strategy with prioritization in poverty-stricken regions. The construction of roads has been extended to poverty-stricken areas, connecting counties and towns with national and provincial highways. Infrastructure projects have been urged to use labor force in poverty-stricken areas to increase their cash income. With a focus on rural poverty alleviation, China has successively issued a series of regional development policies to promote the social and economic development of the Tibetan areas in Sichuan, Yunnan, Gansu and Qinghai Provinces, as well as the regions of Xinjiang, Guangxi, Chongqing, Ningxia, Gansu, Inner Mongolia and Yunnan.

Fourth, China has strengthened basic public services in rural areas. In 2007, China decided to implement the minimum subsistence allowance system in rural areas across the country, with rural residents that have a per capita annual income lower than the pre-set standard as the target of allowance. Through this, China sought to resolve the subsistence issues of the rural poor in a stable, lasting and effective manner. The minimum subsistence allowance was determined by local governments above the county-level in accordance with the average food, clothing, water and electricity expenditures required to support local rural residents annually. As of the end of 2010, the minimum subsistence allowance has covered 25.287 million households with 52.14 million people nationally. In 2010, 44.5 billion yuan of minimum subsistence allowance for rural areas have been granted, among which 26.9 billion yuan were subsidized by the central government. The average minimum subsistence allowance in rural areas nationally was 117 yuan per person per month, with a per capita of 74 yuan per month. For farmers who have lost the ability to work, and those who were old, weak, orphaned, widowed or disabled, the policy of "five guarantees" have been implemented, which provides living and material support in terms of food, clothing, housing, medical care and funeral expenses. Within 10 years, the "five guarantees" gradually achieved a transition from a collective welfare system funded by farmers to a modern social security system funded by national finance. By the end of 2010, the total number of households in rural areas across the country that had received the "five guarantees" reached 5.34 million, with 5.563 million people, thus basically ensuring that "everyone who is entitled to such allowances receives them". The total funding of the "five guarantees" by all levels of finance has also reached 9.64 billion yuan. In 2009, China began to develop pilot areas for the new rural social pension insurance. By July 2011, this work had been carried out in 60% of the country's rural areas, with 493 key national poverty alleviation counties included as pilot areas, achieving coverage of 83%. The new rural social pension insurance used a combination of individual contribution, collective subsidy and government subsidy as the financing method, and a combination of basic pension and personal account pension as the method of payment. The central-western regions were granted full subsidies in accordance with the basic pension determined by the central government while the eastern regions received 50% subsidies. In 2010, the central government subsidized 11.1 billion yuan for the basic pension of the new rural social pension insurance, while the local governments subsidized 11.6 billion yuan. In 2004, China introduced a standardized minimum wage system, which played a positive role in safeguarding the labor compensation rights of laborers with migrant workers as the main entity.

Source Extracted from *New Progress in Development-Oriented Poverty Reduction Program for Rural China* issued by the Information Office of the State Council of the People's Republic of China in 2011.

At the same time, China has regarded contiguous poor areas as the main focus of poverty alleviation. Clause 10 of the *Outline of China's Rural Poverty Alleviation and Development Program (2011–2020)* specifies that: the focus of China's poverty alleviation shall be placed on contiguous poor areas such as the Liupan Mountain Area, Qinba Mountain Area, Wuling Mountain Area, Wumeng Mountain Area, Yunnan-Guangxi-Guizhou Rocky Desertification Area, Mountain Area at the Border of Western Yunnan, south of the Greater Khingan Mountains, Yanshan-Taihang Mountain area, Lvliang Mountain area, Dabie Mountain area, and Luoxiao Mountain area; in addition to areas where special policies will be implemented including Tibet, the Tibetan areas in Sichuan,

Yunnan, Gansu and Qinghai provinces, as well as Kashgar, Hotan and Kezilesu Kirgiz Autonomous Prefecture in Xinjiang. According to statistics, among the 14 contiguous poor areas in China, the average per capita net income of farmers is 2676 yuan, which is equivalent to half of the national average per capita income; among the 600 counties ranked lowest in the overall national ranking, 521 are in contiguous poor areas, accounting for 86.8%. The Chinese government has made it clear that it will increase support to contiguous poor areas, by allocating a majority of the newly added special funds for poverty alleviation to these areas, focusing on implementing a series of livelihood projects for the people, striving to improve the production and living conditions, cultivating a group of characteristic industries with local advantages, accelerating the construction of key regional infrastructure, enhancing ecological construction and environmental protection, focusing on resolving the bottleneck problems that restrict development, and promoting the equalization of basic public services, in order to bring about fundamental changes to contiguous poor areas.

2.5.2 Supporting the Development of Old Revolutionary Base Areas

China has further increased the support to old revolutionary base areas. In recent years, China has successively issued a series of regulatory documents to accelerate the development of and poverty alleviation in old revolutionary base areas, including *Several Opinions of the State Council on Supporting the Revitalization and Development of Former Central Soviet Areas Including Southern Jiangxi Province*, *Plan for Revitalizing the Old Revolutionary Base Areas in the Regions of Shaanxi, Gansu and Ningxia*, *Plan for Revitalizing the Zuoyoujiang Old Revolutionary Base Area*, *Plan for Revitalizing the Dabie Mountain Old Revolutionary Base Area*, as well as the *Plan for Revitalizing the Old Revolutionary Base Areas in Sichuan and Shaanxi Provinces* which is still being formulated.

In terms of fiscal and taxation policies, the central government has further increased the transfer payments to the old revolutionary base areas; through methods such as fiscal discounts and fee subsidies, it has encouraged and guided financial institutions to increase credit and financing support to key construction projects in the old base areas.

In terms of investment policy, the central government has increased their support while central and local fiscal investment have given priority to old revolutionary base areas in fields such as people's livelihood, infrastructure and ecological environment; for projects that comply with national industrial policies, priority has been given in terms of planning layout and project approval. The government has also implemented differentiated land policy and emphasized on the old base areas in terms of the annual land use planning indicators; under the premise of strictly protecting forest land, the rational development and utilization of unused land such as barren hills, barren slopes and sandy land have been encouraged. In addition, corresponding support measures have been proposed in terms of eco-environmental policies, social support and talent cultivation.

[Column 1-22]
Planning outlines of the former central Soviet areas including Southern Jiangxi Province, old revolutionary base areas in the regions of Shaanxi, Gansu and Ningxia, and Zuoyoujiang Old Revolutionary Base Area issued by the central government

1. Former Central Soviet Areas Including Southern Jiangxi Province.
The Former Central Soviet Areas Including Southern Jiangxi Province covers Jiangxi, Fujian and Guangdong Provinces and it is one of the largest and most important revolutionary bases established by the Communist Party of China during the Agrarian Revolutionary War (1927–1937). It was the temporary central government of the Chinese Soviet Republic, the cradle of the People's Republic and the birthplace of the Soviet Spirit. This region has made significant contributions to and great sacrifices for the Chinese revolution. The Former Central Soviet Areas Including Southern Jiangxi Province is not only subject to difficulties and issues such as heavy historical burdens and weak realistic foundations, but also boasts favorable conditions and major opportunities for accelerating development. The region also has relatively superior locational conditions. It is the direct hinterland of the Pearl River Delta and the areas of Xiamen, Zhangzhou and Quanzhou, and an important passage that connects the inland areas with the southeast coast; it is rich in characteristic resources and is known as the world's tungsten and rare earth kingdom. As the region is currently in the stage of accelerated industrial transfer, industrialization and urbanization, it possesses great potential for market development. At present, the Former Central Soviet Areas Including Southern Jiangxi Province has entered a critical period of accelerated development. Therefore, it is a necessity to firmly seize this historical opportunity, strive to overcome difficulties and make every effort to achieve comprehensive revitalization and leap-forward development. We must carry forward the Soviet Spirit, increase support, speed up the process of new industrialization and urbanization, take the tackling of prominent livelihood issues as the starting point, and focus

on improving urban and rural production and living conditions; we must accelerate the development of infrastructure such as transportation, energy and water conservancy and strengthen the support capacity for development; we must take the undertaking of industrial transfer as the leverage and focus on cultivating and strengthening industries with local advantages; we must regard the development of social undertakings as the focus on improving the basic standard of public service; with the protection of ecological environment as the premise, we must focus on promoting sustainable development. We must also view reform and opening up as the driving force, focus on breaking the constraints of the system and mechanisms, and strive to create a new path of leaping development in underdeveloped regions, so that people in the former central revolutionary areas can enjoy a prosperous and happy life and thus ensuring that they become a part of the well-off society in all aspects at the same time as the whole country. Furthermore, we must speed up the construction of national poverty alleviation demonstration areas in the old revolutionary base areas, as well as national rare metal industrial bases, advanced manufacturing bases and deep processing bases for characteristic agricultural products, important regional comprehensive transportation hubs, important ecological barriers in southern China, and red cultural heritage and innovation zones.

2. Old Revolutionary Base Areas in the Regions of Shaanxi, Gansu and Ningxia.

The Old Revolutionary Base Areas in the Regions of Shaanxi, Gansu and Ningxia was formerly the command base of the Red Revolution established by the Communist Party of China during the Agrarian Revolutionary War. It was the destination of the Chinese Red Army's Long March and the place of departure for the Eighth Route Army to proceed to the frontlines during the War of Resistance against Japanese Aggression. This region was once a place where the older generation of proletarian revolutionaries fought and lived; it was an education base for patriotism, revolutionary tradition and the Yan'an Spirit (a revolutionary spirit originated from Yan'an and created by the Communist Party of China). The people of this region have made tremendous sacrifices and indelible contributions to the liberation of the Chinese nation and the establishment of New China. Despite having achieved great results in economic and social development since the reform and opening up and in particular since the implementation of the Western Development Strategy, there are still many special difficulties and problems that exist in this region. With the deepening promotion of the new round of Western Development and the acceleration of building a well-off society in all aspects, this region is in a critical period of exerting its advantages and accelerating its development. We must improve the transport infrastructure, build a water-conserving society, strengthen ecological construction and environmental protection, build national energy and chemical industry bases, further develop characteristic industries, promote new rural construction, upgrade the standards of public service, and deepen reform and opening up. It is also necessary to speed up the construction of key projects such as roads, railways, power grids, pipelines, agriculture and rural areas. We must strive to develop the Old Revolutionary Base Areas in the Regions of Shaanxi, Gansu and Ningxia into a demonstration area for the ecological civilization of the Loess Plateau, a national key energy and chemical base, a national key red tourism region, a modern dry farming demonstration area, and a pilot area for basic equalization of public service.

3. Zuoyoujiang Old Revolutionary Base Area.
The Zuoyoujiang Old Revolutionary Base Area is one of the earliest revolutionary command bases established by the Communist Party of China during the Agrarian Revolutionary War. The region has numerous advantages as well as weaknesses. On the one hand, it enjoys distinct regional advantages, abundant resources, beautiful ecological environment, abundant tourism resources, as well as harmony and stability; on the other hand, the region has a weak infrastructure, the potential of its industries has not been fully exploited, ecological restoration and environmental protection efforts are arduous, development of the tourism industry is low, and there is a lack of basic public services. We must further carry forward the spirit of hard work and self-reliance, increase support, focus on strengthening the development of infrastructure and developing characteristic industries, create a vigorous region with industrial agglomeration and economic prosperity; we must focus on strengthening the construction of ecological civilization, innovate the institutional mechanism of ecological construction, resource conservation and environmental protection, and build a beautiful region with gorgeous sceneries; we must make efforts to strengthen security and improve people's livelihood, increase the standards of basic public services, and build a happy region where people live and work in peace and contentment; we must focus on promoting rural-urban coordinated development, advocate the revolutionary spirit and ethnic culture of the region, and build a cultural region that is a model of tourism nationwide. Through our efforts, we will develop the Zuoyoujiang Old Revolutionary Base Area into a frontier region for all-round opening to Southeast Asia and South Asia, a key deep processing base for resources, a well-known destination for red culture and leisure tourism, an ecological civilization demonstration area, as well as an inter-provincial and interconnected pilot area.

Source Extracted from *Several Opinions of the State Council on Supporting the Revitalization of Former Central Soviet Areas Including Southern Jiangxi Province* (2012) issued by the State Council, *Outline of the Plan for Revitalizing the Old Revolutionary Base Areas in the Regions of Shaanxi, Gansu and Ningxia* (2012) issued by the National Development and Reform Commission, and the *Plan for Revitalizing the Zuoyoujiang Revolutionary Old Base Area* (2015).

2.5.3 Supporting the Development of Minority Regions

China is a unified and multi-ethnic socialist country. Since the founding of New China, the total number of ethnic groups as confirmed by the central government is 56. These ethnic groups include: Han, Mongol, Hui, Tibetan, Uyghur, Miao, Yi, Zhuang, Bouyei, Korean, Manchu, Dong, Yao, Bai, Tujia, Hani, Kazakh, Dai, Li, Lisu, Wa, She, Gaoshan, Lahu, Sui, Dongxiang, Nakhi, Jingpo, Kyrgyz, Tu, Daur, Mulao, Qiang, Blang, Salar, Maonan, Gelao, Xibe, Achang, Pumi, Tajik, Nu, Uzbek, Ethnic Russian, Evenki, De'ang, Bonan, Yugur, Gin, Tatars, Derung, Oroqen, Hezhen, Monba, Lhoba and Jino. Among these, the Han population accounts for the vast majority, while the 55 other ethnic groups have relatively small populations, and is therefore collectively referred to as "ethnic minorities".

To support the development of ethnic minority regions, China has set the development of advantageous resources and modern industry as key measures to accelerate the development of ethnic minorities and minority regions. During the "First Five-Year Plan" period (1953–1957), China allocated 40 of the "156" large construction projects to minority regions, such as the Baotou Iron and Steel Base in Inner Mongolia, Karamay Oilfield in Xinjiang Province, and Gejiu Tin Company in Yunnan Province. In the 1960s, China relocated a number of large industrial enterprises along the coast and in inland areas to minority regions, thus laying the foundation for the development of modern industries. Since the reform and opening up, China has prioritized the development of a large number of major construction projects in minority regions, such as the Xinjiang Tarim Oilfield, Guangxi Pingguo Aluminum Plant, Qinghai Potash Fertilizer Project, and the Large Coal Power Base of Inner Mongolia, thus allowing minority regions to form numerous important resource development and deep processing industrial bases. As a result, a road to industrialization based on resource advantages and distinct characteristics has been initially formed.

Since the implementation of the Western Development Strategy in 2000, China has placed the accelerated development of ethnic minorities and minority regions as the primary task of western development. In order to allow ethnic minorities and minority regions to receive practical benefits from the Western Development Strategy, China has introduced a number of policies, including prioritizing resource development and deep processing projects in minority regions, giving certain benefits and compensation to the ethnic autonomous areas that export natural resources, guiding and encouraging enterprises from economically developed regions to invest in minority regions, and increasing financial support to minority regions. All of this has been an effort to support minority regions in developing their economy and building their strengths. In recent years, the State Council has successively issued *Several Opinions of the State Council on Further Promoting the Economic and Social Development of Xinjiang Province* (September 2007), *Opinions of the State Council on the Recent Support of Tibet's Social and Economic Development* (July 2008), *Several Opinions of the State Council on Further Promoting the Economic and Social Development of Ningxia Hui Autonomous Region* (September 2008), *Several Opinions of the State Council on Supporting the Economic and Social Development of the Tibetan Areas in Qinghai and Other Provinces* (November 2008), *Several Opinions of the State Council on Further Promoting the Economic and Social Development of Guangxi Province* (December 2009) and *Several Opinions of the State Council on Supporting Sound and Fast Development of Inner Mongolia's Economy and Society* (June 2011). To support the development of minority regions such as Guizhou, Gansu and Yunnan Provinces, China has also introduced regulatory documents such as *Several Opinions of the State Council on Further Promoting the Economic and Social Development of Guizhou Province*, *Several Opinions of the State Council on Further Supporting the Economic and Social Development of Gansu Province*, and *Opinion of the State Council on Supporting Yunnan to Accelerate the Construction of an Important Bridgehead that Opens to Southwestern China*. In March 2010, China decided to launch a nationwide aid program for Xinjiang Uyghur Autonomous Region.

At present, 5 ethnic autonomous regions, 30 ethnic autonomous prefectures and 120 ethnic autonomous counties have been included in the scope of the Western Development Strategy or have enjoyed preferential policies. The Western Development Strategy has brought about practical benefits for minority regions and has led to the establishment of a series of key projects such as the "West-East Gas Pipeline" and "West-East Electricity Transmission Project", as well as a series of infrastructure projects such as airports, highways, and hydro-junctions. Lhasa was included as a part of the Qinghai–Tibet Railway, thus ending Tibet's history of having no railways.

[Column 1-23]

Summary of policies in support of ethnic minority areas development

First, when planning infrastructure projects located in the minority areas, the local governments should either be exempted from contributing capital or contribute less; when developing resources or building enterprises in these areas, due consideration must be given to local interests and the production and life of the ethnic minorities; and appropriate compensation must be granted to places exporting natural resources or doing their bit for the eco-balance and environmental conservation. In 1994, the state adjusted the ratio between the amount of capital from the central budget and that from autonomous region governments to 4:6, while the ratio between the central government and the government of other provinces was fixed at 5:5. In 2004, the state adopted the compensation mechanism for ecological construction and environmental protection. When tapping the rich oil and gas resources in Xinjiang, attention is paid to the stimulation effect on local development. The West-East Gas Pipeline alone can bring in over one billion yuan of revenue to Xinjiang a year.

Second, poverty problems of ethnic minorities need resolving. Since 1990, the state has set up a fund to assure the basic needs of people living in poverty-stricken minority areas, and 141 impoverished counties were listed as the first batch to gain this support. In 1994, the Seven-Year Priority Poverty Alleviation Program (a program designed to lift 80 million people out of absolute poverty in the seven years from 1994–2000) was carried out, and, with the assistance threshold lowered, 116 more poverty-stricken minority counties were covered by state preferential policies. In 2001, the *Outline of China's Rural Poverty Alleviation and Development Program (2001–2010)* was implemented, with ten more minority counties included, and Tibet as a special region covered. In 2005, the comprehensive development of poor minority villages became the focus of national poverty-relief efforts. In 2007, the state formulated the *11th Five-Year Plan for the Development of Ethnic Minorities*, containing 11 key projects. In 2009, the state announced new standards for poverty-relief work and expanded the coverage to low-income rural people in the minority areas. Other efforts include: providing work as a form of relief, relocating people from places with poor conditions, building settlements for formerly nomadic people, repairing dilapidated housing for rural residents, supplying safe drinking water in rural areas, and providing minimum living allowances to rural and urban residents. Thanks to continuous efforts in these endeavors, the impoverished population in the minority areas shrank from some 40 million in 1985 to 7.7 million in 2008.

Third, the state has worked out preferential policies for the production of and trade in goods to satisfy the special needs of ethnic minorities. In 1963, the state introduced preferential policies for ethnic minority enterprises regarding profit retention, self-owned funds and price subsidies. In 1997, it enacted new preferential policies, set up special loans with discounted interest and exempted some enterprises from paying value-added tax, benefiting 1760 designated producers of special commodities needed by the ethnic minorities. In 1991, a mechanism for national brick-tea reserves was established to guarantee the supply of brick tea. In 2007, the state established a fund to ensure the production and promotion of the special commodities needed by the ethnic minorities, as well as related personnel training.

Fourth, priority has been given by the state to improving medical and health care for the ethnic minorities and in the minority areas. Since the introduction of reform and opening-up policies, the state has built or renovated township hospitals, and county-level epidemic-prevention stations and health centers for women and children, thus greatly improving the healthcare services in the minority areas. More than 80% of the counties in Tibet now have epidemic-prevention stations. Through various channels, the state has trained healthcare workers for ethnic minorities and expanded the contingent of medical professionals. In Xinjiang, one-third of all medical workers are from ethnic minorities.

Fifth, the state has strongly supported the construction of pasturing and border areas and granted poverty-relief loans with discounted interest to support the pasturelands. In 2005, the state abolished taxes on agriculture and animal husbandry. After decades of unremitting endeavors, the minority areas have grown into important production bases of agriculture and animal products. Inner Mongolia now produces one-fifth of the nation's total milk, ranking first in China in milk production, and Xinjiang is the country's second-biggest producer of wool and cashmere. Most of China's borderlands are inhabited by ethnic minorities. In 1979, the state worked out *The Borderlands Construction Plan (Draft)*, allocating 40 billion yuan for the construction of these areas over eight years. In 1992 China implemented its frontier opening-up strategy, designating 13 open cities and 241 first-grade open ports, and establishing 14 border economic and technological cooperation zones. In 1996, the State Council worked out preferential policies for promoting border trade and economic cooperation with other countries. In 1999, the state initiated a program to boost the borderlands' economy and help the local residents raise their incomes. This was followed by the formulation and execution of the *11th Five-Year Plan for the Economic Development of the Borderlands*, starting in 2005. In 2009, the government decided to expand the program to all frontier counties and the frontier farms under the Xinjiang Production and Construction Corps.

Sixth, the state has strengthened the protection and construction of ecological environment in the minority areas. Especially since the launch of the "Western Development Strategy", a series of policies and measures have been executed, including prohibiting tree felling on the upper reaches of major rivers, returning farmlands to forests and grasslands and closing hillsides for afforestation. As compensation, the state has disturbed grain to farmers and herdsmen to make up for their losses in returning their farmlands to forests or grasslands, and subsidies to places where revenue has shrunk because of the restriction on tree felling.

Seventh, the state has increased its support for the sparsely populated minority areas with poor conditions. In 2005, it formulated and implemented the *Program to Support the Ethnic Minorities with Small Populations (2005–2010)*, and listed 640 ethnic minority villages as recipients of assistance.

Eighth, the state has increased efforts to extend fiscal transfer payments to the minority areas. In the 1950s, the state began to implement preferential fiscal policies for these areas, such as "unified collection of revenues and allocation of expenditures and subsidies for the needy", and raising the proportion of the financial reserve fund (two percentage points higher than in other regions). From 1980 to 1988, the central financial authorities adopted a quota subsidy system with a yearly increase of 10% for the five autonomous regions and the three provinces with large ethnic minority populations—Guizhou, Yunnan and Qinghai. In 1994, the state began to adopt a tax-sharing system, and introduced the system of policy-related transfer payments to the minority areas. In 2000, China initiated transfer payments for the minority areas on top of the general transfer payments and special-fund transfer payments as prescribed by relevant regulations. From 1978 to 2008, the total transfer payments by the central financial authorities to the minority areas totaled 2088.94 billion yuan, with an annual increase of 15.6%. In 2008 alone the amount was 425.3 billion yuan, making up 23.8% of the nation's total transfer payments. From 1955, when the Xinjiang Uyghur Autonomous Region was established, to 2008, the fiscal assistance from the central budget to Xinjiang reached 375.202 billion yuan, with an annual increase of 11%, the sum in 2008 being 68.56 billion yuan.

Ninth, the state has vigorously organized and encouraged paired-up assistance between the economically developed areas and the less-developed minority areas. In 1979, it decided to pair up such areas, for example, getting Beijing to assist Inner Mongolia, Hebei to assist Guizhou, Jiangsu to assist Guangxi and Xinjiang, Shandong to assist Qinghai, Shanghai to assist Yunnan and Ningxia, and the whole nation to assist Tibet. In 1996, the State Council determined to organize the 15 developed provinces and cities along the eastern coast to provide aid to 11 western provinces (autonomous regions and municipalities directly under the central government), and mobilized all departments of the central government to provide pair-up aid to the impoverished areas. In order to promote the development of Tibet, the central government has held four forums on work in that region.

Source *China's Ethnic Policy and Common Prosperity and Development of All Ethnic Groups* from the State Council Information Office, P.R.C.

2.5.4 Promoting the Transformation of Resource-Exhausted Cities

The resource-based city (the resource-based district included) is a kind of city whose dominated industries are exploitation and processing of natural resources such as local mineral products and forest. For a long time, as supplying places for primary energies and important raw materials, resource-based cities have made a prominent commitment to economic and social development of our country. However, for many reasons such as lacking overall planning and reduction of resources, a great deal of conflicts and problems has been accumulated during the development of these cities.

Resource-based cities in our country involve 28 provinces (autonomous regions, municipalities), whose resource exploitation and economic and social development are at different levels. Although these cities are faced with different contradictions and problems, all of them are challenged by problems such as having a single economic structure and prominent historical problems resulted from resource exploitation.

Since the establishment of the People's Republic of China (PRC), resource-based cities of our country have produced 52.9 billion tons of raw coal, 5.5 billion tons of raw petroleum, 5.8 billion tons of iron ore and 2 billion cubic meters of wood; they have provided the country with over 93% coal, over 90% petroleum, over 80% iron ore and 70% natural gas and have made significant contributions to economic construction and pushing forward industrialization. With intensive resource exploitation, the resources of some resource-based cities have gradually exhausted, and historical problems become prominent. As of the end of 2011, of the 69 identified resource-based cities in the country, 140 thousand hectares of coal mining subsidence area still needed to be restored, and there were over 100 thousand mine disaster hazard spots including earth fissures, abandoned mining pits, coal waste piles and large tailing heaps. The number of unemployed persons reached 600 thousand, most of which were unemployed miners and "4050" people (women aged above 40 and men aged above 50 who cannot find work due to poor employment conditions) with great difficulty in re-employment. The number of urban residents who benefited from the minimum living standard guarantee system was 2.156 million in total, making up 10.5% of urban population and double the national average. Moreover, as a result of unresolved historical problems such as collectively owned factories and the relief of mining enterprises from their obligation to perform social functions, there have been frequent cases of filed petitions and thus affecting the stability of society. Meanwhile, industrial development still relied heavily on resources; the extractive industry accounted for over 20% of the secondary industry while alternative industries such as the modern manufacturing and high technology industries were still at their start-up stages.

To accelerate the transformation of resource-based cities and effectively address prominent problems faced during development, in 2001, the State Council determined Fuxin, Liaoning Province as the first pilot of economic transformation of resource-exhausted cities. In 2007, based on the experience of transformation pilots of resource-based cities in northeast China, the State Council issued *Several Opinions of the State Council on Promoting the Sustainable Development of Resource-dependent Cities*, proposing that the compensation system for resources development and the aid system for declined industries would be generally established across the whole country by 2015 so that the economy and society of resource-based cities can become sustainable.

In March 2008, relevant departments such as the National Development and Reform Commission (NDRC) published the first list of twelve resource-exhausted cities. In March 2009, the second list of thirty-two resource-exhausted cities was published. In 2012, the third list of twenty-five resource-exhausted cities was published (see Table 7). The central government has supported these 69 resource-exhausted cities with financial transfer payment, which was beyond 80 billion yuan in total by 2014. These funds have been used to construct infrastructure, carry out livelihood projects and develop new industries in resource-exhausted cities. The NDRC has set up new alternative industries and attracted special projects to increase employment for resource-based cities; it has supported 272 projects in total and directly attracted over 40 thousand laid-off workers to be re-employed. The Ministry of Finance and Ministry of Land and Resources have implemented major projects of mine geology environment administration and allocated a budget of 6.84 billion yuan. Currently, the country is considering establishing pilots of sustainable development in resource-based areas while the establishment of systems such as the Sustainable Development Reserve Fund System for Resource-based Enterprises and Legislation of Sustainable Development of Resource-based Cities is proceeding in an orderly fashion. The 23 provinces (districts, cities) where the resource-exhausted cities are located

Table 7 List of nationwide resource-exhausted cities

Prefecture-level Cities (Districts): Fuxin, Liayuan, Jiaozuo, Pingxiang, Baiyin, Shizuishan, Yichun, Baishan, the Greater Khingan Range, Zaozhuang, Tongchuan, Fushun, Wansheng District, Tongling, Huangshi, Huaibei, Jingdezhen, Qitaihe, Puyang, Nanchuan District, Xinyu, Hegang, Luzhou, Wuhai, Shuangyashan, Shaoguan
County-level Cities: Daye, Gejiu, Wudalianchi, Jiutai, Shulan, Dunhua, Beipiao, Arxan, Yumen, Qianjiang, Zhongxiang, Leiyang, Zixing, Lengshuijiang, Huaying, Heshan, Lingbao, Huozhou, Xintai, Songzi, Lianyuan, Changning, Genhe, Yakeshi, Ergun, Zhalantun, Tieli
Counties (Autonomous Counties, Banners): Dayu, Tongguan, Yimen, Changjiang, Wangqing, Oroqen Autonomous Banner, Jiayin, Xunke
Municipal Districts (Administrative Districts): Yingshouyingzi Mining District, Yangjiazhangzi Development Area, Xiahuayuan, Wanshan Special Zone, Nanpiao, Gongchangling, Dongchuan, Jingxing Mining District, Shiguai, Erdaojiang, Jiawang, Honggu, Zichuan, Pinggui Administrative Area, Aihui

Source The website of the Department of Revitalization of Old Industrial Bases in Northeast China of the NDRC of the PRC: http://www.dbzxs.ndrc.gov.cn

have successively set up working mechanisms such as steering groups and joint sessions. 13 provinces (districts, cities) including Jiangsu, Hubei, Shandong, and Guangxi have published policies and measures which supported sustainable development of local resource-based cities. 8 provinces (districts, cities) including Liaoning, Inner Mongolia, Jiangxi, and Chongqing have created provincial financial transfer payment or special aid funding, among which the Inner Mongolia Autonomous Region allocated special funding of 1.8 billion yuan in total to support the sustainable development of resource-based cities during 2009–2011. Almost all resource-exhausted cities have established special institutions of transformation, drew up transformation plans, carried out every task in earnest, developed new alternative industries and strengthened the capability of sustainable development.

In December 2013, the State Council printed and distributed *Sustainable Development Plan for Nationwide Resource-based Cities (2013–2020)*, which specified 262 resource-based cities across the country, including 126 prefectural-level divisions (consisting of prefecture-level cities, districts, autonomous prefectures, leagues, etc.), 62 county-level cities, 58 counties (consisting of autonomous counties, forest zones, etc.), and 16 municipal districts (consisting of development areas and management districts). According to differences in guarantee capacity of resources and capacity of sustainable development, resource-based cities were classified into four types: growing cities, mature cities, declining and regenerative cities. The *Plan* specified to make overall plans and take all factors into consideration and implement policies by types, to guide all types of resource-based cities to accelerate their transformation and development, and especially to support the transformation of resource-exhausted cities. It proposed major missions in five respects: exploiting and comprehensively utilizing resources in order, establishing diversified industrial system, practically guaranteeing and improving people's livelihood, strengthening the governance of environment and protection of ecology, and strengthening the construction of capacity of support and guarantee. Moreover, it specified the overall goal to push forward sustainable development, namely, till 2020, to generally accomplish the mission of transforming resource-exhausted cities; to generally form the pattern of which the resource exploitation is in harmony with economic and social development and ecological environment protection in resource-rich areas; and to establish and perfect long-acting mechanisms that benefit the sustainable development of resource-based cities, such as systematic restraints, product pricing, resource development and compensation, interest distribution and sharing, and support for new alternative industries. The *Plan* also specified to continue increasing the transfer payment funding from the central government and support for resource-exhausted cities within central budget; to launch sustainable development pilots in resource-rich areas; to accelerate the formulation of laws on sustainable development of resource-based cities; to gradually establish a multiple-layer policy guarantee system of sustainable development; to research and formulate classified guiding opinions of sustainable development for nationwide resource-based cities as well as coordinated assessment methods of resource exploitation and urban sustainable development; to establish a statistical system of sustainable development of resource-based cities; and to strengthen the guidance and dynamic supervision of sustainable development.

[Column 1-24]
List of national resource-dependent cities

1. Thirty-one Growing Cities
Twenty prefecture-level administrative regions: Shuozhou, Hulun Buir, Erdos, Songyuan, Hezhou, Nanchong, Liupanshui, Bijie, Qiannan Buyei and Miao Autonomous Prefecture, Qianxinan Buyei and Miao Autonomous Prefecture, Zhaotong, Chuxiong Yi Autonomous Prefecture, Yan'an, Xianyang, Yulin, Wuwei, Qingyang, Longnan, Haixi Mongol and Tibetan Autonomous Prefecture, Altay Prefecture;

Seven county-level cities: Holingol, Xilinhot, Yongcheng, Yuzhou, Lingwu, Hami, Fukang;

Four counties: Yingshang County, Dongshan County, Changle County, Shanshan County.

2. One hundred and forty-one Mature Cities:
Sixty-six prefecture-level administrative regions: Zhangjiakou, Chengde, Xingtai, Handan, Datong, Yangquan, Changzhi, Jincheng, Xinzhou, Jinzhong, Linfen, Yuncheng, Lyuliang, Chifeng, Benxi, Jilin, Yanbian Korean Autonomous Prefecture, Heihe, Daqing, Jixi, Mudanjiang, Huzhou, Suzhou, Bozhou, Huainan, Chuzhou, Chizhou, Xuancheng, Nanping, Sanming, Longyan, Ganzho, Yichun, Dongying, Ji'ning, Tai'an, Laiwu, Sanmenxia, Hebi, Pingdingshan, Ezhou, Hengyang, Chenzhou, Shaoyang, Loudi, Yunfu, Baise, Hechi, Guangyuan, Guang'an, Zigong, Panzhihua, Dazhou, Ya'an, Liangshan Yi Autonomous Prefecture,

Anshun, Qujing, Baoshan, Pu'er, Lincang, Weinan, Baoji, Jinchang, Pingliang, Karamay, Bayingolin Mongol Autonomous Prefecture;

Twenty-nine county-level cities:

Luquan, Renqiu, Gujiao, Diaobingshan, Fengcheng, Shangzhi, Chaohu, Longhai, Ruichang, Guixi, Dexing, Zhaoyuan, Pingdu, Dengfeng, Xinmi, Gongyi, Xingyang, Yingcheng, Yidu, Liuyang, Linxiang, Gaoyao, Cenxi, Dongfang, Mianzhu, Qingzhen, Anning, Kaiyuan, Hotan;

Forty-six counties (including autonomous counties and forestry district):

Qinglong Manchu Autonomous County, Yi County of Hebei Province, Laiyuan County, Quyang County, Kuandian Manchu Autonomous County, Yi County of Liaoning Province, Wuyi County, Qingtian County, Pingtan County, Xingzi County, Wannian County, Baokang County, Shennongjia Forestry District, Ningxiang County, Taojiang County, Huayuan County, Lianping County, Longan County, Longsheng Pan-Ethnicities Autonomous County, Teng County, Xiangzhou County, Qiongzhong Li and Miao Autonomous County, Lingshui Li Autonomous County, Ledong Li Autonomous County, Tongliang County, Rongchang County, Dianjiang County, Chengkou County, Fengjie County, Xiushan Tujia and Miao Autonomous County, Xingwen County, Kaiyang County, Xiuwen County, Zunyi County, Songtao Miao Autonomous County, Jinning County, Xinping Yi and Dai Autonomous County, Lanping Bai and Pumi Autonomous County, Maguan County, Qusong County, Lueyang County, Luonan County, Maqu County, Datong Hui and Tujia Autonomous County, Zhongning County, Baicheng County.

3. Sixty-Seven Declining Cities:
Twenty-four prefecture-level administrative regions:
Wuhai, Fuxin, Fushun, Liaoyuan, Baishan, Yichun, Hegang, Shuangyashan, Qitaihe, Daxing'anling Prefecture, Huaibei, Tongling, Jingdezhen, Xinyu, Pingxiang, Zaozhuang, Jiaozuo, Puyang, Huangshi, Shaoguan, Luzhou, Tongchuan, Baiyin, Shizuishan;

Twenty-two county-level cities:

Huozhou, Arxan, Beipiao, Jiutai, Shulan, Dunhua, Wudalianchi, Xintai, Lingbao, Zhongxiang, Daye, Songzi, Qianjiang, Changning, Leiyang, Zixing, Lengshuijiang, Lianyuan, Heshan, Huaying, Gejiu, Yumen;

Five counties (including autonomous counties):

Wangqing County, Dayu County, Changjiang Li Autonomous County, Yimen County, Tongguan County;

Sixteen municipal districts (including development zones and administrative districts):

Jingxing Mining District, Xiahuayuan District, Yingshouyingzi Mining District, Shiguai District, Gongchangling District, Nanpiao District, Yangjiazhangzi Development Zone, Erdaojiang District, Jiawang District, Zichuan District, Pinggui Administrative District, Nanchuan District, Wansheng Economic Development Zone, Wanshan District, Dongchuan District, Honggu District.

4. Twenty-three regenerative cities:
Sixteen prefecture-level administrative regions:

Tangshan, Baotou, Anshan, Panjin, Huludao, Tonghua, Xuzhou, Suqian, Ma'anshan, Zibo, Linyi, Luoyang, Nanyang, Ngawa Tibetan and Qiang Autonomous Prefecture, Lijiang, Zhangye;

Four county-level cities:

Xiaoyi, Dashiqiao, Longkou, Laizhou;

Three counties:

Anyang County, Yunyang County, Shangri-La County

Source Excerpt from *Notice of the National Resource-Dependent City Sustainable Development Plan (2013–2020)* issued by the State Council in 2013.

CHAPTER 2

Major Achievements and Problems of Promoting Regional Development

Since the implementation of the strategy of coordinated regional development, prominent problems of every region have been effectively alleviated. Guided by the strategy of coordinated regional development, the proportion of economy of the central and the western regions in the national economy has remarkably increased. Comparable with the Beijing-Tianjin-Hebei Region, Yangtze River Delta Region and Pearl River Delta Region, a host of new regional economy growth poles such as the middle reaches of the Yangtze River, Chengdu-Chongqing, Central Plains, Central-Southern of Liaoning, Shandong Peninsula, the West Coast of the Taiwan Straits have emerged. At the same time, on the basis of the four major regions, the country has implemented special support policies on areas with difficulties such as poverty-stricken areas and primarily established policy system for cross-administrative regions with difficulties.

While fully recognizing the progress of strategy of coordinated regional development, we also have to realize that there is still a long way to accomplish the true coordinated regional development: Firstly, big absolute gaps still remain among regional economic development. Secondly, gaps are not narrowed among regional basic public service. Thirdly, problems of disorder in regional development are still relatively prominent. Fourthly, different regional economic development is not coordinated with population distribution and ecological environment. As a result, the strategy of coordinated regional development is also faced with underlying problems of transformation.

X. Song et al., *The Great Change in the Regional Economy of China under the New Normal*, The Great Transformation of China,
https://doi.org/10.1007/978-981-32-9475-2_2

1 Achievements Since the Implementation of the Strategy of Coordinated Regional Development

1.1 *Major Changes in Regional Growth Pattern*

1.1.1 *Gradually Narrowed Relative Gap Among the Eastern, Central and Western Regions*

Since the twenty-first century, as the implementation of the strategy of coordinated regional development deepens, great changes have occurred to the growth pattern in which the eastern region takes the lead. In 2007, the economic growth rate of the western region reached 14.6%, surpassing the eastern region for the first time. In 2008, the overall economic development of the central and western regions and the northeast region accelerated, entirely exceeding the growth speed of the eastern region; such a tendency continued from 2009 to 2013. During the "Eleventh Five-Year Plan" period, all the annual growth speed of regional gross domestic product of the central, the western and the northeastern regions surpassed 13%, 0.5 to 1 percentage points higher than that of the western region, which was the first time in over thirty-year history of the reform and opening-up policy and a significant change of regional growth pattern.[1] As the implementation of the strategy of coordinated regional development deepens, the trend of continually expanding regional gap has been repressed to some degree.

From the perspective of economic aggregate, in 1978, the beginning of the reform and opening up, the economic aggregate of the eastern region was 151.439 billion yuan, taking up 41.54% of the national economic aggregate. The economic aggregate of the western region was 65.423 billion yuan, taking up 17.95% of the national economic aggregate; in 2000, the economic aggregate of the eastern region was 5274.281 billion yuan, taking up 53.16% of the national economic aggregate, and the economic aggregate of the western region was 1708.857 billion yuan, taking up 17.22%; in 2013, the economic aggregate of the eastern region reached 32,225.9 billion yuan, taking up 51.51% of the national economic aggregate, and the economic aggregate of the western region was 12,600.3 billion yuan, taking up 20.00% of

[1] Du Ying: *2013 China Regional Economy Development Yearbook*, China Financial & Economical Publishing House, 2013, pp. 316–317.

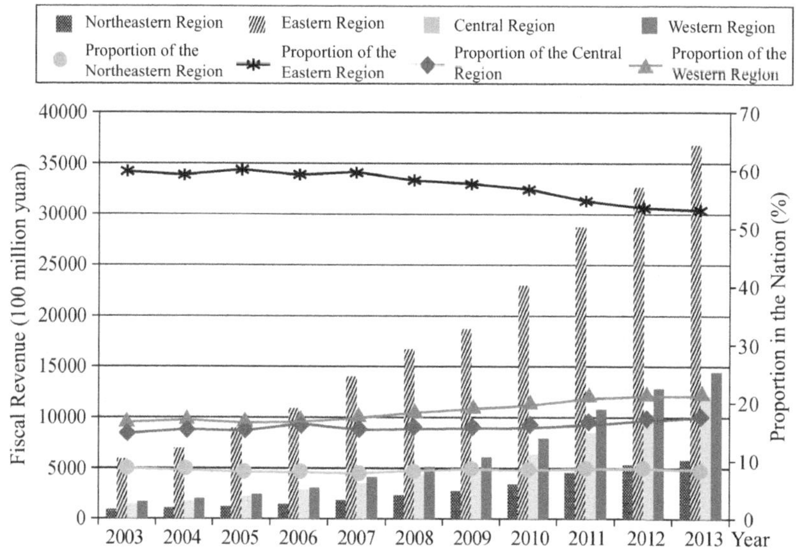

Fig. 1 四大区域板块 GDP 总量及占比变化 (2003–2013年) (GDP aggregate of the four major regions and changes in proportion [2003–2013])

- 财政收入 (亿元): Fiscal Revenue (100 million yuan)
- 全国占比 (%): Proportion in the Nation (%)
- 东北地区: Northeastern Region
- 东北占比: Proportion of the Northeastern Region
- 东部地区: Eastern Region
- 东部占比: Proportion of the Eastern Region
- 中部地区: Central Region
- 中部占比: Proportion of the Central Region
- 西部地区: Western Region
- 西部占比: Proportion of the Western Region
- 年份: Year
- 数据来源: 根据 2003–2013 年《中国统计年鉴》计算。(*Source* Calculated based on the *China Statistical Yearbook 2003–2013*)

the national economic aggregate. Compared with the data of 2000, in 2013, the proportion of the western region in the national economy rose by 2.78 percentage points. From 2003 to 2013, the proportions of the central and the western regions in national economy remarkably rose. In general, the achievements of coordinated regional development were remarkably effective (see Fig. 1 and Table 1).

Table 1 Regional gross domestic product growth speed of every major region from 2003 to 2013

		Nationwide	*Northeastern region*	*Eastern region*	*Central region*	*Western region*
2013	Absolute amount (100 million yuan)	568,845	54,442	322,259	127,306	126,003
	Proportion in national GDP (%)	–	8.64	51.15	20.21	20.00
	Growth Rate (%)	7.7	8.4	9.1	9.7	10.7
2012	Absolute amount (100 million yuan)	518,942	50,477	295,892	116,278	113,905
	Proportion in national GDP (%)	–	8.76	51.32	20.17	19.76
	Growth rate (%)	7.7	10.2	9.3	10.9	12.4
2011	Absolute amount (100 million yuan)	473,104	45,378	271,355	104,474	100,235
	Proportion in national GDP (%)	–	8.70	52.04	20.04	19.22
	Growth rate (%)	9.3	12.6	10.5	12.8	14.0
2010	Absolute amount (100 million yuan)	401,513	37,493	232,031	86,109	81,408
	Proportion in national GDP (%)	–	8.58	53.09	19.70	18.63
	Growth rate (%)	10.4	13.7	12.4	13.9	14.2
2009	Absolute amount (100 million yuan)	340,903	31,078	196,674	70,578	66,973
	Proportion in national GDP (%)	–	8.51	53.84	19.32	18.33
	Growth rate (%)	9.2	12.7	10.9	11.8	13.5
2008	Absolute amount (100 million yuan)	314,045	28,196	177,580	63,188	58,257
	Proportion in national GDP (%)	–	8.62	54.27	19.31	17.80
	Growth rate (%)	9.6	13.4	11.1	12.2	12.4

(continued)

Table 1 (continued)

		Nationwide	*Northeastern region*	*Eastern region*	*Central region*	*Western region*
2007	Absolute amount (100 million yuan)	265,810	23,373	152,346	52,041	47,864
	Proportion in national GDP (%)	–	8.48	55.27	18.88	17.37
	Growth rate (%)	14.2	14.1	14.4	14.3	14.6
2006	Absolute amount (100 million yuan)	216,314	19,715	128,593	43,218	39,527
	Proportion in national GDP (%)	–	8.53	55.66	18.70	17.11
	Growth rate (%)	12.7	13.5	14.2	13.1	13.2
2005	Absolute amount (100 million yuan)	184,937	17,141	109,925	37,230	33,493
	Proportion in national GDP (%)	–	8.67	55.58	18.82	16.93
	Growth rate (%)	11.3	12.0	13.5	12.7	13.1
2004	Absolute amount (100 million yuan)	159,878	14,545	92,823	31,616	28,603
	Proportion in national GDP (%)	–	8.68	55.39	18.87	17.07
	Growth rate (%)	10.1	12.3	14.4	13.0	12.9
2003	Absolute amount (100 million yuan)	135,823	12,722	76,965	25,871	23,696
	Proportion in national GDP (%)	–	9.14	55.27	18.58	17.02
	Growth Rate (%)	10.0	10.8	13.4	10.8	11.5

Source Calculated based on the *China Statistical Yearbook 2003–2013*

From the perspective of per capita GDP, in 1978, the per capita GDP in the eastern region was 465 yuan, while that in the western was 263 yuan, with the former being 1.77 times as the latter. In 2000, the per capita GDP in the eastern region was 12,125 yuan, while that in the western was 4718 yuan, with the former being 2.57 times as the latter. In 2013, the per capita GDP in the eastern region was 62,405 yuan, while that in the western was 34,491 yuan, with the former being 1.81 times as the latter. In history, the maximum gap in per capita GDP between the eastern and western regions was in 2003, namely 2.7 times, and the minimum was in 2013, namely 1.81 times (see Table 2).

Table 2 Growth of per capita local GDP of every major region from 2003 to 2013

		Nationwide	*Northeastern region*	*Eastern region*	*Central region*	*Western region*
2013	Absolute amount (yuan)	41,908	49,606	62,405	35,357	34,491
	Growth rate (%)	7.1	8.2	8.0	9.3	10.1
2012	Absolute amount (yuan)	38,420	46,014	57,722	32,427	31,357
	Growth rate (%)	7.1	10.5	8.1	10.6	11.6
2011	Absolute amount (yuan)	35,198	41,400	53,350	29,229	27,731
	Growth rate (%)	8.8	12.5	8.8	12.0	13.1
2010	Absolute amount (yuan)	30,015	34,301	46,356	24,154	22,471
	Growth rate (%)	9.9	13.2	10.4	13.9	13.4
2009	Absolute amount (yuan)	25,608	28,538	40,047	19,862	18,443
	Growth rate (%)	8.7	12.4	9.0	11.1	12.0
2008	Absolute amount (yuan)	23,708	25,956	36,654	17,860	16,109
	Growth rate (%)	9.1	13.4	9.1	11.9	12.2
2007	Absolute amount (yuan)	20,169	21,573	31,894	14,754	13,277
	Growth rate (%)	13.6	13.9	12.5	14.4	13.9
2006	Absolute amount (yuan)	16,500	18,277	27,318	12,269	10,991
	Growth rate (%)	12.0	13.4	12.4	12.7	12.7
2005	Absolute amount (yuan)	14,185	15,945	24,048	10,383	9163
	Growth rate (%)	10.7	12.0	11.7	12.2	11.8
2004	Absolute amount (yuan)	12,336	13,548	20,755	8683	7725
	Growth rate (%)	9.4	12.1	12.7	12.7	11.9
2003	Absolute amount (yuan)	10,542	11,866	17,405	7147	6438
	Growth rate (%)	9.3	10.4	11.4	10.9	11.0

Source Calculated based on the *China Statistical Yearbook 2003–2013*

From the perspective of local fiscal revenue, in 1978, the local fiscal revenue of the eastern region was 50.604 billion yuan, taking up 52.91% of the national local fiscal revenue; in 2000, the local fiscal revenue of the eastern region was 365.139 billion yuan, taking up 57.00% of the national local fiscal revenue; in 2013, the local fiscal revenue of the eastern region was 3675.3 billion yuan, taking up 53.31% of the national local fiscal revenue. As for the western region, it was 9.29 billion yuan in 1978, the beginning of the reform and opening-up policy, taking up 9.71% of the national local fiscal revenue; in 2000, it was 112.729 billion yuan, taking up 17.6% of the national local fiscal revenue; it reached 1444.5 billion yuan in 2013, taking up 20.93%. In all, the gap in local fiscal revenue budget between the eastern and western regions is getting narrowed (see Table 3).

Table 3 Growth of local fiscal revenue of every major region from 2003 to 2013

		Nationwide	*Northeastern region*	*Eastern region*	*Central region*	*Western region*
2013	Absolute amount (100 million yuan)	69,011	5778	36,753	12,035	14,445
	Proportion in national GDP (%)	–	8.37	53.26	17.44	20.93
	Growth rate (%)	13.0	8.8	12.5	16.5	13.2
2012	Absolute amount (100 million yuan)	61,078	5310	32,679	10,327	12,763
	Proportion in national GDP (%)	–	8.69	53.50	16.91	20.90
	Growth rate (%)	16.2	18.2	13.7	21.5	18.0
2011	Absolute amount (100 million yuan)	52,547	4491	28,741	8496	10,819
	Proportion in national GDP (%)	–	8.55	54.70	16.17	20.59
	Growth rate (%)	29.4	33.5	24.9	33.3	37.4
2010	Absolute amount (100 million yuan)	40,613	3363	23,005	6371	7873
	Proportion in national GDP (%)	–	8.28	56.65	15.69	19.39
	Growth rate (%)	24.6	23.6	22.5	26.4	30.0
2009	Absolute amount (100 million yuan)	32,603	2720	18,787	5040	6056
	Proportion in national GDP (%)	–	8.34	57.62	15.46	18.58
	Growth rate (%)	13.8	15.4	12.3	14.4	17.4
2008	Absolute amount (100 million yuan)	28,650	2357	16,730	4404	5159
	Proportion in national GDP (%)	–	8.23	58.39	15.37	18.01
	Growth rate (%)	21.5	27.8	19.0	22.7	26.3
2007	Absolute amount (100 million yuan)	23,573	1844	14,053	3590	4085
	Proportion in national GDP (%)	–	7.82	59.62	15.23	17.33
	Growth rate (%)	28.8	27.2	29.6	21.7	33.5
2006	Absolute amount (100 million yuan)	18,304	1450	10,844	2950	3059
	Proportion in national GDP (%)	–	7.92	59.25	16.12	16.71
	Growth rate (%)	23.0	20.7	21.1	30.3	24.1

(continued)

Table 3 (continued)

		Nationwide	*Northeastern region*	*Eastern region*	*Central region*	*Western region*
2005	Absolute amount (100 million yuan)	14,884	1201	8955	2264	2465
	Proportion in national GDP (%)	–	8.07	60.16	15.21	16.56
	Growth rate (%)	27.3	21.8	29.2	26.0	24.3
2004	Absolute amount (100 million yuan)	11,693	985	6929	1797	1983
	Proportion in national GDP (%)	–	8.43	59.25	15.36	16.96
	Growth rate (%)	18.7	15.9	17.3	24.6	20.2
2003	Absolute amount (100 million yuan)	9850	850	5909	1441	1650
	Proportion in national GDP (%)	–	8.63	59.99	14.63	16.75
	Growth rate (%)	15.7	11.4	16.8	14.1	15.3

Source Calculated based on the *China Statistical Yearbook 2003–2013*

From the perspective of per capita local fiscal revenue, in 1978, the per capita local fiscal budget revenue of the eastern region was 156 yuan, while that of the western region was 37 yuan, with the former being 4.22 times as the latter; in 2000, the per capita local fiscal budget revenue of the eastern region was 839 yuan, while that of the western region was 311 yuan, with the former being 2.7 times as the latter; the year 2003 marked the biggest gap, 2.98 times, and afterwards, the gap continued to narrow; in 2013, the per capita local fiscal budget revenue of the eastern region was 7092 yuan, while that of the western region was 3942 yuan, with the gap narrowed to 1.8 times.

From the perspective of local fiscal budget expenditure, in 1978, the local fiscal budget expenditure of the eastern region was 21.489 billion yuan, taking up 36.42% of the national local fiscal budget expenditure; in 2000, the local fiscal budget expenditure was 475.842 billion yuan, taking up 45.90% of the national local fiscal budget expenditure; in 2013, the local fiscal budget expenditure of the eastern region was 4737 billion yuan, taking up 39.56% of the national local fiscal budget expenditure. At the beginning of reform and opening up, the local fiscal budget expenditure of the western region was 13.686 billion yuan, taking up 23.20% of the national local fiscal budget expenditure; in 2000, the local fiscal budget expenditure was 260.109 billion yuan, taking up 25.09% of the national local fiscal budget expenditure; in 2013, the local fiscal budget expenditure of the eastern region decreased to 39.56% across the country while that of the western region rose to 29.7%. The achievements of coordinated regional development were remarkably effective (Table 4).

Table 4 Growth speed of local fiscal budget expenditure of every major region from 2003 to 2013

		Nationwide	*Northeastern region*	*Eastern region*	*Central region*	*Western region*
2013	Absolute amount (100 million yuan)	119,740	11,311	47,370	25,495	35,564
	Proportion in national GDP (%)	–	9.45	39.56	21.29	29.70
	Growth rate (%)	11.7	10.9	12.5	12.7	10.2
2012	Absolute amount (100 million yuan)	107,188	10,201	42,093	22,625	32,269
	Proportion in national GDP (%)	–	9.52	39.27	21.11	30.11
	Growth rate (%)	15.6	14.6	13.0	17.9	17.8
2011	Absolute amount (100 million yuan)	92,734	8902	37,250	19,186	27,397
	Proportion in national GDP (%)	–	9.60	40.17	20.69	29.54
	Growth rate (%)	25.5	23.0	23.4	27.4	28.0
2010	Absolute amount (100 million yuan)	73,884	7236	30,182	15,062	21,404
	Proportion in national GDP (%)	–	9.79	40.85	20.39	28.97
	Growth rate (%)	21.0	19.8	21.0	20.8	21.7
2009	Absolute amount (100 million yuan)	61,044	6039	24,952	12,473	17,580
	Proportion in national GDP (%)	–	9.89	40.87	20.43	28.80
	Growth rate (%)	24.0	23.9	20.3	26.4	27.7
2008	Absolute amount (100 million yuan)	49,248	4876	20,738	9869	13,766
	Proportion in national GDP (%)	–	9.90	42.11	20.04	27.95
	Growth rate (%)	28.5	27.1	22.3	28.1	39.7

(continued)

Table 4 (continued)

		Nationwide	*Northeastern region*	*Eastern region*	*Central region*	*Western region*
2007	Absolute amount (100 million yuan)	38,339	3835	16,950	7704	9850
	Proportion in national GDP (%)	–	10.00	44.21	20.09	25.69
	Growth rate (%)	26.0	23.3	24.7	26.2	29.2
2006	Absolute amount (100 million yuan)	30,431	3110	13,591	6104	7627
	Proportion in national GDP (%)	–	10.22	44.66	20.06	25.06
	Growth rate (%)	21.0	18.5	17.5	29.5	22.0
2005	Absolute amount (100 million yuan)	25,154	2623	11,564	4714	6253
	Proportion in national GDP (%)	–	10.43	45.97	18.74	24.86
	Growth rate (%)	22.2	22.8	21.7	23.4	21.8
2004	Absolute amount (100 million yuan)	20,593	2137	9503	3820	5133
	Proportion in national GDP (%)	–	10.38	46.15	18.55	24.93
	Growth rate (%)	19.5	21.5	18.9	21.8	18.1
2003	Absolute amount (100 million yuan)	17,230	1759	7990	3136	4345
	Proportion in national GDP (%)	–	10.21	46.38	18.20	25.22
	Growth rate (%)	12.8	10.9	17.3	11.8	6.6

Source Calculated based on the *China Statistical Yearbook 2003–2013*

From the perspective of per capita local fiscal expenditure, in 1978, the per capita local fiscal budget expenditure of the eastern region was 1.2 times as that of the western region.[2] In 2000, the per capita local fiscal budget expenditure of the eastern region was 1094 yuan, while that of the western region was 719 yuan, with the former being 1.52 times as the latter. Under the imbalanced development strategy, the gap between the eastern and the western regions had obviously widened over the decade and the year 2004 marked the biggest gap, 1.53 times. Afterwards, the gap in per capita local fiscal budget expenditure between the eastern and the western regions began to narrow continuously. In 2013, given the

[2] In 1978, the local fiscal budget revenue of Sichuan Province was missing.

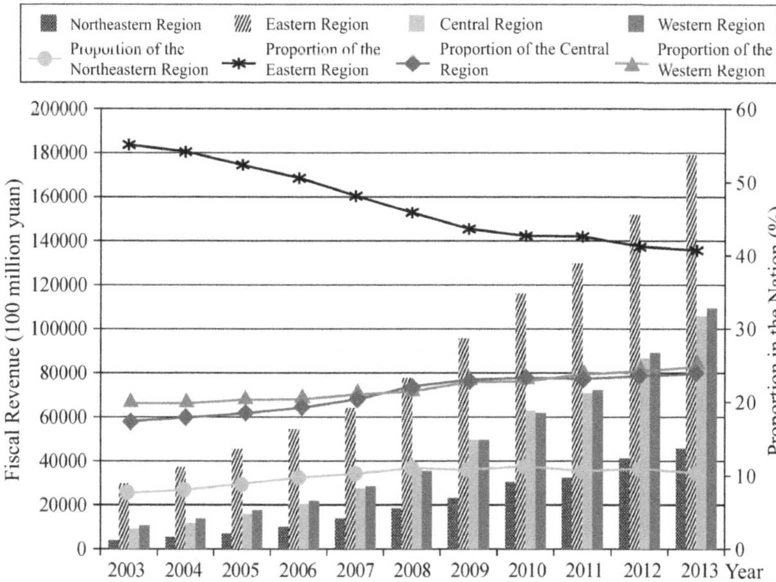

Fig. 2 四大区域板块全社会固定资产投资总量及占比变化 (2003–2013年) (Total investment in fixed assets and changes in proportion of the four major regions [2003–2013])

- 财政收入 (亿元): Fiscal Revenue (100 million yuan)
- 全国占比 (%): Proportion in the Nation (%)
- 东北地区: Northeastern Region
- 东北占比: Proportion of the Northeastern Region
- 东部地区: Eastern Region
- 东部占比: Proportion of the Eastern Region
- 中部地区: Central Region
- 中部占比: Proportion of the Central Region
- 西部地区: Western Region
- 西部占比: Proportion of the Western Region
- 年份: Year
- 数据来源: 根据 2003–2013 年《中国统计年鉴》计算。(*Source* Calculated based on the *China Statistical Yearbook 2003–2013*)

central transfer payment, the per capita local fiscal budget expenditure of the eastern region was 9141 yuan while that of the western region was 9707 yuan; the per capita fiscal expenditure of the western region had surpassed that of the eastern region.

From the perspective of total investment in fixed assets, in 1982, the total investment in fixed assets of the eastern region was 53.501 billion yuan, taking up 43.48% of the national total investment in fixed assets; in 2000, the total investment in fixed assets of the eastern region was 1748.49 billion yuan, taking up 53.12% of the national total investment in fixed assets. In 1982, the total investment in fixed assets of the western region was 21.915 billion yuan, taking up 17.81% of the national total investment in fixed assets; in 2000, the total investment in fixed assets of the western region was 611.07 billion yuan, taking up 18.56% of the national total investment in fixed assets. After 2000, the proportion of the total investment in fixed assets of the eastern region in the whole country continuously decreased, reaching 40.64% in 2013; while the proportion of the total investment in fixed assets of the western region in the whole country began to rise continuously after implementing the Western Development Strategy, reaching 24.80% in 2013 (see Fig. 2 and Table 5).

Table 5 Growth speed of total investment in fixed assets of every major region from 2003 to 2013

		Nationwide	*Northeastern region*	*Eastern region*	*Central region*	*Western region*
2013	Absolute amount (100 million yuan)	446,294	46,540	179,098	105,740	109,261
	Proportion in national GDP (%)	–	10.56	40.64	24.00	24.80
	Growth rate (%)	19.1	13.4	17.9	22.1	22.8
2012	Absolute amount (100 million yuan)	374,695	41,043	151,922	86,615	89,009
	Proportion in national GDP (%)	–	11.14	41.22	23.50	24.15
	Growth rate (%)	20.3	25.7	16.6	22.3	23.4
2011	Absolute amount (100 million yuan)	311,485	32,643	130,263	70,824	72,104
	Proportion in national GDP (%)	–	10.67	42.59	23.16	23.58
	Growth rate (%)	23.8	6.2	12.4	12.6	16.5

(continued)

Table 5 (continued)

		Nationwide	*Northeastern region*	*Eastern region*	*Central region*	*Western region*
2010	Absolute amount (100 million yuan)	251,684	30,726	115,854	62,891	61,892
	Proportion in national GDP (%)	–	11.32	42.69	23.18	22.81
	Growth rate (%)	12.1	29.5	21.3	26.2	24.6
2009	Absolute amount (100 million yuan)	224,599	23,733	95,548	49,852	49,686
	Proportion in national GDP (%)	–	10.85	43.67	22.78	22.71
	Growth rate (%)	30.0	26.8	22.9	35.9	38.2
2008	Absolute amount (100 million yuan)	172,828	18,714	77,735	36,695	35,949
	Proportion in national GDP (%)	–	11.07	45.97	21.70	21.26
	Growth rate (%)	25.9	34.4	19.8	32.3	27.2
2007	Absolute amount (100 million yuan)	137,324	13,920	64,876	27,746	28,251
	Proportion in national GDP (%)	–	10.33	48.13	20.58	20.96
	Growth rate (%)	24.8	32.3	18.7	32.8	28.4
2006	Absolute amount (100 million yuan)	109,998	10,520	54,637	20,897	21,997
	Proportion in national GDP (%)	–	9.74	50.57	19.34	20.36
	Growth rate (%)	23.9	27.0	19.7	29.4	24.7
2005	Absolute amount (100 million yuan)	88,774	7679	45,626	16,146	17,645
	Proportion in national GDP (%)	–	8.82	52.39	18.54	20.26
	Growth rate (%)	26.0	37.6	21.9	28.9	28.3
2004	Absolute amount (100 million yuan)	70,477	5580	37,432	12,529	13,754
	Proportion in national GDP (%)	–	8.05	54.02	18.08	19.85
	Growth rate (%)	26.8	32.5	24.5	32.1	26.8
2003	Absolute amount (100 million yuan)	55,567	4212	30,064	9486	10,844
	Proportion in national GDP (%)	–	7.71	55.06	17.37	19.86
	Growth rate (%)	27.7	20.8	33.2	27.2	27.3

Source Calculated based on the *China Statistical Yearbook 2003–2013*

1.1.2 New Economic Growth Poles continue to emerge

In the past ten years, with the implementation of the strategy of coordinated regional development, the development vitality of each region had continuously increased. Apart from the traditional Beijing-Tianjin-Hebei Region, Yangtze River Delta Region and Pearl River Delta Region, a batch of new growth poles such as the middle reaches of the Yangtze River, Chengdu-Chongqing, and central plains have emerged in the central and western regions; central-southern Liaoning, Shandong Peninsula and Western Taiwan Straits Economic Zone in the eastern region have developed and expanded as well.

The region in the middle reaches of the Yangtze River, located at the junction of the horizontal axis of the Yangtze River channel and vertical axis of Beijing-Guangzhou channel, and including Wuhan city circle in Hubei Province, Xiangyang-Jingmen-Jingzhou-Yichang city cluster, Changsha-Zhuzhou-Xiangtan city cluster in Hunan province and Boyang Lake Ecological Economic Zone in Jiangxi province, has developed into an important high-tech, advanced manufacturing and modern service base, as well as an important integrated transport hub across the country.

Chengdu-Chongqing economic zone, located at the junction of the horizontal axis of the Yangtze River channel and the vertical axis of Baotou-Kunming channel, and including Chongqing economic zone and Chengdu economic zone, has developed into an important high-tech, advanced manufacturing and modern service base of the country, as well as the center of technology, education, trade, logistics, finance and integrated transport hub.

The central plains economic zone, located at the junction of the horizontal axis of the Eurasian Continental Bridge Passageway and the vertical axis of Beijing-Guangzhou channel, and including part of the central plains city circle centered around Zhengzhou in Henan Province, has developed into an important base for the advanced manufacturing industry, modern service industry and energy raw materials across the country.

The central-southern Liaoning region, located in the north wing of Bohai Economic Rim and including parts of central and southern Liaoning province, has developed into an important advanced equipment manufacturing and new raw materials base of the country, as well as an important base of technological innovation and technology research development.

The Shandong Peninsula Region is located in the south wing of Bohai Economic Rim and includes Jiaodong Peninsula of Shandong province and parts of the Yellow River Delta Region. It has developed into an important advanced manufacturing and high-tech base of the country.

Western Taiwan Straits Economic Zone, located in the western coast of Taiwan Straits and including Fujian Province and parts of Zhejiang Province, Jiangxi Province and Guangdong Province, has developed into the base of export-oriented manufacturing and harbor logistics in coastal regions.

1.2 The Comparative Advantages of the Four Major Regions Have Been Given Full Play

The strategy of coordinated regional development is oriented towards issues. For solving major issues faced by different regions, such as the issue of poverty in the western region, industry recession in the northeastern region and out-of-order development in the eastern region, the strategy is of great maneuverability and strongly targeted at those issues, basically realizing "one region one policy" for each typical region, fully mobilizing the initiative of the central and the local governments, powerfully playing the comparative advantages of each region, and effectively solving prominent problems faced by every region.

1.2.1 Positive Progress Has Been Made in Infrastructure Construction, Ecological Environment Construction and Development of Featured Industries in the Western Region

The development foundation of the western region is relatively weak. Therefore, the Western Development Strategy formulated by the country has regarded infrastructure, ecological environment and featured industries as the key directions for development of the western region. Over the past decade, the western region has made remarkable achievements in these fields.

Firstly, the construction of infrastructure has accelerated significantly. Over the past decade, the country has successively carried out more than 100 major projects of western development in the western region, mainly covering fields such as the highway, railway, civil aviation, hydroelectricity and development of social undertakings. The mileage of highways in the western region has increased rapidly, from 533,000 kilometers in 1999 to 1,420,000 kilometers in 2008; the mileage of expressways rose from 2529 kilometers to 16,456 kilometers, and the mileage of secondary roads rose from 35,131 kilometers to 99,478 kilometers.

Great achievements have been made in the construction of civil aviation airports, reconstruction and expansion of some airline hubs and construction of feeder airports. Remarkable improvements have been made to the railways. The Qinghai–Tibet railway has opened to traffic, while major projects such as the Lanzhou–Chongqing railway has been under construction. Four major projects, such as the construction of communications infrastructure including the communications corridor of the western region, digital cities, broadband access and general telephone service, have been progressing smoothly. Construction of the West–East Gas Pipeline has been completed and it is now supplying gas to its targeted regions. A batch of large-scale hydro projects has been successively accomplished and gone into operation.

Secondly, ecological construction has been constantly strengthened. The country has carried out a batch of major ecological construction projects to reverse the trend of deteriorating ecology of the western region, such as returning the grain plots to forestry, returning grazing land to grassland, protection of natural forest, control of the sources of sandstorms, territorial management of Three Gorges Reservoir Region, water pollution control, ecological protection of the Yangtze and Yellow River headwaters, treatment of stony desertification and construction of ecological shelters. Great ecological changes have taken place in some areas, realizing the transition from the trend of "overall deterioration, partial improvement" to "overall containment, partial improvement". The implementation of the returning the grain plots to forestry project has achieved distinct ecological, social and ecological benefits. The forest coverage rate has increased by an average of 2 percentage points, which has promoted the rehabilitation of meadows, transformation of the production management methods of the animal husbandry industry, and the adjustment of the economic structure of pasturing areas. The natural forest protection project has been comprehensively carried out; the Beijing–Tianjin Sandstorm Sources Control Project has obtained primary effects, and the comprehensive control of karst rocky desertification has started.

Thirdly, featured advantageous industries have rapidly developed. Great progress has been made in the secondary industry, especially the energy industries such as coal, petroleum, natural gas and electricity; in the tertiary industry such as transportation and traffic, culture and tourism; as well as in the development of featured agriculture. Six major featured advantageous industries have enjoyed sound momentum of growth, including the energy and chemical industry, advantageous mining resource exploitation and processing industry, featured farm and pasture product processing industry, equipment manufacturing industry, high-tech industry and tourism industry, which led to the formation of a batch of featured advantageous industry bases and a batch of brands and enterprises that are famous home and abroad and of strong competitiveness. The production and processing capacity of commodity grain, high-quality cotton, sugar crop, tobacco, vintage wine and melon and fruit continued to strengthen. Additionally, high-tech industrialization projects such as biological technology, new energy, modern pharmacy and modern agriculture have been successfully carried out, while the promotion of advanced applied technology and transformation of scientific and technological achievements have also been accelerated. The effect of high tech in boosting economic growth has continuously increased. The high-tech industries of Chengdu-Chongqing region and Guanzhong region, such as information, biology, aeronautics and astronautics, have continuously gotten stronger; the coal electricity integration and coal chemical industry base construction of many provinces and districts including Inner Mongolia, Xinjiang, Shaanxi, Ningxia have been progressing smoothly. Xinjiang has become the biggest output area of natural gas in the country and an important petrochemical base. With furthering reform of resource pricing, more development space and system guarantee have been obtained in resource-rich areas and output areas in the western region, the exploitation of advantageous resources has significantly accelerated, and relevant industries have realized sustainable and rapid development.

[Column 2-1]
Implementation of the Western Development Strategy (taking the Chengdu-Chongqing Region as an example)
The Chengdu-Chongqing Economic Zone, located in the upper reaches of the Yangtze River in the western region, is an important population, urban and industrial cluster in the country. It is a region in the west with relatively good basic conditions and fast economic growth, and it is shouldering the responsibility of developing into an "important economic center of the western region". Since the implementation of the Western Development Strategy, the Chengdu-Chongqing region has made remarkable progress in economic and social development.

Firstly, economic aggregate has increased significantly. From 2006 to 2012, the economic aggregate of Chongqing rose from 390.7 billion yuan to 1141 billion yuan, and the per capita local gross product value reached

39,083 yuan, exceeding the national average and ranking second in the western region and 12th in the country; the proportion of added value in the non-agricultural industries reached 91.2%. From 2007 to 2012, the GDP of Chengdu jumped from 336.478 billion yuan to 813.894 billion yuan, and annual average growth reached 19.32%; the per capita GDP rose from 26,849 yuan to 57,624 yuan, and annual average growth reached 16.5%; the total fiscal revenue rose from 99.661 billion yuan to 233.126 billion yuan, and annual average growth reached 18.52%.

Secondly, the urban–rural gap has been effectively reversed. In 2012, the urbanization rate of Chongqing rose to 57%. The income of urban and rural residents grew in step with GDP growth, reaching 22,968 yuan and 7383 yuan, respectively, 2391.6 yuan and 1321.3 yuan more than the average of the western region. The urban–rural income gap shrunk from 3.6:1 in 2006 to 3.11:1 in 2012. From 2007 to 2012, the urbanization rate of Chengdu rose from 62.58% in 2007 to 68.44% in 2012, while the rural per capita net income rose from 5642 yuan to 11,501 yuan, and annual average growth rate was 15.3%; the urban–rural income gap shrank from 2.63:1 to 2.36:1. At the same time of rapid development of the urban and rural areas, urban–rural income gap was further narrowed.

Thirdly, an urban–rural integrated employment, census register and social security system, as well as public service systems such as education, medical treatment and public health and culture that covered both urban and rural areas have been initially formed, which pushed forward the balanced resource distribution of resources such as transportation and traffic, water supply, electricity, gas, information networks and municipal services between the urban and rural areas. A mechanism where urban and rural residents co-construct and share the fruits of reform and development has been primarily established. Rural residents have been enjoying increasing benefits.

Fourthly, major projects have been successfully carried out. Significant progress has been made in a batch of projects in transportation and traffic, energy, commerce and trade, social undertaking, etc. Significant projects have been accomplished, including the Chengdu-Chongqing high-speed railway, Xi'an–Chengdu high-speed railway, Xiangyang–Chongqing double-track railway and Yichang–Wanzhou railway. A batch of projects has been under construction, including the Lanzhou–Chongqing railway, Chengdu-Harbin railway, Chongqing–Guizhou railway, Zhengzhou–Wanzhou railway, new airport of Chengdu and Chongqing Jiangbei airport. Chongqing Liangjiang New Area and Chengdu Tiandu New Area have been approved as national new areas.

Source Organized based on public documents.

1.2.2 Significant Progress Have Been Made in the Reform of Major Fields such as the State-Owned Enterprises of Old Industrial Bases Including the Northeastern Region, Development of Significant Technology Equipment, and Transformation of Resource-Exhausted Cities

Old industrial bases including the northeast region are heavy industrial bases and raw material bases of national importance, with a high proportion of state-owned enterprises, heavy industries and energy raw materials. Since the implementation of the revitalization of old industrial bases including the northeastern region, the country has supported the northeastern region to further reforms in major fields such as state-owned enterprises and actively supported the development of significant technology equipment and major livelihood projects such as shantytowns transformation, which effectively promoted the transformation of old industrial bases.

Firstly, the reform of state-owned enterprises has been accelerated. The country supported state-owned industrial enterprises of the old industrial base of the northeastern region to comprehensively launch the reform of property rights system. Through policies such as policy-mandated bankruptcy, cancelation of bad and doubtful debts after verification, relief of enterprises from their obligation to operate social programs, stripping off bad assets, exemption of historical tax debt, and disposal of bad loans, state-owned enterprises have been able to remove their heavy historical burden. During the ten years from 2003 to 2012, the three provinces of the northeastern region had accumulated 320 policy-mandated bankruptcy enterprises and helped 833,000 employees to settle down, which accounted for 1/5 of the national aggregate. Over 250 enterprises totally relieved over 1700 enterprises of their obligation to operate social programs, involving 170,000 employees.

Secondly, industrial competitiveness has been gradually shaped. The country attached greater support to the autonomization of significant technology equipment of the old industrial base of the northeastern region. Over the past ten years, a batch of significant technology equipment had been successfully developed in the old industrial base of the northeastern region, such as the gigawatt (GW) nuclear power unit, thermal power generation set, extra-high voltage (EHV) equipment for power transmission and transformation, large-scale hydraulic turbine set, large-scale wind turbine generator, megaton ethylene unit, large-scale shield tunneling machine, China Railway High-Speed (CRH) bullet train, advanced ship and marine drilling platform, high-end numerically controlled production center, and heavy numerical control (NC) machine tool. The region has continued to play a pillaring effect in fields such as major technology equipment and national defense industry. Within the ten years, the old industrial base of the northeastern region had introduced a series of influential foreign capital projects such as Dalian Intel and Shenyang BMW. The "Going Out" policy of enterprises proved to be highly effective and a batch of enterprises such as Shenyang Machine Tool had successfully merged with and acquired well-known foreign enterprises.

[Column 2-2]
Development of the equipment manufacturing base in the northeastern region
The northeastern region is one of the nationally-important bases of equipment manufacturing. After ten years of implementing the revitalization strategy, autonomization has been realized in the fields of GW nuclear power, ultra-supercritical thermal power, ±800KVDC and one-million-volt alternating current EHV equipment for power transmission and transformation complete equipment, 700,000 kilowatt large-scale hydraulic turbine set, 300,000 kilowatt pumped storage set, 5 billion large-scale wind turbine generator, megaton ethylene set, large-scale shield tunneling machine, 350 km/h high-speed train, high-end five-axis linkage processing center urgently needed in the field of aeronautics and astronautics and military industry, as well as heavy NC machine tool. Advanced equipment manufacturing bases with international competitiveness have taken shape in cities such as Shenyang, Dalian, Harbin and Qiqihar, among which the output value of the equipment manufacturing industry of Shenyang and Dalian ranks high in the country.

Shenyang Machine Tool, Northern Heavy Industries Group (NHIG), Shenyang Blower Works Group (SBW), Sany Heavy Industry, TBEA and other heavy equipment companies of national importance are based in Shenyang, whose products cover mining equipment, power station equipment, smelting equipment, rolling equipment, petrochemical equipment, cement equipment, jack-up equipment, numerically controlled machine tool, forge and press equipment, artificial board set equipment, bulk cargo transportation equipment, environmental protection equipment, engineering machinery, transmission machinery, agriculture machinery, metal cutting machine tool, large-scale electric transmission and transformation equipment, etc. These products have been extensively applied in various fields such as the mining, petrochemical, metallurgy and electric power industries, national defense and scientific research. As a result, Shenyang has been known as the "Oriental Ruhr". In November 2008, with joint evaluation of the periodical office of *China Equipment* and the equipment industrial development research center, Shenyang Tiexi New District was selected as an important agglomeration area of the equipment manufacturing industry and was ranked first.

Dalian possesses national famous leading enterprises such as Dalian Machine Tools Group (DMTG), Sinovel Wind Group, Dalian Shipbuilding Industry Co. (DSIC) and Dalian Marine Crankshaft Factory. Dalian has a relatively sound technology foundation in high-end numerically controlled machine tools and relevant products; major technical equipment such as wind power generation equipment, marine engineering equipment, large-scale marine crankshaft, shield tunneling machine, nuclear power product and high-end machine tools; as well as high-end locomotives and city rapid rail vehicles, high-end bearing products and high-end refrigeration products.

Qiqihar possesses leading enterprises such as China First Heavy Industries (CFHI), Qiqihar Heavy CNC Equipment Corp. and Qiqihar No. 2 Machine Tool (Group) Co. (QIER), with advantage in numerically controlled machine tool, rail traffic equipment and nuclear power equipment.

Harbin possesses key enterprises such as Harbin Measuring & Cutting Tool Group Co. (HMTC Group), Harbin Electric Corporation and Avic Harbin Aircraft Industry Group Co., Ltd., with advantage in fields such as general tools and measuring instruments, power generation equipment and aircraft manufacturing.

Changchun possesses leading enterprises such as CRRC Changchun Railway Vehicles Co., Ltd., with strong technology advantage in fields such as rail traffic equipment and agricultural machinery equipment.

In 2012, the output of power generation equipment of the three provinces of the northeastern region took up 1/3 of the national aggregate; output value of numerically controlled machine tool took up 1/3 of the national aggregate; output of internal combustion engine took up 1/5 of the national aggregate; capacity of oil refining reached 1/5 of the national aggregate; output of ethylene took up 1/3 of the national aggregate; output of steel took up over 1/10 of the national aggregate; output of automobiles took up around 1/7 of the national aggregate; total capacity of shipbuilding reached 1/5 of the national aggregate. The three provinces played a pillar role in the national equipment manufacturing industry and the production of important industrial products.

Source Organized based on public documents.

Thirdly, support has been given to the transformation of resource-exhausted cities and implementation of major livelihood projects such as shantytowns transformation. In 2001, the State Council confirmed Fuxin as the first experimental city of economic transformation of resource-exhausted cities in the country. In 2005, the country confirmed five experimental cities of resource-based cities of economic transformation in the northeastern region, and they were Fuxin, Yichun, Liaoyuan, Baishan and Panjin. The country put greater efforts in supporting resource-exhausted cities to develop new alternative industries, accelerate the construction of major livelihood projects and restore the ecological environment. In 2005, Fushun and Fuxin took the lead in conducting shantytowns transformation project. In 2006, the northeastern region took the lead in conducting shantytowns transformation project in the whole country. In the past ten years, the northeastern region transformed over 300 million square meters of various shantytowns, from which over 10 million people with difficulty benefited. Additionally, on the basis of pilots in the northeastern region, the country also actively supported old industrial cities and old industrial areas of urban area to accelerate transformation. 21 pilots of removal and transformation of old industrial areas in urban areas were confirmed, such as Shougang of Beijing, Hongdu of Nanchang, Gutian of Wuhan, Qingshuitang of Zhuzhou, Gulou of Xuzhou, Jianxi of Luoyang and Qilihe of Lanzhou. The country organized old industrial pilot areas to actively explore in the methods of organization and implementation, capital raise, land utilization, governance of land polluted by industry, transformation and utilization of old factory, old workshop and old facility, protection and utilization of industrial heritage and promotion of green architecture, thus setting an example for removal and transformation of other old industrial areas in other urban areas across the country.

1.2.3 The "Three Bases One Hub" Construction of the Central Region Has Been Actively Promoted

The advantage in transportation is prominent in the central region with huge population and good industrial foundation. Since the implementation of the rise of central region strategy, the country has supported the central region to accelerate the construction of modern equipment manufacturing, high-tech industry base, raw material of energy base, food production base and comprehensive transportation and traffic hub.

Firstly, the construction of modern equipment manufacturing and high-tech industry base has been accelerated. The country arranged special funding for the central region to develop the equipment manufacturing industries such as clean power technology equipment with high efficiency, high-tension power transmission and transformation equipment, high-power electric motor car, large-scale construction machinery, numerically controlled system and new agriculture equipment. The country promoted the research, development and industrialization of high tech such as electronic information, biological engineering and modern traditional Chinese medicine. During the "11th Five-Year Plan" period, the country supported the central region to establish 22 new national major labs, 13 national major lab breeding bases that were co-set up by the provincial and central governments, and 16 national engineering technology research centers.

Secondly, the construction of energy raw material base has been sturdily pushed forward. The country constructed a batch of projects in areas such as steel, nonferrous metals and ethylene, including major projects such as the expansion of Wuhan Iron & Steel Corporation (WISCO), the stainless steel seamless steel tube assembly line of Shanxi Taigang Stainless Steel Co., Ltd., and auto sheet and electrical steel that were jointly constructed by Hunan Valin Steel Co., Ltd. Special funds for industrial structure adjustment such as the revitalization and technology transformation of major industries, and adjustment and transformation of old industrial bases were utilized to support relevant projects in fields such as the equipment manufacturing, automobile, petrochemical, electromechanical and light textile of the central region.

Thirdly, the construction of food production has been supported. The central government strengthened fiscal support to the six provinces of the central region through a direct subsidy for grain, comprehensive direct subsidy for agricultural capital, allowance for purchasing agricultural machinery and superior crop varieties, which improved the financial incentives of granary counties and supported the construction of food production base. During the "11th Five-Year Plan" period, the six provinces of the central region were supported to construct farmland with high standard of over 1.33 million hectares in accumulative total with nearly 1000 agricultural projects.

Fourthly, the construction of a comprehensive traffic and transportation hub has been actively pushed forward. The construction of passenger transport lines, inter-region communication channel and coal transportation channel has been accelerated, and greater efforts have been put in the construction of provincial highways and transformation of national highways and provincial highways. During the "11th Five-Year Plan" period, various transportation projects were carried out, including the construction of passenger transport lines such as Beijing-Wuhan-Guangzhou and Zhengzhou to Xi'an; express railroads such as Shijiazhuang to Taiyuan and Hefei to Wuhan to Yichang to Chongqing; inter-region trunk lines and coal transportation channels such as Taiyuan to Zhongwei, the Wuhan to Xiangyang to Ankang double-track line, Chongqing to Huaihua, south section of Luozhan railway, upgrading project of the Datong–Qinhuangdao railway, upgrading project of the Houma–Yueshan railway and Baotou-Xi'an channel; and passenger transport lines such as Zhengzhou to Xuzhou, Hangzhou to Changsha to Kunming, Bengbu to Hefei to Fuzhou and Datong to Xi'an. Various railway projects were completed, including the upgrading of the Ganzhou to Longyan railway, the railway lines of Ganzhou to Shaoguan, Loudi to Shaoyang, Hengyang to Chaling to Ji'an, Fuyang to Liu'an, Suzhou to Huai'an and Taiyuan to Xingxian, and the intercity railway of Nanchang to Jiujiang; intercity railways such as Wuhan to Huangshi, Wuhan to Xiaogan, Wuhan to Xianning, Changsha to Zhuzhou to Xiangtan, Zhengzhou to Kaifeng, Zhengzhou to Jiaozuo and Nanjing to Anqing have been under construction. The transformation and upgrading projects of the five airports of Nanchang, Zhengzhou, Wuhan, Changsha and Taiyuan of the central region were carried out while 12 branch line airports, such as Huangshan, Jingdezhen, Luoyang and Zhangjiajie, were under construction; projects such as the construction of Datong airport and Nanchang airport, transformation and expansion of Fuyang airport, and construction of Lvliang airport, Jiuhuashan airport and Shennongjia airport were also carried out. The construction of the golden waterway of the Yangtze River was continuously promoted and the construction of Wuhan New Port, Yichang Port, Hefei Port, Wuhu Port, Bengbu Port and Nanchang Port were taken place.

Fifthly, breakthroughs have been made in the development of major urban clusters. Wuhan metropolitan area took the lead in obtaining progress in important fields and key links such as structure optimization, energy conservation and emission reduction, and independent innovation. The demonstration and radiation effect of Wuhan has been obviously strengthened. The central urban cluster took the lead in the accomplishment of breakthroughs in promoting the coordinated development of agriculture modernization, industrialization and urbanization by seizing the strategic opportunity of the country supporting the construction of the Central Plains economic region. Important transportation arterial lines such as passenger transport lines and intercity rapid rail transport were seen as the linkages, while the construction of Zhengdong New District, Bianxi New District and Luoyang New District were regarded as the carriers. The Changsha-Zhuzhou-Xiangtan city group actively explored new mechanisms that benefited resource-saving and environment protection and the new pattern of urban agglomeration development. The construction of advanced equipment manufacturing base, electric information industry base and culture creativity industry base were also implemented. The Wanjiang City Belt actively promoted cities along the Yangtze River to engage in cross-river cooperation and linkage development and accelerated the formation of industrial agglomeration area. It has since become an important demonstration area of carrying industry transfer in the country. Poyang lake city cluster is targeted at establishing the Poyang lake ecological and economic zone, specifying function division and optimizing space distribution. Taiyuan city cluster took the lead in economic transformation of resource-based cities, steadily pushing forward urban integration development in fields such as public transportation, telecommunication, finance and municipal administration, centered by Tai(yuan)Yu(ci).

[Column 2-3]
Construction of city clusters in the central region (taking the Wuhan City Cluster as example)
Wuhan is the central city of the central region. In recent years, Wuhan city cluster has played a key role in the rising of central region and regional development.

Firstly, the tendency of industrial chain and integrated development has gradually become obvious. The photoelectronic industry of Wuhan has gradually extended to other cities such as Xiaogan and Xianning; steel and deep processing enterprises have mainly extended to Ezhou and Huangshi; medicine and chemical engineering industries have mainly transferred to Qianjiang, Xiaogan and Huanggang; textile, clothing and dyeing industries have mainly transferred to Xiaogan, Xiantao and Tianmen; automobile industry and spare parts industry have mainly extended to Xiaogan, Xiantao and Qianjiang. In the architectural material industry, Huaxin Cement Group has gathered its business and research institutions in Wuhan, and has invested and established three companies in Wuhan, which are Huaxin Wuhan Qingshan Co., Ltd. (cement grinding station of 300,000 tons), Huaxin Wugang Co., Ltd. (utilize blast furnace slag of Wugang Company to process grinding deeply), and Huaxin Concrete (Wuhan) Co., Ltd. Product bases have been established in Chibi of Xianning City, Wuxue of Huanggang City, and Xiantao City. Wuhan Tobacco Group has successively acquired three cigarette factories, which were Sanxia, Hongan and Guangshui, and bought plan targets of three cigarette factories, which were Jiangling, Dawu and Xianning, greatly enhancing the annual production of Wuhan Tobacco Group. Additionally, industries such as machine manufacturing of the inner circles, electronics and food processing have gradually shown a trend of mass development, thus initially forming featured industry belts which include the photoelectron industry, steel industry, chemical engineering industry, textile and clothing industry and automobile and spare parts industry.

Secondly, the effect of the integration of major service industries such as tourism, commerce and trade, finance and information has become obvious. In tourism, the Wuhan city cluster has formulated *Overall Planning of Tourism Development of the Wuhan City Cluster*, realizing integrated tourism development of nine cities. By relying on the resources of city cluster, eight major tourist products such as scientific education culture, hot spring holiday, red culture and ecological leisure were elaborately arranged and organized, forming a series of tourism brands within the city cluster. In trade, commerce and logistics, the three major groups, Wuhan Wushang Group Co., Ltd., Wuhan Zhongbai Group Co., Ltd., and Wuhan Zhongshang Group Co., Ltd., have continuously extended chain outlets into every city within the cluster. Among them, Wuhan Wushang Group Co., Ltd. has developed over 700 chain outlets within the cluster, with total business area reaching 0.95 million square meters. In finance, the status of Wuhan as a regional financial center has gradually become prominent, with financial institutions such as the People's Bank of China (PBC), Industrial and Commercial Bank of China (ICBC), Agricultural Bank of China (ABC) and China Construction Bank (CCB) setting up regional headquarters, branches or national financial backstage service centers in Wuhan, and introducing 35 foreign-invested financial enterprises in total and setting up over 40 micro-loan companies. Wuhan Commercial Bank was renamed as Hankou Bank, and has set branches in Ezhou. In information transmission, software and information technology service industry, the communication fee within the city cluster has continuously decreased. The Communications Admission of Hubei Province has taken the lead in setting pilots of communication fee reform between Wuhan and Ezhou, implementing the "discount package within the city cluster", lowering the communication fee of fixed-line telephone and cellphone between the two cities, and adjusting the call charge standard to nearly the same as the local communication standard.

Thirdly, the platform of transregional investment and financing within the city cluster has been gradually perfected. Joint Development Investment Group Ltd. of Hubei Province was established, and financing and construction by means of sponsors was conducted. Till now, Joint Development Investment Group Ltd. of Hubei Province has constructed and financed major projects such as the ecological water networks of Dadong Lake, Wuhan New District and Huashan New City. The City Cluster Construction and Development Fund has been established, which is co-founded by Joint Development Investment Group Ltd. of Hubei Province, China Development Bank Capital Co., Ltd. (CDBC), and the Hubei branch of China Development Bank. The government of Hubei province has invested three hundred million yuan every year to support the nine cities within the city cluster to carry out comprehensive projects that are led and constructed by the concept of reform and innovation. Such projects are determined by open tendering and encourage the injection of social capital.

Fourthly, in traffic infrastructure construction, "one-hour transport circle" has been basically accomplished. The Sui(zhou)Yue(yang) highway; highway ramps of Qing(ling)Zheng(dian) of Wuhan, (Wu)hanying(shan), Han(yang)Cai(dian), (Wu)hanma(Cheng) and (Wu)hanhong(hu); the Guan(shan)Ge(dian) first-class highway; and the Yangluo Yangtze River Bridge have been completed and in operation. The whole 188-kilometer outer ring of Wuhan has been completed and in operation; the mileage of highway within the city cluster has reached 2000 kilometers, and the framework of highway that "links the eastern and western region and connects the southern and northern region" has taken shape. Four urban railways have been constructed and in operation, which are Wuhan to Xiaogan, Wuhan to Huangshi via Ezhou, Wuhan to Xianning and Wuhan to Huanggang. The passenger line of Wu(han)Guang(zhou), the railway of Wuhan to Hefei and the second line of Wu(han)Xiang(yang)An(kang) have been completed and in operation. The transformation of Wuchang railway station and Wuhan railway station have been in operation. The phase 3 expansion of and the construction of a new international building at Wuhan Airport have been progressing. The largest comprehensive three-dimensional transportation hub, which integrates the highway, railway, waterway and airway in central China, has primarily taken shape. In electricity, the 500 kV looped network power transmission and transformation project of eastern Hubei Province has been accomplished. With its annual transmission capacity of thirty billion kilowatt-hours, it has provided strong electricity support for the construction and development of the city cluster.

Fifthly, the integration of public service has been accelerated. In education, the city cluster has actively pushed forward the joint-schooling of ministry-affiliated and local colleges and universities in Wuhan. It has actively pushed forward the paired assistance of elementary education between Wuhan and the nearby eight cities and construction of vocational education areas, boosting co-construction and share of educational resource. In culture, the library alliance website of the nine cities within the city cluster has been officially launched and the interflow reading service among public libraries of every city within the cluster has been carried out comprehensively. The show business alliance within the city cluster has been primarily formed while free entries have been actively promoted by museums and memorial halls. In health and sanitation, the emergency command system for public health within the nine cities of the city cluster has been under construction, of which the first stage of provincial health emergency decision-making and command information system has been completed. The maternal and childcare service centers of the nine cities have been exchanging information, sharing resources, complementing each other's advantages and reducing running cost.

Source Organized based on public documents.

1.2.4 The Quality of Development in the Eastern Region Has Been Further Improved

The eastern region is China's most economically developed region. Since the implementation of the coordinated regional development strategy, the state has focused on supporting the eastern region to continuously improve the quality and efficiency of economic development. The eastern region is at the forefront of the country in transforming the economic development pattern.

First, the economic strength and overall quality of the eastern region have been further improved. The GDP of the eastern region increased from 5274.28 billion yuan in 2000 to 32,225.9 billion yuan in 2013, with an average annual growth rate of 9.1%. The per capita GDP increased from 14,397.3 yuan in 2000 to 62,405 yuan in 2013, exceeding 10,000 US dollars and reaching the level of moderately developed countries, with an average annual growth rate of 8.1%.

Second, the radiation-driven capacity of the core area has been significantly improved. In 2013, the GDP of the three major metropolitan economic circles in the Yangtze River Delta, the Pearl River Delta, and the Beijing-Tianjin-Hebei region accounted for 42.6% of the national GDP. The total import and export volume accounted for 76.2% of the country's total. The actual use of foreign capital accounted for 85.2% of the country. The three major metropolitan areas continued playing the core engine of China's economic development and opening up. At present, the city clusters of the Pearl River Delta, the Yangtze River Delta and the Beijing-Tianjin-Hebei region in the eastern coastal areas have initially acquired global competitiveness. The city clusters of Shandong Peninsula and the Western Taiwan Strait have also become important platforms for leading regional competition. Among the 10 cities with competitiveness in the country, the eastern coastal areas accounted for 6. The city clusters in the eastern coastal areas have become an important platform for leading the Chinese economy to participate in global competition.

Third, the industrial structure and independent innovation of the eastern region have taken the lead in the country. The proportion and level of high-tech industries such as electronic information, biomedicine, new energy, and new materials, as well as services industries such as modern logistics, financial services, technology services, information services, tourism, cultural creativity, and leisure and entertainment have further increased. The added value of the tertiary industry in the 10 provinces and cities in the eastern region has increased from 57.2% in 2005 to 57.9% in 2006 and 59.1% in 2013. At the same time, the eastern region has actively promoted independent innovation, extensively used high-tech and advanced practical technologies to transform and upgrade traditional industries, and accelerated the transformation and transfer of processing and manufacturing industries. The proportion of exports of high-tech products, mechanical and electrical products and other high-value-added products increased significantly. After strenuous efforts, the eastern region has initially established an industrial structure with the modern service industry and high-tech industry as the main body. At the same time, the eastern coastal city clusters have become a region with high concentration of innovation factors. In 2012, the eastern region accounted for nearly 70% of China's invention patent authorization, and the concentration of innovation factors has exceeded the economic concentration.

1.3 Positive Progress in the Development of Poor Areas

On the basis of the differentiated policies of the four major regions, the state has also implemented special assistance policies for poor areas, and has initially established a regional policy system to solve the special difficulties of discrete areas across administrative regions through establishing type areas and functional areas.

First, the development conditions in poverty-stricken areas have been improved. The national standard for poverty alleviation in rural areas has gradually increased from 865 yuan in 2000 to 1274 yuan in 2010 and to 2300 yuan in 2011. The number of poor people in rural areas measured by this standard decreased from 94.22 million at the end of 2000 to 26.88 million at the end of 2010. The proportion of poor people in rural residents dropped from 10.2% in 2000 to 2.8% in 2010. Economic development in poor areas is in full swing. The industrial structure in poor areas has been further optimized, the industries with advantages and characteristics have developed rapidly, and the comprehensive strength of the county economy has been continuously strengthened. From 2001 to 2010, the per capita GDP of 592 key counties in the country's poverty alleviation and development work increased from 2658 yuan to 11,170 yuan, an average annual growth of 17%. The per capita general budget revenue of local finance increased from 123 yuan to 559 yuan, with an average annual growth rate of 18.3%. The per capita net income of farmers increased from 1276 yuan in 2001 to 3273 yuan in 2010, an average annual increase of 11% (excluding price factors). The growth rate of the above data is higher than the national average. Production and living conditions in poor areas have been improved significantly. From 2002 to 2010, 592 key counties in the country's poverty alleviation and development work added 3.497 million hectares of basic farmland, 952,000 kilometers of newly built and renovated roads, 35.061 million square meters of newly built educational and health facilities, and solved the drinking water problem for 56.757 million people and 49.993 million large livestock. By the end of 2010, the proportion of rural households drinking tap water and deep water wells in key counties of the national poverty alleviation and development work reached 60.9%, the proportion of natural villages connecting roads was 88.1%, the proportion of electricity supply was 98%, the proportion of telephone calls was 92.9%, the per capita housing area of rural households was 24.9 square meters, the proportion of rural households using dry toilets and water flushing toilets reached 88.4%, and the rural landscape in poor areas changed significantly. Social undertakings in poverty-stricken areas have made continuous progress. By the end of 2010, the enrollment rate of school-age children aged 7–15 in key counties of the national poverty alleviation and development work reached 97.7%, close to the national average. Illiteracy among young adults was 7%, 5.4 percentage points lower than 2002, and the average years of schooling for the young adults labor force has reached 8 years. The new rural cooperative medical insurance has achieved full coverage, and the construction of primary medical and health service system has been continuously strengthened. By the end of 2010, 93.3% of the farmers in the key counties of the national poverty alleviation and development work have participated in the new rural cooperative medical system, 91.4% have been able to seek medical treatment in time for illness, township hospitals have been built, and the vast majority of administrative villages have health clinics. Population and family planning work and the construction of public cultural service systems in poor areas have continued to be strengthened. Ecological deterioration in poor areas has been initially curbed. From 2002 to 2010, 9.949 million hectares of farmland were converted to forests and grasslands and 15.096 million hectares of economic forests were added in key counties of the national poverty alleviation and development work. The proportion of farmers whose drinking water sources are polluted in key counties of the national poverty alleviation and development work decreased from 15.5% in 2002 to 5.1% in 2010, and the proportion of farmers who have difficulty in obtaining fuel decreased from 45 to 31.4%.

Second, ethnic minority areas have experienced accelerated development. The total economic volume of ethnic minority areas increased from 5.79 billion yuan in 1952 to 3062.62 billion yuan in 2008, an increase of 92.5 times at comparable prices. The per capita disposable income of urban residents increased from 307 yuan in 1978 to 13,170 yuan in 2008, an increase of more than 30 times at comparable prices. The per capita net income of farmers and herdsmen increased from 138 yuan in 1978 to 3389 yuan in 2008, a 19-fold increase at comparable prices. Inner Mongolia's economic growth rate once topped that of the whole country for 7 consecutive years, while Xinjiang's economic growth rate maintained double-digit growth for 6 consecutive years. Tibet's GDP reached 39.591 billion yuan in 2008, increased by 65 times from 1959. Inner Mongolia, Tibet, Guangxi and other ethnic regions have relied on their advantages in resources and location to speed up their development in an all-round way. Inner Mongolia Autonomous Region has actively developed advantageous resources while its dairy, energy, chemical, iron and steel industries have continued to grow at a high level. The economic growth rate of Inner Mongolia has remained the highest in the country for many years, and at the same time, its energy consumption of industrial added value and the emission of chemical oxygen demand have decreased significantly. Driven by the opening and operation of the Qinghai–Tibet Railway, tourism and consumption in Tibet Autonomous Region grew strongly. Guangxi Zhuang Autonomous Region has accelerated its economic growth by promoting the development and opening up of Beibu Gulf. Economic exchanges between Xinjiang, Yunnan, Guangxi, Jilin and other border provinces and regions and neighboring countries have continued to expand. The import and export trade between Xinjiang and Central Asia has developed steadily. The total import and export volume of Yunnan, Guangxi and ASEAN countries has increased rapidly.

Third, the prominent problems faced by resource-exhausted cities have been effectively alleviated. From 2007 to 2011, the average annual growth rate of GDP in the first two batches of 44 urban areas was 3.5 percentage points higher than the national average, and the average annual growth rate of local general budget revenue was 20.6%, more than double that of 2007. Alternative industries have developed rapidly, the industrial structure has been continuously optimized, and diversified industrial systems in resource-exhausted cities are gradually taking shape. The development of alternative industries according to local conditions has gradually reduced the proportion of the added value of extractive industries in regional GDP. Panjin's petroleum equipment, Tongling's electronic information, Fuxin's hydraulic equipment and other industries have already had a rough competitive advantage. Jiaozuo and Zaozhuang's tourism have become the pillar industries of the city. People's livelihood has been continuously improving. By the end of 2011, 69 resource-exhausted cities had renovated 87 million square meters of shantytowns, benefiting nearly 2 million families. Solid progress has been made in ecological management. A total of 76,000 hectares of mine geological environment have been restored and treated. Coal gangue and smelting waste residue have gradually been comprehensively utilized. Environmental problems such as soil erosion and heavy metal pollution have been preliminarily controlled. Vegetation has been restored and its environmental carrying capacity has been significantly enhanced. Resource-exhausted cities have also been actively exploring their own distinctive transformation models. Fushun and Baiyin opened up new paths for economic transformation through coordinated development with Shenyang and Lanzhou, respectively. Jiaozuo and Zaozhuang started from a high starting point to develop tourism and have gradually reduced their dependence on mineral resources. Fuxin, Liaoyuan, Panjin and Huaying strengthened the construction of industrial parks, and the trend of replacing industrial clusters has begun to emerge. Pingxiang has carried out a pilot project of sustainable development reserve for resource-based cities to explore the establishment of a long-term mechanism for sustainable development.

[Column 2-4]
Progress in the transformation of resource-exhausted cities (taking Fuxin as an example)

In December 2001, the state approved Fuxin, Liaoning Province, to become the first pilot city for economic transformation as a resource-exhausted city. For more than 10 years, Fuxin has actively explored the sustainable development path of resource-based cities, cracked the development problems, made great efforts to improve people's livelihood, and embarked on a new journey of transformation and revitalization.

From 2002 to 2012, Fuxin's GDP rose from 7 billion yuan to 46 billion yuan, with an average annual growth rate of 6 percentage points higher than that of the whole country. The general budget revenue of local finance increased from 420 million yuan to 5 billion yuan, tripling and a half. The total investment in fixed assets of the whole society has reached 150 billion yuan, with an average annual growth rate of more than 30%. In the past decade, Fuxin's development has always run through a main line: people first, people's livelihood first, that is, people's livelihood has always been guaranteed and improved, and people's livelihood improvement has been the most concerned, direct and realistic issue of interests, thus leading the transformation of leading industries, and improving urban functions and ecological environment management.

Improve employment and address possible layoffs. At the beginning of the twenty-first century, 23 mines in Fuxin City were closed down one after another. A large number of industrial workers were unemployed. The number of unemployed workers in Fuxin City reached 156,000 which accounted for 36.7% of all workers. The registered unemployment rate of the urban population was as high as 7%. The employment situation was grim and became a top priority. Employment is the foundation of people's livelihood. In the decade, governments at all levels have done everything possible to promote employment and reemployment. A total of 677,000 people has been employed under the real-name system. The stable employment rate has reached more than 65%, ensuring that every family has at least one bread earner. The registered unemployment rate of the urban population has dropped to 3.9%, basically solving the problem of reemployment left over from history.

Expand industry and lay a solid foundation for improving people's living standards. Fuxin has formed a single industrial structure dominated by coal for more than 50 years, which makes the local economic foundation very weak and the people's life very difficult. In 2000, Fuxin's GDP per capita was only 31% of Liaoning Province's average. Since the transformation, Fuxin has insisted on the adjustment of the industrial structure as the core of economic transformation and has made great efforts to change the single industrial structure dominated by coal. It vigorously promoted food and agricultural products processing, new energy, coal chemical industry "three bases" and "six key industrial clusters" such as hydraulic, leather, sheet home, and foundry, fluorine chemical and new materials. A diversified industrial pattern has been formed, and the framework of alternative industries has been established. From 2002 to 2012, the single industrial structure dominated by coal was adjusted, and the proportion of the coal industry in the above-scale industries fell from 33.4 to 22.2%. The proportion of equipment manufacturing industry in the industry increased from 3 to 27.8%, historically surpassing the proportion of coal industry in 2009, ranking first.

Optimize the environment and build a modern city that is livable and happy. Fuxin City was built on the basis of mines, with a mixed layout between urban and rural areas and lagging infrastructure construction. Since the transformation of resource-exhausted cities, Fuxin City has taken the improvement of urban functions, expansion of urban space and improvement of ecological environment as important measures to promote the transformation, and has implemented the "trinity" planning of the central district, Fumeng County and Xinqiu District. According to the development idea of one industry and one new town, five new towns, including "Yulong New Town" and "Shenzhang New Town", have been planned and constructed. Efforts to build infrastructure have been stepped up. Six expressways have passed through the city, with the total mileage and density ranking first in the province. Efforts have been made to promote the construction of forestry ecology, afforestation and greening totaled 650,000 hectares in ten years, and the forest coverage rate increased from 21.7 to 32.1%.

Renovate shantytowns so that residents have their own houses. Fuxin is the largest shantytown area in Liaoning Province, which could be considered as "The area of shantytowns equals to that of mining". The city has a total of 6.32 million square meters of shantytowns, accounting for nearly half of the city's residential area, involving 440,000 people, accounting for two-thirds of the city's population. Moreover, these houses are in disrepair and many have become dilapidated buildings. Going out of shantytowns is the dream of several generations of Fuxin people. Since the transformation, Fuxin has promoted the renovation of shantytowns as the city's "No.1 People's Livelihood Project". In 2005, the shantytown renovation project with the largest area, the heaviest task and the most outstanding difficulties in the whole province was launched. A total of 4.91 million square meters of shantytowns have been demolished, 6.92 million square meters of new resettlement buildings have been built, and the living conditions of 400,000 people have been thoroughly improved. As a result, the per capita housing area in the whole city has increased from 7.6 square meters to 22.5 square meters, and the living environment of nearly half of the citizens has undergone earth-shaking changes.

Strengthen the protection to ensure that the elderly have a sense of security and the sick have a sense of medical care. Before the transformation of resource-exhausted cities, Fuxin had only 170,000 endowment insurance participants. Employees in non-state-owned economic units did not enjoy medical treatment and their social security capacity was very weak. Since the transformation, Fuxin City has grasped the opportunity of the state carrying out a pilot program to improve the social security system in Liaoning and has continuously strengthened the construction of social security and relief systems. In the past decade, the pension standard for urban residents has been raised 9 times, from 330 yuan to 1117 yuan. The participation rates of the new type of social endowment insurance for rural and urban residents have reached 80 and 83%, respectively. The number of all kinds of employees in the endowment insurance in the whole region has reached 410,000. The urban medical insurance system has achieved full coverage, and the participation rate of the new rural cooperative medical system has reached 93%.

Source Extracted from http://www.chinaeast.gov.cn/2012/10/12/C-131902.

2 Main Problems in Regional Development

While great achievements have been made, we should also see that there are still some prominent contradictions and problems in the current regional development of our country.

2.1 The Absolute Gap Between Regional Economic Developments Is Still Relatively Large

In recent years, although the gap in regional development speed tends to narrow, the absolute gap in regional development is still large and the imbalance problem is still very prominent. Taking the per capita GDP gap as an example, from a vertical perspective, the absolute differences between the per capita GDP of the eastern region and the western region in 1978, 2000, 2010 and 2013 were 202 yuan, 7407 yuan, 23,885 yuan and 27,914 yuan, respectively. The absolute differences in per capita GDP are still on the trend of expansion. Compared with other countries, the difference in GDP per capita between different regions is not only significantly larger than that of major developed countries but also exceeds that of some developing countries. If measured by the administrative region ratio of the highest and lowest GDP per capita, it is 2.41 times in the United States, 2.62 times in Japan and 3.61 times in India, while Tianjin had the highest GDP per capita of all provinces (autonomous regions and municipalities) in China in 2013, 99,607 yuan, while Guizhou province had the lowest GDP per capita, 22,922 yuan, a difference of 4.3 times. Even excluding the three municipalities directly under the central government of Beijing, Tianjin and Shanghai, the highest Jiangsu Province reached 74,607 yuan, still 3.3 times that of Guizhou Province.

Moreover, in recent years, the trend of narrowing the growth gap of GDP per capita in the eastern, central and western regions is still unstable. After the outbreak of the international financial crisis in 2008, the international market demand was weak at that time, foreign demand suddenly declined, the coastal areas were the first to bear the brunt, and the eastern region was greatly impacted. The northeast region and the central and western regions were relatively stable in overall development due to the underdeveloped export-oriented economy, delayed transmission and the subsequent large-scale expansion of domestic demand policies by the state. However, since 2013, the economic situation faced by the eastern, central, western and northeastern regions is obviously different from that faced after the outbreak of the international financial crisis in 2008. The eastern region is developing more steadily and the growth rate is still rising. However, the problems in the central and western inland regions are more prominent. The growth rate in the northeast region is lower than the national and

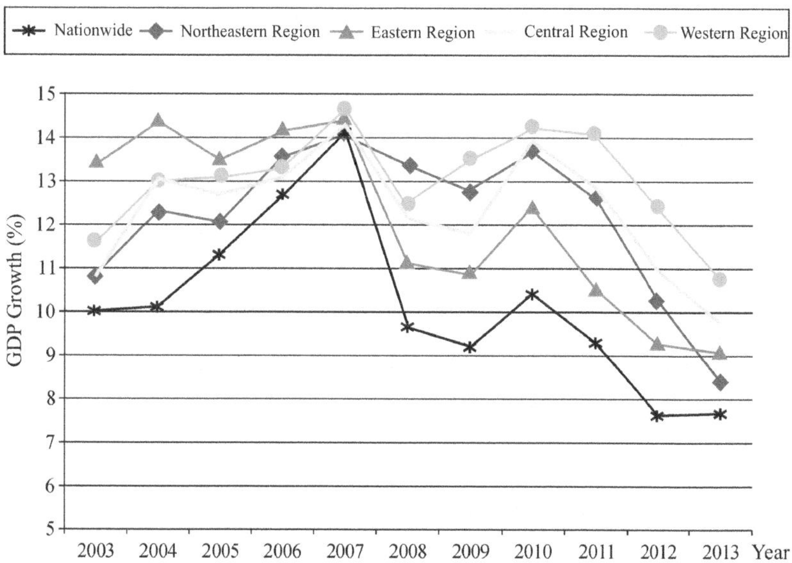

Fig. 3 2003–2013 年四大区域板块经济增速及变化 (2003–2013 Economic growth and changes of the four major regions)

- GDP 增速 (%): GDP Growth (%)
- 全国: Nationwide
- 东北地区: Northeastern Region
- 东部地区: Eastern Region
- 中部地区: Central Region
- 西部地区: Western Region
- 年份: Year
- 数据来源: 根据 2003–2013 年《中国统计年鉴》计算。(*Source* Calculated from *China Statistical Yearbook 2003–2013*)

eastern average. The economic growth rate in the western and central regions is also significantly lower than that in previous years, and the relative growth advantage with the eastern region is also significantly reduced (see Fig. 3). Through industrial upgrading in recent years, the economic growth in the eastern coastal areas has gradually stabilized and picked up since 2014, while the downward pressure on economic growth in the central and western regions and the northeast region has continued to increase and the economic growth momentum is insufficient. In 2014, the GDP of the eastern, central, western and northeastern regions increased by 8.1, 8.9, 9.1 and 5.9% year on year, respectively, showing the new situation and new trend of "the eastern region is slowly stabilizing while the central and western regions are experiencing difficulties while the northeast region is under greater pressure". Especially in recent years, as Guangdong, Jiangsu, Zhejiang and other eastern provinces have stepped up their economic transformation and upgrading efforts, under the influence of market forces, various factors and industries will still gather in those regions with better conditions, especially in the metropolises and city clusters in the eastern region. If this situation continues, the narrowing of the regional economic growth gap may be reversed.

[Column 2-5]
Changes in economic growth rate in all regions of China since 2013
In 2013, China's GDP reached 56,884.5 billion yuan, up 7.7% year-on-year, while the GDP of the eastern, central, western and northeastern regions reached 32,225.9 billion yuan, 12,730.6 billion yuan, 12,600.3 billion yuan and 5444.2 billion yuan, respectively, increased by 9.1, 9.7, 10.7 and 8.4% year-on-year.

In 2014, the national gross national product (GNP) was 62,646.3 billion yuan, up 7.4% year-on-year, of which the eastern, central, western and northeast regions' gross national product reached 35,005.3 billion yuan, 13,867.1 billion yuan, 13,807.3 billion yuan and 5747 billion yuan, respectively, increased by 8.0, 8.9, 9.0 and 5.9% year-on-year.

In 2015, the vast majority of provinces lowered their economic growth expectations. According to government work reports published by provinces (cities, districts) across the country, 30 other provinces (cities, districts) except Tibet have all lowered their GDP growth rate for 2015. Five provinces (cities, districts) including Tibet, Guizhou, Shaanxi, Chongqing and Fujian have set their GDP growth rates for 2015 at 12, 10, 10, 10 and 10%, respectively, maintaining double-digit growth forecasts, while the other 26 provinces (cities, districts) are all expected to have single-digit growth. In terms of local general public budget revenue indicators, with the exception of Tibet, Jiangxi, Chongqing and Guangdong provinces (cities, districts), the other 27 provinces (cities, districts) have all lowered their planned growth rates for 2015. On the whole, the northeast region has the lowest economic index set in the country, and the western region has a lower index than the eastern region on average.

Source Based on public data.

2.2 *The Gap in the Level of Basic Public Services Between Regions Continues to Widen*

Basic public service level is an important indicator to measure the level of regional development. Since entering the twenty-first century, with the continuous deepening of the transformation of government functions, improving the protection and improvement of people's livelihood, establishing a basic public service system, and promoting the equalization of basic public services have increasingly become the major strategic principles of the party and the state, as well as the contents of regional policies. In July 2012, the State Council issued China's first national-level special plan in the field of basic public services, the *12th Five-Year Plan for the National Basic Public Service System*. It identified 44 categories and 80 items of basic public services in 8 major areas during the "12th Five-Year Plan" period, covering different stages of citizens' survival and development as well as the basic needs of food, clothing, housing, health and sports throughout their lives. It also made it clear that the basic public service system will be provided to the whole population as a public product.

The plan defines basic public services as services provided by the government on the basis of a certain social consensus and adapted to the level and stage of economic and social development, aiming at ensuring the survival and development of all citizens' basic needs. It is pointed out that the scope of basic public services generally includes services in the fields of education, employment, social security, medical and health care, family planning, housing security, culture and sports, etc. which guarantee basic livelihood needs, and broadly includes services in the fields of transportation, communications, public facilities, environmental protection, etc. which are closely related to people's living environment and services in the fields of public safety, consumer safety, national defense safety, etc. which guarantee safety needs.

[Column 2-6]

Plans for equalization of basic public services issued by various regions in recent years

In November 2009, Guangdong Province issued the *Outline for Equalization of Basic Public Services in Guangdong Province (2009–2020)*, dividing basic public services into two categories and eight items, namely, basic services, including public education, public health, public culture and sports, and public transportation; and basic security, including living security (including endowment insurance, minimum living security and five guarantees), housing security, employment security and medical security. In 2014, Guangdong Province revised the *Outline of the Plan for Equalization of Basic Public Services in Guangdong Province (2009–2020)*. The new outline defined basic public services as public education, public health (including population and family planning), public culture and sports, public transportation, public safety and living security (including pension insurance, minimum living security, five guarantees, and protection for the disabled), housing security, employment security, medical security, and ecological environment security. Compared with the country, Guangdong Province has added the content of safety and ecological environment.

In August 2011, Guangxi Zhuang Autonomous Region promulgated the *12th Five-Year Plan for the Equalization of Basic Public Services in Guangxi Zhuang Autonomous Region*, which defined the scope of basic public services in the 12th Five-Year Plan period as two major categories and ten items: first, basic services, including six items of public education, public health, population and family planning, food and drug safety, public culture and sports, and public transportation; The second is the basic security category, including living security (including endowment insurance, minimum living security and rural five guarantees), employment security, medical security (including medical assistance) and housing security.

In October 2011, Beijing issued the *Beijing 12th Five-Year Plan for the Development of Social Public Services*, distinguishing basic public services from non-basic public services, proposing the concept of "social public services" and summarizing "social public services" as "public education, health and basic medical care, employment, social security, social welfare and social assistance, culture, sports, safety and other services". In addition, Beijing has also put forward the "spatial concept" of social public services, which mainly includes the construction of a convenient living service network, and the construction of social public service functional areas and gathering areas.

In December 2012, Zhejiang Province promulgated the *12th Five-Year Plan for Zhejiang's Basic Public Service System*, which divided the basic public service system into four categories, namely, basic living services (employment promotion, social security, housing security), basic development services (education, medical and health care, population and family planning, culture and sports), basic environmental services (living infrastructure, public information infrastructure, environmental protection), and basic safety services (life and production safety, disaster prevention and mitigation, and emergency management).

In December 2012, Jiangxi Province issued the *12th Five-Year Plan of Jiangxi Province's Basic Public Service System*, which focused on strengthening the integration of urban and rural basic public service planning and implementing the basic public service policies in the main functional areas; promoting the convergence of basic public service systems between urban and rural areas, increasing support for basic public services in old revolutionary base areas, ethnic minority areas and poverty-stricken areas; increasing support for basic public services in rural areas and establishing and improving a coordination mechanism for the equalization of basic public services in the region.

In March 2013, Fujian Province issued the *12th Five-Year Plan for Promoting the Equalization of Basic Public Services in Fujian Province*, which was innovative in terms of "equalization" and mainly included two aspects: first, to increase support for the former Central Soviet Area and the old revolutionary base areas; The second was to promote the equalization of basic public services in urban and rural areas, regions and groups.

In August 2013, Shandong Province issued the *Action Plan for the Construction of Basic Public Service System in Shandong Province (2013–2015)*, incorporating public safety services into the action plan for the construction of basic public service system, and focusing on food safety, drug safety, social security, traffic management, fire safety, campus safety, etc.

In August 2013, Jiangsu Province issued the *12th Five-Year Plan for the Basic Public Service System of Jiangsu Province*. First, it added the connotation of basic public service, including public transportation and environmental protection into the scope of basic public service. Second, it summarized mechanism innovation into six categories, namely financial guarantee mechanism, service supply mechanism, management and operation mechanism, supervision and inspection mechanism, urban and rural overall planning mechanism, and regional coordination mechanism. In addition, Jiangsu Province also placed special emphasis on legalizing the supply of basic public services.

In January 2014, Shanghai issued the *Shanghai Basic Public Service System and Construction Plan for 2013–2015*, which clearly defined the basic public service system as "a systematic and integrated system arrangement consisting of basic public service scope and standards, resource allocation, management and operation, supply mode and performance evaluation". In terms of mechanism, Shanghai emphasized to play an important role in the division of labor and coordination among various departments.

Source Extracted from the *Research Report on Perfecting the Basic Public Service System in the 13th Five-Year Plan* commissioned by the National Development and Reform Commission.

It can be seen that although the definition of basic public services in different regions is not completely consistent, regional education, health care and social security are the core of the basic public service level, and the gap between the central and western regions and the eastern region of these indicators is still widening. Specifically, there is a large gap in economic and social development between the eastern and western regions, between the coastal and inland regions, and between developed and underdeveloped regions. These gaps have led to the coexistence of modernization and poverty and backwardness in the supply of basic public services in China. For example, it is difficult to make an equal comparison between the supply level of basic public services in Beijing and the supply level of basic public services in western regions such as Gansu Province.

For example, from the point of view of compulsory education, in 1998, the extremum ratio of "average budget expenditure per student" in compulsory education in all provinces and autonomous regions was 3.41, i.e. the highest province was 3.41 times that of the lowest province. By 2005, the ratio had risen to 11.57. Among them, the average budget for junior high school students was 27.4 times higher in Shanghai than in Anhui. The average budget for primary school students was 31.5 times higher in Shanghai than in Guangxi.[3] After 2005, the absolute disparity of average education expenditure between the central and western regions and the northeast region and the eastern region continued to widen. In 2011, the disparity of average education expenditure between the eastern region, the central region and the western region in the compulsory education stage further widened (see Table 6). The average budgeted expenditure for all kinds of students in Shanghai and Beijing exceeded the national average by four times.

[3]Jiang Aiping, *Current Situation and Development Trend of Unequal Basic Public Services Among Regions in China*, *Guangxi Social Sciences*, 2010, 8.

Table 6 Expenditure of education funds per student in the compulsory education stage in each region (Unit: Yuan)

	2009	*2010*	*2011*
Nationwide	9199	11,089	13,680
Average of western region	6946	8457	10,612
Average of eastern region	11,135	13,418	16,504
Average of central region	5727	6821	8768
Average of northeastern region	10,782	12,849	16,185

Source Calculated based on *China Statistical Yearbook 2009–2011*

From the perspective of higher education, the regional difference of "average budget expenditure per student" is also expanding. In 1998, the Gini coefficient for the average budget expenditure of higher education students in all provinces and autonomous regions was only 0.054, with little regional difference. From 1999 to 2005, the Gini coefficient increased year by year (except in 2001), reaching the maximum value of 0.380 in 2005. Since 2006, the Gini coefficient fluctuated around 0.3 and rose to 0.343 in 2010, becoming the second-largest value after the enrollment expansion of colleges and universities. In 2011, the Gini coefficient dropped again, with a figure of 0.328, but it was still at a relatively high level.[4]

Judging from the medical field, the gap between regions is still widening day by day. In 2010, the average number of health technicians per 1000 populations in the eastern region was 6.3, while the average number of health technicians per 1000 populations in the central, western and northeastern regions was 3.9, 3.9 and 5.2, respectively. There was a significant gap in the development level.[5] The "2012 China Social Development and Social Attitude Survey" conducted by the Chinese Academy of Social Sciences showed that there are significant differences in medical and health care in the eastern, central and western regions. Judging from the distribution of resources, the medical resources (the number of medical institutions per capita) in the eastern region were 1.13 times of the national average, while those in the central and

[4]Yue Changjun: How to Promote Fair Opportunities in College Education from the Perspective of Investment in Funds, *Guangming Daily*, July 24, 2013, 16th Edition.

[5]National Natural Resources and Geospatial Basic Information Database Project Office: *China Regional Planning and Sustainable Development Analysis Report*, April 2013.

Table 7 Development of basic public services in different regions during the 12th Five-Year Plan period (2012)

Area	*Indicator*	*Nationwide*	*Eastern region*	*Central region*	*Northeastern region*	*Western region*
			Jiangsu	*Hubei*	*Heilongjiang*	*Guizhou*
Basic public education	Teacher ratio of ordinary primary school students	17.36	(+) 16.74	(+) 17.04	(+) 12.95	(−) 19.2
	Net primary school enrolment rate (%)	99.85	(+) 99.98	(+) 99.97	(−) 99.77	(−) 99.34
Labor employment service	Urban registered unemployment rate (%)	4.09	(+) 3.1	(+) 3.8	(−) 4.2	(+) 3.3
Social insurance	Urban and rural endowment insurance coverage rate (%)	59.26	(+) 66.61	(−) 55.91	(−) 40.72	(−) 40.97
	Urban and rural medical insurance coverage rate (%)	96.56	(+) 100.77	(+) 97.68	(−) 78.16	(−) 496.11
Social services	Coverage rate of social service and community service institutions (%)	29.5	(+) 98.3	(−) 25.9	(−) 18.5	(+) 57.9
Basic medical care and health services	No. of health technicians per thousand populations	4.94	(+) 5	(+) 5	(+) 5.25	(−) 3.72
	Health care management rate for children under 7 years old (%)	88.9	(+) 98.8	(+) 90.4	(+) 94.3	(−) 78.8
	Category A & Category B legally reported infectious disease mortality rate (1/100,000)	1.24	(+) 0.47	(+) 0.77	(+) 0.79	(−) 2.09
Public culture	Per capita book volume of public libraries	0.58	(+) 0.82	(−) 0.44	(−) 0.48	(−) 0.4

Note (+) indicates that the corresponding indicators are better than the national average, and (−) indicates that the corresponding indicators are behind the national average. The social insurance data is the annual data of 2011, and other data are the annual data of 2012

Source Calculations by the Research Group on Perfecting the Basic Public Service System in the 13th Five-Year Plan of Renmin University of China western regions were 90.85% and 91.47% of the national average. Beijing, Shanghai and Tianjin were the three regions with the most abundant medical resources in our country. Jiangxi, Anhui and Guizhou provinces had the lowest medical resources in the country. In 2011, the per capita financing of Shanghai and Beijing's new rural cooperative medical care reached 987 yuan and 637 yuan, respectively, while the provinces in the central and western regions were mainly concentrated between 230 and 240 yuan. The imbalance in health care is the most serious problem of inequality in basic public services among regions. At the same time, the imbalance between regions will not improve much in the next three years, and the superiority of developed regions will continue to be maintained.[6]

If you select a typical province from the eastern, central, northeast and western regions, such as Jiangsu, Hubei, Heilongjiang and Guizhou, respectively, and compare the development of basic public services in different regions during the 12th Five-Year Plan period, you can see that the basic public service indicators in all fields in the eastern region are better than the national average, most indicators in the eastern region are better than the national average, while most indicators in the northeast and western regions are behind the national average, significantly lagging behind the development level in the eastern region (see Table 7).

2.3 Regional Development Disorder Remains a Serious Problem

As various administrative districts continue to focus on economic development, many places equate the strategy of coordinated regional development with the improvement of the economic growth rate of the district. In order to pursue the growth of GDP, they are keen on developing the heavy chemical industry regardless of their own resources and environmental conditions and the carrying capacity and comparative advantages of the ecological environment. They are racing to launch some "two high and resource-dependent projects" of high consumption, high pollution and resource processing type, causing serious problems of resource destruction and environmental pollution, and thus causing problems such as administrative blockade, prominent administrative barriers and the inability of free flow of production factors. In recent years, the steel, automobile, petrochemical, nonferrous metal and building materials industries have

[6]Institute of Social Development Strategy of the Chinese Academy of Social Sciences: *Survey Report on Basic Public Services in China [2012]*, 2013.

proliferated everywhere and presented low efficiency and poor concentration, which are typical reflections of this problem. Take the steel industry as an example. China's steel output has exceeded the sum of the world's top 15 countries, but some provinces and autonomous regions are still building new steel production capacity. There are also some places that develop water-intensive industries in areas where water resources are seriously scarce and some that develop energy-intensive industries in areas where energy resources are scarce, which not only damages the local resource ecosystem, but also leads to the homogenization of industrial structure among regions, intensifies vicious competition among regions, and leads to prominent problems of regional blockade and compartmentalization. In recent years, the form of administrative barriers has shown a trend of concealment. The problem of creating local barriers under the pretext of attracting investment and technical standards has become more and more prominent. It has directly led to the decentralization and fragmentation of the economy, contributed to the emergence of similar economic structures of regions and repeated construction, and seriously hindered the free flow of capital, talents, information, technology and other factors of production and the optimal allocation of resources among regions.

[Column 2-7]
Cases of disordered competition in some regions
The National Audit Office of the People's Republic of China recently found that some counties have reduced or exempted their fiscal revenues in disguised form in attracting investments. Of the 54 counties audited, 53 counties issued 221 preferential policies for attracting investment from 2008 to 2011, which were obviously contrary to the national policies. They reduced or exempted 7.043 billion yuan of fiscal revenue that should be collected in a disguised form by means of fiscal expenditure, of which 3.336 billion yuan was exempted in a disguised form in 2011, equivalent to 5.81% of the general budget revenue of that year. Attracting investment is bound to be linked with preferential policies, which is common sense nowadays. So, 53 of the 54 counties audited have preferential policies that violate national policies, which should be quite normal in the context of "attracting investment", while the remaining county does not have this problem, instead, it is somewhat inconceivable—without preferential policies, how can it attract investment? The concept of "attracting investment" has deviated from its original meaning and turned into vicious competition among regions. Originally, attracting investment meant publicizing regional advantages, attracting investment and complementing

advantages among regions. However, if there is a demand for investment in many regions with the same advantages and conditions, and the investment is in short supply, competition is inevitable. At this time, if the economic development tasks faced by local governments are all hard targets and the more investment one wins, the more outstanding one's achievements are, then vicious competition will be inevitable. As a result, preferential policies such as tax reduction and exemption, tax collection, financial refund, and even financial subsidies, which violate regulations, have been issued. In addition, all localities also give "enterprises that successfully attract investment" super-national treatment and even the privilege of breaking away from laws. Such enterprises would often have a "talisman" from the local government, such as "exemption from inspection", that is affixed to the entrance gate. As a matter of fact, the preferential policies for attracting investment are very much the same across the country. There is nothing new except tax reduction and privileges. As far as the whole society is concerned, the waste of social resources and the loss of public finance caused by investment are very serious. Some people describe vicious competition as meaningless and inefficient, just like the audience watching a performance in a theater. If the audience in the front rows stand up and watch, the audience in the back rows would have to stand up as well. But in fact, everyone could simply remain seated and continue watching, thus it would be meaningless for everyone to stand and waste physical strength. From the perspective of national economic development, attracting investment cannot increase the total amount of investment and economic development. However, the vicious competition caused by it wastes a large amount of social resources, loses a large amount of local taxes, loses fiscal revenue, and exacerbates environmental pollution and destruction of natural resources. The more serious problem is the destruction of legal order. So, what we need to reflect on first is not the seriousness of the reduction or exemption of fiscal revenue in disguised form in attracting investment, but attracting investment itself—how did it deviate from its original meaning?

Source Extracted from *People's Daily*, June 10, 2012, 2nd Edition.

2.4 The Regional Economy and Population Distribution, Ecological Environment Is Not Coordinated

Economic development and population aggregation are not necessarily synchronized, resulting in differences in population distribution and economic distribution between regions. The economic agglomeration in the eastern coastal areas of China is higher than the population agglomeration, and the economic agglomeration in the western areas is lower than the population agglomeration. There are objective reasons for the differences in natural conditions and ecological environment. Moderate regional differences have certain rationality. In 1935, Chinese scholar Hu Huanyong proposed the Heihe (Aihui)-Tengchong line, or Hu Huanyong line, to reveal the law of population distribution in the country. That is, a straight line is drawn from Aihui in Heilongjiang to Tengchong in Yunnan. 36% of the land in the southeast half of the line supports 96% of the population. 64% of the land in the northwest half supports only 4% of the population. The average population density ratio of the two is 42.6:1. The data of the third and fourth population censuses conducted in 1982 and 1990 show that the basic pattern of population distribution in China has remained basically unchanged since 1935. Take the southeastern region as an example, in 1982, it accounted for 42.9% of the total area and 94.4% of the population. In 1990, the proportion of the population was 94.2%. After 55 years, the proportion of population in the east and west has not changed much. The fifth national census in 2000 found that the proportion of the population in the southeast and northwest was still 94.2%: 5.8%.

[Column 2-8]
Hu Line

"Hu Line", also named as the "Aihui-Tengchong Line" or "Heihe-Tengchong Line", is a contrast line dividing the population density of China raised by Hu Huanyong, a Chinese geographer, in 1935. "Aihui-Tengchong Line", as a crucial line of the population geography of China, is widely recognized and cited by domestic and foreign demographers and geographers. The Hu Line is not only a contrast line in population geography but also one that loads and splits many natural and social elements.

At the 60th anniversary of the founding of PRC and the 100th anniversary of the founding and development of modern and contemporary geography in China, 30 great geographical discoveries were published during the Great Geographical Discoveries of China in 100 Years Selection, sponsored by the Geographical Society of China and the *Chinese National Geography Magazine*. "Hu Line" was listed among the 30 discoveries, right after Everest Measurement.

Based on the natural resources, Hu Line is a product of climatic change. It is nearly coincident with the 400 mm isohyet discovered in modern times, which is also the demarcation line of semi-humid and semi-arid areas in China, indicating the close connection between climate and population density. Lands in the Northwest of China have no choice but to develop animal husbandry economy on the steppes, deserts and plateaus because of desertification, where the annual precipitation is less than 400 mm; while the Southeast of China develops agriculture economy well thanks to the abundant precipitation.

According to the analysis of the National Conditions Analysis Study Group from the Chinese Academy of Sciences on the bases of the documents in 2000, with 43.18% land of the whole China, the southeast of the Hu Line hosts 93.77% population and 95.70% GDP of China, indicating its overwhelming high-density economic and social functions. Nevertheless, the northwest of the Line holds vaster lands but sparse population. Under ecological stress, it is weak in economic development and population attraction; its major functions are ecological restoration and preservation. Dividing suitable areas for human survival, the Hu Line is also the northwestern boundary of the corn belt, flanked by ecotones of agriculture and pasture and water sources for many rivers. What's more, most of the impoverished counties are located on its sides. As we talked in the former paragraph, this Line is coincident with the 400 mm isohyet: the southeast of the line is dominated by plains, water networks, hills, karst and Danxia landforms. Since ancient times, farming has been this area's economic basis. The northwest of the line, with a very low population density, is the world of grasslands, deserts and snowy plateaus, and has been traditionally occupied by nomadic nations.

Source Based on public data.

However, while the population structure of the two parts of the southeast and northwest of the Hu Line remains basically unchanged, the population distribution of provinces in China has undergone tremendous changes (see Table 8). Large differences between the proportion of the

Table 8 Changes in permanent residents in various provinces from 2000 to 2010[a]

Region	*No. of permanent residents in 2010*[b]	*Proportion*[c] *(%)*	
		2010	*2010*
National total[d]	1,339,724,852	100	100
Beijing	19,612,368	1.09	1.46
Tianjin	12,938,224	0.79	0.97
Hebei Province	71,854,202	5.33	5.36
Shanxi Province	35,712,111	2.60	2.67
Inner Mongolia Autonomous Region	24,706,321	1.88	1.84

(continued)

Table 8 (continued)

Region	*No. of permanent residents in 2010*[b]	*Proportion*[c] *(%)*	
		2010	*2010*
Liaoning Province	43,746,323	3.35	3.27
Jilin Province	27,462,297	2.16	2.05
Heilongjiang Province	38,312,224	2.91	2.86
Shanghai	23,019,148	1.32	1.72
Jiangsu Province	78,659,903	5.88	5.87
Zhejiang Province	54,426,891	3.69	4.06
Anhui Province	59,500,510	4.73	4.44
Fujian Province	36,894,216	2.74	2.75
Jiangxi Province	44,567,475	3.27	3.33
Shandong Province	95,793,065	7.17	7.15
Henan Province	94,023,567	7.31	7.02
Hubei Province	57,237,740	4.76	4.27
Hunan Province	65,683,722	5.09	4.90
Guangdong Province	104,303,132	6.83	7.79
Guangxi Zhuang Autonomous Region	46,026,629	3.55	3.44
Hainan Province	8,671,518	0.62	0.65
Chongqing	28,846,170	2.44	2.15
Sichuan Province	80,418,200	6.58	6.00
Guizhou Province	34,746,468	2.78	2.59
Yunnan Province	45,966,239	3.39	3.43
Tibet Autonomous Region	3,002,166	0.21	0.22
Shaanxi Province	37,327,378	2.85	2.79
Gansu Province	25,575,254	2.02	1.91
Qinghai Province	5,626,722	0.41	0.42
Ningxia Hui Autonomous Region	6,301,350	0.44	0.47
Xinjiang Uyghur Autonomous Region	21,813,334	1.52	1.63
Active duty military personnel	2,300,000	–	–
Difficult to determine the permanent place of residence	4,649,985	–	–

[a]The data in this table is from the Sixth National Census Report

[b]Permanent residents include: those who live in the streets of local township and whose household registrations are made in the streets or are to be determined; those who live in the streets of local township and have left the township street where their household registrations are made for more than half a year; those whose household registration are in the streets of the local township, but go out for work within half a year, or go overseas to work or study. "Overseas" refers to outside the customs of our country

[c]This refers to the proportion of permanent residents of all provinces, autonomous regions, and municipalities directly under the central government to the country's total resident population (including active military personnel and people who have difficulty determining their permanent residence)

[d]The national total of this table does not include the population of the Hong Kong Special Administrative Region, the Macao Special Administrative Region and Taiwan

economy and that of the population exist in many provinces. At present, the number of provinces with abnormal economic-population distribution is far greater than the number of "normal" ones, resulting in a large amount of labor force flowing across provinces year in year out. Estimated by the GPR of the economic-population distribution (the specific value of the proportion of the population of the domestic administrative region to the national population and the proportion of the economy aggregate of the administrative region to the economy aggregate of the country, the more the GPR value deviates from 1, the more economic-population distribution is uncoordinated), in 2012, among the 323 provincial-level regions of 16 developed countries, there are 264 regions with GPR values ranging from 0.75 to 1.25, accounting for 81.4% of the total. Among China's 31 provinces, autonomous regions, and municipalities directly under the Central Government, taking 2013 data as an example, there are only 10 regions with GPR values between 0.75 and 1.25, accounting for 32% of the total regions, 6 regions with a much higher regional economic agglomeration than population concentration, accounting for 19% of the total, 15 with a far lower regional economic agglomeration than population concentration, accounting for 48% of the regions. The terrible and abnormal proportion distribution of regions in China leads to the typical "dumbbell" characteristics of regional development, indicating that the regional economic development still has an inconsistency with the ecological environment and population distribution, and the overall layout of land development still needs to be optimized, which is also a major reason for the large-scale labor mobility across the provinces in recent years.

3 Main Problems of Regional Policies

3.1 *Regional Policies Need to Be More Systemic and Holistic*

First, there is a lack of laws on national spatial planning and regulation at the national level. At present, China's legislation is dominated by industry legislation, and there are few legislations on comprehensive space areas and few laws related to land space planning. The existing laws are mainly focused on housing and urban and rural construction, such as *The Urban and Rural Planning Law of the People's Republic of China*, etc., and the current law system lacks a national, comprehensive national land space planning law like Japan's *Comprehensive National*

Land Development Law and *Land Use Planning Law*. The land spatial planning function is scattered among several ministries and commissions, so it is difficult to coordinate transportation, industry, energy and environment and it's hard to improve the comprehensive benefits in regional development and jointly solve complex issues concerning urban and rural regional development and land and space planning.

Second, the regional management and regional policies have played insufficient roles in regulating macroeconomic development and the layout of major national industries. There is a lack of overall planning and coordination. At present, regional planning is greatly affected by the division of local administrative regions; and regional policies rely greatly on local governments' enthusiasm, which led to the partial alienation of national regional policies into administrative region policies, which has stimulated the provincial and regional governments to pursue GDP goals, ignoring the realization of tasks such as equalization of basic public services. At the same time, China's current socialist market economic system is still in the stage of perfection; the barriers to the free flow of resource elements have not been completely eliminated; the unified, open, competitive and orderly national socialist market still needs to be improved. There are still many issues to be solved among regions, for instance, the benefit compensation and industrial division, which, to a certain extent, has also weakened the guiding role of regional strategies.

Third, the fiscal and taxation system that promotes coordinated regional development is still not perfect. The fiscal and taxation policies have not played its full role in regional development. At present, there are basically no differentiated fiscal and taxation policies for the different regions. For example, in regions with weak economic foundation and fragile ecological environment, the general transfer payment and special transfer payments scale are too small to meet and adapt to the needs of narrowing the gap in basic public services. At the same time, the levying method in the tax field and the rule for the headquarters to pay the tax have led to the taxation still focusing on the production field and the headquarters area, which is not conducive to resource origin and underdeveloped areas, stimulating the local regions to blindly develop the heavy chemical industries which have big revenue increase effect, and attract enterprises to register their place of business and headquarters, regardless of resources and environmental conditions. In this way, the local governments fail to play a role in guiding the attention of all regions to basic public services.

Fourth, there are conflicts between other policies and regional ones. As China introduced regional policies, a series of policies and measures for regional distribution have also been introduced in industries, finance, and land, among which fiscal and taxation policies and industrial policies are core policies, which may promote regional economic structure optimization and interregional industrial division. However, because of different value goals, regional policies are not coordinated with fiscal and taxation and industrial ones in the face of different regional economies and complex, diverse issues. Regional policies focus on achieving coordinated development of the regional economy, supporting underdeveloped regions, and paying more attention to supporting regions to play comparative advantages, while industrial policies focus more on effectively allocating resources and production factors across the country according to different stages of development of industries. Fiscal and taxation policies also attach importance to the whole national situation.

3.2 Regional Planning Is Subject to Further Focus

In the absence of national land space planning laws at the national level, national-level regional planning has increased in recent years. Since 2006, under the regional framework of the eastern, central, western, and northeastern regions, the relevant state ministries and commissions have separately issued a series of special regional policies for some provinces, the Yangtze River Delta, the Pearl River Delta, and Tianjin Binhai New District (see Appendix 1). According to preliminary statistics, since 2006, China has issued more than 100 regional planning and policy documents, including over 60 regional plans and more than 40 regional policy documents. From the perspective of geographical units, some are based on four major sectors (west, northeast, central, and eastern); some span provincial-level administrative regions (the Yangtze River Delta, Guanzhong-Tianshui, the West Bank of Taiwan Straits, Chengdu and Chongqing City Group, and Tibetan residences in Qinghai, Sichuan, Yunnan and Gansu Provinces); some regard provincial administrative regions as a unit, and others regard the key areas in the provincial administrative regions as a unit. From the perspective of coverage, in the past 10 years, regional planning and policy documents have been introduced intensively, and even can be said to have flourished unprecedentedly, which basically achieved full coverage of every region. This special policy has undoubtedly played an important role in supporting the development of specific regions, but it should be noted that such excessive regional preferential or supportive policies may easily cause negative effects while stimulating the development of specific regions.

First, it has an impact on the state regional policy system. The state has no strict unified standard or basis on implementing preferential policies and supportive policies for a certain region. In practice, it often depends on the recent policy intentions and local demands, which will undoubtedly have a strike on the formation of a reasonable state regional policy system. From concentrated advantages to decentralized advantages and from limited areas to national inclusiveness, this series of national development plans has stimulated repeated competition of local governments, and has led some regions to face more intense competition of resources, policies and development.

Second, it is easy to induce "getting funding by running relationship". Because the policy lacks clear standards and is closely related to the negotiation and public relations capabilities of various places, it will naturally induce the local regions to conduct public relations and lobbying activities through various channels and methods. In particular, many places are keen to accelerate the pace of business attraction and investment in the name of national-level regional planning. Since 2009, nine regional development plans have been upgraded to national-level plans, including the Pearl River Delta, Western Taiwan Straits Economic Zone, Shenzhen Comprehensive Reform Experimental Zone, Jiangsu Coastal Area, Hengqin Island, Guanzhong-Tianshui, Liaoning Coastal Area, Changchun-Jilin-Tumen Open Pilot Zone, and Yellow River Delta. Almost at the same time as this round of national-level regional planning "great leap forward", the "great leap forward" of investment by local provincial governments also began. Guangdong has established 2.3 trillion yuan of investment in the next five years, and Yunnan's five-year investment plan has reached 3 trillion yuan.

Third, the "generalization" of regional policies. Under the market economy, in order to promote coordinated regional development, the state should pay more attention to fairness, and should give priority support and assistance to problem-stricken areas facing various difficulties, especially impoverished and backward areas. However, regional planning "spreads everywhere", which means there is no emphasis and the policy cannot focus on the major task. Almost every province and city is supported by this policy. Many areas are covered by several national-level regional plans and some provinces even put forward the slogan "Strive for all provincial cities to be covered by the national strategy".

Fourth, it is easy to create new unfair issues. Since the policy is "one-to-one", the state's preferential policies and support for a particular region will inevitably create unfairness for other similar regions, resulting in an unfair regional competition circumstance. Moreover, regional planning and policies are still based on administrative divisions and administrative regions, which have weakened the national regional strategy to a certain extent and contributed to the provincial GDP competition.

4 The Deep Cause Analysis of the Problem

4.1 Local Government Competition System and Assessment Mechanism Aiming at Economic Growth

Since the Reform and Opening-up, the central government has been relatively decentralized, and the local government's authority has been relatively expanded. Under the mechanism in which GDP growth is stressed on, a local government competition system has been formed and a very unique phenomenon has emerged, that is, local governments allocate resources and participate in the market competition directly. Some scholars believe that this "local competition" pattern is one of the drivers of China's rapid economic growth and is a unique practice in the "China model". Following the American scholar Ramo, Zhang Wuchang proposed that the key for China's rapid economic growth lies in "county competition."[7] That is to say, the local government has promoted the local economic growth by giving preferential policies to attract investment. He also theoretically demonstrated this with *the Theory of Share Tenancy*, pointing out that local governments are "landlords", and enterprises that attract investment are "farmers". When the local government sells land, the land price is a fixed rent, and the subsequent value-added income is the share of land rent. Shi Zhengfu believes that the local government has become the three major market players involved in market competition. "In China, the city and county governments in particular have competed for a long time at the frontier of economic development and have grown into a symbiotic interaction with the business community. There is a living force that has

[7] Zhang Wuchang: *China's Economic System*, CITIC Publishing House, 2012 edition, pp. 3–5.

become one of the engines of China's economic and social development".[8] From the perspective of GDP growth, local government competition is highly successful, but local government competition has also accumulated a series of problems, such as redundant construction, overcapacity, and environmental pollution. Governments at all levels "manage cities, lands and state-owned assets". A secretary is like a chairman of the board, a mayor is a general manager. The local government's main focus is on investment promotion, industrial development, and development zone construction. What is particularly serious is that since the local government acts as the main body of resource allocation, the state's macroeconomic regulation and control has been seriously distorted. The target of regulation is not the market but the local government. The regional strategies and policies of the country are also alienated to promote the development of the administrative region to a certain extent. It can be said that the local government competition system aiming at GDP growth has gradually become an important obstacle to the coordinated development of China's regions, and has formed a great constraint on the realization of coordinated regional development and industrial division.

First, the fierce competition among local governments has damaged the market order of fair competition and blocked the implementation of national regional strategies. Under the effect of fiscal decentralization and the performance mechanism of GDP assessment, local governments have launched fierce "tax source game", "resource benefit game", "environmental benefit game" and "reputational performance game" for economic development. At the same time, local governments have the right to control and supervise land and resources on account of their administrative power. They can carry out "institutional subsidy competition" by competing to sell the land and resources. The combination of the assessment pressure and the means of local government has led local governments to be keen on pursuing GDP growth and expanding investment, leading many local governments to use the banner of "promoting economic development in this area and this region" and administrative means to intervene in fair market competition. They took measures to protect local enterprises and products, or implement special preferential policies to attract enterprises, which has seriously affected the rational circulation of products and factors. In some localities where

[8] Shi Zhengfu: *Supernormal Growth: China's Economy from 1979 to 2049*, Journal of Fudan University (Humanities and Social Sciences Edition), No. 2, 2014.

protectionism is rampant, police, industry and commerce, taxation, epidemic prevention, and technical supervision departments have created obstacles for the entry of foreign products. Under the pattern of "local competition", it is difficult to establish a unified national market order because of the vicious competition between the regions.

Second, local government competition has seriously aggravated overcapacity and blocked regional cooperation and regional industrial division. As early as 2000, scholars pointed out that, "The country has 31 provinces, autonomous regions and municipalities altogether. If each of them has its own plan-making power and set the main goal so as to accelerate the pace of economic growth, and to compete with each other, it will inevitably result in a large number of repetitive production and repeated construction."[9] But over the years, local governments have been trapped in a "prisoner's dilemma" in the GDP competition. If a local government lags behind others in major projects and heavy chemical industries, it will not only affect local fiscal revenue and employment, but also the promotion of local officials. This has led local governments to devote little or no consideration to environmental and social costs when attracting investment and expanding production capacity, and to strive to pursue GDP growth and industrial project construction in the region. The preferential policies that local governments routinely use in vicious competition include low-cost transfer of industrial land, tax rebates, illegal loans, lower labor costs and water and electricity prices. These policies distorted factor prices and brought malformed resource allocation. Sometimes, local governments will also undermine the market mechanism for enterprises to enter and exit freely, force loss-making enterprises to continue to operate, and give "blood transfusions" to such enterprises through financial subsidies or government guarantees. All these have further exacerbated overcapacity, so it is very hard to achieve the regional cooperation and regional industrial division.

Third, local government competition has intensified the deterioration of the ecological environment, making it impossible to establish ecological compensation and joint protection mechanisms among regions. Due to more attention to regional GDP growth, the local government "accepts any project" and generally pursues heavy industrialization, which runs counter to the concept of green, low-carbon and recycling. Some regions

[9] Fang Weizhong: *Analysis of Economic Reform and Development*, China Planning Press, 2013, p. 21.

do not care about the direction of local leading industries when they undertake transfer, and do not care whether they have the conditions for this development. Many areas are therefore suffering from "investment thirst". As long as the economic benefits of the investment project are good, as long as it can increase local fiscal revenue, boost GDP growth, or even bring in funds or projects, the local government will give them land and exempt taxation from them, ignoring environmental protection. While attracting investment, a large number of high-pollution and energy-intensive enterprises have also been introduced.

Since the ecological environment has certain public product attributes, industries can be developed and revenue can be increased just by destroying the environment, but if we put environmental protection as the priority, we cannot get any benefit. Therefore, it is difficult to form a synergy for ecological protection among regions, let alone to build an ecological compensation and joint protection mechanism among them. Instead, it forms the paradox of "those who destroy get benefits", "those who protect remain poor".

In general, under the influence of local government competition and assessment system aiming at economic growth, local governments have focused on narrowing the gap in economic growth to narrow the disparity among regions, especially the GDP gap, while ignoring the gap of residents' living and welfare levels among regions. These local governments are typical of pursuing high GDP growth, carrying out various forms of investment promotion through various preferential means (such as tax reduction or tax rebate, subsidy, and certain monopoly management rights). They compete to set up all kinds of development zones or parks, develop those heavy chemical industries and enterprises that can increase the local economic aggregate and fiscal revenue relatively quickly, acquire large-scale land, launch the "city-building movement", and obtain various titles like special zones, experimental zones, demonstration zones, new zones, etc. They all focus on the government's economic growth rate, so that it is hard to achieve the goals of saving energy resources, protecting the ecological environment, and ensuring the improvement of people's livelihood. What's more, the negative impact will be greater and greater, and will eventually disrupt the improvement of residents' living and welfare levels and even the regional economic development itself.

Moreover, under the baton of pursuing GDP growth, coordinated regional development is more reflected in the more balanced regional GDP growth rate which is equivalent to "accelerated GDP growth".

However, in the short-term, technological innovation and industrial upgrading in the central and western regions are difficult to make major breakthroughs. Lacking obvious new growth highlights, accelerating growth still mainly depends on large investment and increasing material and resource consumption. Therefore, the current changes in the growth rate of various regions actually reflect the shift between capital investment and industrial transfer among regions, instead of the coordinated regional development that has transformed its development mode. The institutional defects in income distribution, household registration, fiscal and taxation, social security, and basic public services are still serious. There are even dangers of "turning back the wheel of the history" in terms of resource conservation and ecological protection. The long-term mechanism for promoting coordinated regional development has not yet been established. In particular, the value of the labor force, the ecological environment and other factors are not rewarded or compensated for their contribution, and it is easy to cause negative incentives for backward areas, further eroding the foundation of sustainable development in these places.

4.2 *The Financial and Administrative Rights of the Central and Local Governments Are Not Clear*

The division of central and local financial and administrative power is an important component of state governance and an important basis for regional development. Generally speaking, administrative power refers to the duties and responsibilities of a government in public affairs and services. According to the connotation of the administrative power, each of the government's powers has a horizontal division among different departments of the same level of government, as well as a vertical division among different levels of government. Financial power refers to the financial expenditure guarantee of a government while performing its powers. The reasonable division of administrative power and financial power enables all levels of government and functional departments to perform their own duties and promote the efficient operation of the government.

The basic pattern of the current division of administrative power and financial power in China is a product of gradual evolution under the circumstance of the changing political and economic background after the founding of New China. At present, the division of administrative power basically follows the pattern before the Reform and Opening-up, and the division of financial power basically follows the pattern determined during the 1994 tax-sharing system reform. In 1994, the central government made a big adjustment to the tax system. The tax-sharing system with universal rules replaced the profit and tax payment system that is determined and negotiated according to the ownership system of different governments. The consumption tax and customs duties are exclusive to the central government, while the business tax and income tax are paid to the local government. For the largest tax—VAT, the central government has a 75% share.

The tax-sharing reform basically redivided the financial power between the central and local governments, which empowered the central government with concentration on the budgetary income and more direct control over local expenditure behaviors. The effect of the tax-sharing system on income concentration is very significant: in 1994, the central government's share of budgetary revenues rose to 56%. After the tax-sharing reform, income tax as a major local tax has increased rapidly, and the central government has further adjusted the rules. In 2002, 50% of the personal income tax was drawn to the central government. In 2003, this ratio was increased to 60%. The tax-sharing system has fixed many loopholes in the old system. As a turnover tax, VAT is hard to evade, and it can effectively prevent local government from plotting with the state-owned enterprises to conduct the accounting operation. In addition, the establishment of an independent national tax system ensures the tax collection. After the tax-sharing system, the newly established national tax system is directly managed by the central government. The wages and office expenses are all from the central government. The State Taxation Administration is responsible for collecting VAT and then giving the place its share (see Fig. 4).

Although the tax-sharing reform concentrated tax revenues, it has not readjusted the administrative powers between the central and local governments. Some of the affairs that should be handled by the central government are handled by local governments, and the central government undertakes the duty of expenditure for local governments' affairs. In general, the central and local responsibilities are overlapped—the local governments had too many administrative powers but too few financial powers.[10] The administrative power of basic public services such as education, health, social security, public safety, and environmental protection is undertaken by the local government, but without corresponding financial power, which increases the local financial pressure.

[10]Yue Feng: Evolution and Problems of Intergovernmental Financial Relations, *Reform Internal References*, No. 1029.

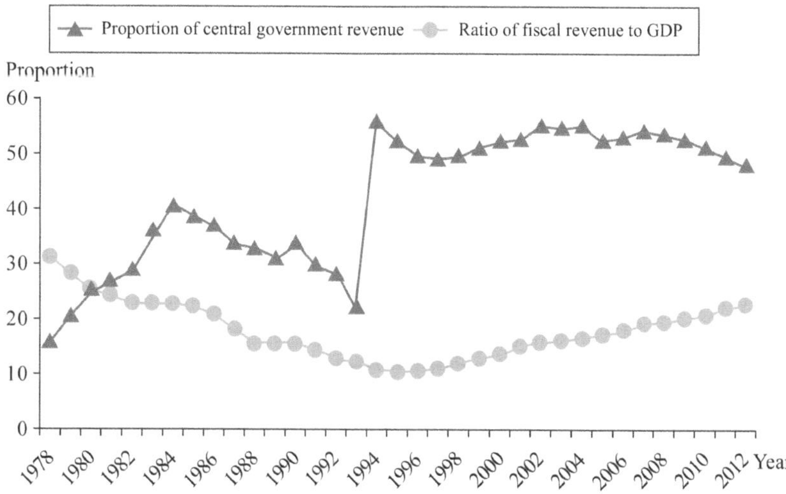

Fig. 4 政府收入占 GDP 比例和中央收入占全部收入比例 (1978–2012年) (Government revenue as a percentage of GDP and central income as a percentage of total income [1978–2012])

- 中央财政收入比重: Proportion of central government revenue
- 财政收入与 GDP 之比: Ratio of fiscal revenue to GDP
- 比重/%: Proportion
- 年份: Year
- 资料来源: 根据国家统计局网站资料整理: http://www.nbs.gov.cn (*Source* The website of the National Bureau of Statistics: http://www.nbs.gov.cn)

The national land space planning and regional compensation mechanism lack top-level design, which further stimulates local excessive competition and to seek local financial growth as an important target in regional development. At the same time, as a unitary state, the central government can appoint tasks to local governments, such as education, health, infrastructure, etc., and ask local governments to pay for these. For example, many small and medium-sized state-owned enterprises in the mid-to-late 1990s bankrupted or were restructured, while local governments paid for social security expenditures for employees who were retired early and laid-off workers. In addition, there are many administrative powers among governments that have not been clarified through legal forms. Instead, they are determined through negotiations between central and local governments, such as rural pensions, health care, rural roads, etc. Usually, the central government decides and the local government implements and both of them pay for the expenditure. This unclear administrative and financial power relations between the central and the local have the following negative effects on coordinated regional development.

First, it has affected the realization of basic public services equalization among regions. Since there is no significant difference in the relative efficiency of input and output of basic public services, the basic public services of the government are "input-type" rather than "efficiency-type". Therefore, the gap in regional public services is mainly reflected in the input. At present, most of the basic public service administrative powers belong to the local governments. There is no national unified basic public service funding guarantee mechanism. The huge gap in local fiscal revenues leads to a large gap in the standard of basic public services, so it is impossible to achieve equalization. Moreover, among different groups and regions, there is also a tendency for secondary allocation to transfer conversely. For example, there is a serious disparity of the basic medical insurance in different places, and the regional differences in basic social security also have the tendency to reverse transfer. For example, the medical insurance which is from social pooling in Beijing and Shanghai, can be reimbursed for 300,000 yuan to 400,000 yuan at most according to the rule of 6 times higher than the salary, but in other cities where people do not have such a high salary only about 100,000 yuan.

Second, the lack of legal basis and top-level design of the division of power and financial power, to a certain extent, result in the "getting funding by running relationship" in various regions and seeking regional preferential policies. In 2012, about 33% of the country's fiscal revenue was transferred from the central government to the local, about nearly 4 trillion yuan of funds. Among them, the total amount of general transfer payments was too large, and the interregional gap was not the main method of measure. The scale of special transfer payments was too large, and the project was too fragmented.[11]

[11] The editorial office of the *Inside Information on Economic Reform: Simplifying the Intergovernmental Financial Relations Strategy* and the *Inside Information on Economic Reform* No. 1029.

Generally speaking, the central and local expenditure responsibilities are divided into various forms, some are divided according to the project, some are divided according to the proportion, and the different items' central subsidy ratio is not the same even in the same place. At the same time, because the simultaneous functional division and administrative division, according to the regional policies, have different standards and dimensions, certain regions belong to more than one policy region, which means it might be in the sectoral regions (like the development strategy of western region, the rising strategy of central region and the revitalizing strategy of northeast region) and the specific functional areas (like the poor areas, ethnic areas, border areas, resource-depleted areas, etc.). So, there is a possibility of selecting policies according to local interests, resulting in repeated enjoyment of two types of policies. However, some types of the fiscal transfer payment policies have inconsistent standards in different administrative regions. This has made all regions keen to "get entitled" and gain new financial transfer payments by being upgraded to a national strategy.

Third, the local government lacks a stable source of income and independent financial sources, which has stimulated local government competition. At present, the income division between the central and local governments is mainly based on shared income. The current local taxes mainly include turnover tax, property tax, resource tax and various local additional taxes. The construction of the local tax system is seriously out of date: the resource taxes and property taxes that are suitable for the local as a big income source have narrow tax bases and light tax burden, which results in insufficient local effective financial sources. Therefore, the local governments are desperate to expand the tax base, often through investment promotion and development of industrial parks. As a result, local governments have a heavy dependence on land transfer fees, and they must continuously expand the scale of urban development and investment scale, further exacerbating excessive competition among local governments.

4.3 Tax Distribution System that Separates Tax Collection Place from Tax Source Place

Since the implementation of the tax-sharing system of the fiscal management system reform in 1994, China's inter-provincial per capita tax revenue gap has shown a significant expansion trend compared with the per capita GDP gap. The specific performance is that the current tax-sharing system lacks the basic institutional norms of horizontal tax distribution among regions. The tax generated by tax source created by the local government has not been collected and enjoyed by the local government, but by another local government. Due to the imperfect taxation, tax collection and management and market economic system, the improper transfer of taxation among different regions has become increasingly fierce. The tax that originally belonged to A has been taken away by B, and the tax belonged to B been transferred to C. According to statistics, more than 90% of all tax revenues have different degrees of "separation problem between tax collection and tax source". The definition of tax collection and tax source separation is cited from the research group on tax collection and tax source issues[12]: This problem caused by the design of the tax system has had a huge impact on regional development. Since most of the corporate headquarters are located in developed areas, especially in large cities, the huge tax revenue generated by those backward areas, raw material producing areas, and central enterprises' production bases was collected by developed regions and central cities, which intensified the damage of equal rights of the different regions and affected the coordinated development of the regions. There are several situations in the problem of "tax collection and tax source separation".

First, the head office and the branches are distributed in multiple regions, so the unreasonable distribution of taxes among regions causes the separation between tax collection and tax source. Specifically, it is divided into two types, one is the parent company type, where the subsidiary company is an independent legal person and account independently. In this case, there is no tax consolidation, but only cross-regional tax transfers by connected transactions, transferring pricing, etc. The other is the head and branch offices type, where the branch company is a non-independent legal person. Therefore, the enterprise pays on a consolidated basis, and the tax is distributed horizontally between the head office and the branch office. China's current tax law determines the taxation location according to the territorial principle. According to the relevant documents of the State Administration of Taxation, 60% of the income tax of the consolidated taxpayer is paid into the central treasury, and 40% is paid into the local treasury where the head office is located. Obviously, under this management system, the local government of the head office obtains the transfer tax revenue from the areas

[12] *Regional Tax Transfer Survey*, China Tax Publishing House, 2007, p. 8.

where the branch offices are located. For example, in Beijing, where the "head offices" are most concentrated, the tax revenue has continuously increased by 20–30% in recent years. The main reason is that there are more than 180 consolidated taxpaying enterprises in the country, more than 90 in Beijing, including 38 in the Xicheng District, accounting for about 20% of all. The 38 companies have nearly 1300 second-tier branch companies, and there are tens of thousands of branch companies at all levels, most of which are distributed in various provinces and cities across the country. These branch companies scattered at all levels in various provinces and cities across the country cannot contribute taxes to their local governments. In addition, the head office of China's largest West-East Gas Transmission Project is in Shanghai, where the tax is collected. Although this great project passes through many western provinces and cities, whose local governments have provided certain public goods and services for the development of the enterprises, they cannot obtain the corresponding tax. Daqing Oilfield in Heilongjiang Province is the production base of central enterprises. During the "Eleventh Five-Year Plan" period, Daqing Oilfield should have paid an annual tax of about 25 billion yuan. However, according to the current tax law, the income tax generated by Daqing Oilfield was collected by China National Petroleum Corporation (CNPC), and the local government of Heilongjiang Province had no right to manage it. It is worth noting that the problem of tax collection and tax source separation did not only exist in the income tax. In recent years, the problem of the separation of VAT has been reflected in various places.

Second, the production and operation sites of enterprises span more than two administrative regions, leading to the separation of regional tax collection and tax sources. For example, the tax distribution issue between the Hubei Province and Chongqing in the Three Gorges Power Station: 84.33% of the current value-added tax of the Three Gorges Power Station belongs to Chongqing City, and 15.67% belongs to Hubei Province. According to the *Research on the Tax Collection and Tax Source Separation of the Three Gorges Power Station,* written by the Hubei Provincial research group of the State Administration of Taxation, it is calculated and estimated that from 2003 to 2009, the Three Gorges Power Station can provide a total of 24.877 billion yuan of various taxes, including 18.312 billion yuan for the Three Gorges Corporation, 4.221 billion yuan for the central government, and 1.977 billion yuan for Chongqing. However, Hubei Province, where the Three Gorges Power

Station is located, can only receive 367 million yuan, less than 1.5% of the total tax revenue (and less than 1/5 of Chongqing's share). A large number of situations similar to this exist across the country. Under the principle of "land management", many regional governments enjoy the legal rights of tax collection and management power and tax revenue power, so how the tax revenue is distributed horizontally among these regions is the key to this issue. In the case of inter-region production and operation, once there is a contradiction in horizontal tax distribution, it is necessary for the two regional governments to resolve through negotiation or the superior government's adjudication. If there is a disparity between the two regions' strength, the underdeveloped regional government may be in a disadvantaged position, and horizontal tax distribution may generally be more conducive to stronger regions. This separation between tax collection and tax source has further weakened the policy capacity of regional governments, and further widened the gap between economic and social development in underdeveloped regions and developed regions.

[Column 2-9]
Tax distribution of the Three Gorges Project and the Three Gorges Hydroelectric Power Station

The full name of the Three Gorges Project is the Yangtze River Three Gorges Hydroelectric Power Station. Located in Yichang, Hubei Province, the whole project consists of dams, hydropower stations and navigation buildings. Started in 1993 and completed in 2009, the estimated total investment of this project is 203.9 billion yuan and its annual power generation equals 84.7 billion yuan.

From 2003 to 2009, the Three Gorges Power Station implemented a special tax policy, which involves the issues of horizontal distribution of taxes among regions and the vertical distribution of central and local taxes. From 2003 to 2009, according to the relevant regulations of the State Council and the relevant documents of the Ministry of Finance and the State Administration of Taxation, the tax distribution policy of the Three Gorges Power Station is: all income tax belongs to the Three Gorges Corporation, the locality retention of VAT, urban construction tax and education surtax are distributed to Hubei Province and Chongqing at the ratio of 15.67:84.33.

The determination of this ratio is based on the calculation of the comprehensive submerged physical indicators in the Three Gorges reservoir area. The land inundation ratio of Chongqing and Hubei in the Three Gorges reservoir area is 80.31:19.69, and the submerged physical ratio is 85.501:14.499. Taking into account these two indicators and also the submerged objects in the dam area, the ratio of 84.33:15.67 was determined. This distribution ratio is widely used in the construction phase to allocate various funds related to the Three Gorges Power Station between Chongqing and Hubei Province, including the distribution of local-level taxes generated by the Three Gorges Hydropower Station, as well as the allocation of the industrial development fund and the funds in the Three Gorges reservoir areas such as the return of imported materials for self-use materials.

From 2003 to 2009, the tax amount payable of the Three Gorges Power Station was 24.877 billion yuan, of which the value-added tax was 11.742 billion yuan, the enterprise income tax was 12.197 billion yuan, and the urban construction tax and education surtax were 938 million yuan. If distributed according to the principle of territorial distribution, the central government should have shared 16.124 billion yuan, and Hubei Province should have shared 8.753 billion yuan. While according to the current tax distribution system, the central government shared 4.221 billion yuan, the Three Gorges Corporation shared 18.312 billion yuan, Chongqing City shared 1.977 billion yuan, and Hubei Province shared 367 million yuan.

After the completion of the Three Gorges Project in 2009, the state did not specify a specific tax distribution method. According to this, Hubei Province believed that since the Three Gorges Dam, the registered place of enterprises and the main production sites are all located in Hubei, the local taxation of the Three Gorges Power Station should be attributed to Hubei Province in accordance with the principle of territorial management. The funds needed for the development of the Three Gorges Reservoir Area in Chongqing will be transferred through financial transfer payment. However, Chongqing believed that the Three Gorges Reservoir Area and the Three Gorges Power Station are both the "production sites" of the Three Gorges Power, and Chongqing has spent a lot on resettlement of the original residents, therefore, the value-added tax should continue to be distributed according to the ratio of 84.33:15.67, and so should the income tax.

Source The Research Group on Tax Collection and Tax Source Issues: *Regional Tax Transfer Survey*, China Tax Publishing House, 2007, pp. 225–257.

Third, the tax collection regulations result in the transfer of tax revenue from the place of production to the place of consumption, and from the place of resource supply to the place of resources utilization. According to the current *Provisional Regulations on Value-Added Tax of the People's Republic of China*, the value-added tax is collected mainly when the products are sold in the place of production, which means the local government can get the locality share of VAT. However, the value-added tax can be finally passed on to the consumers by the production enterprise, and the value-added tax of the consumers should be vested in the local government. In accordance with the internationally accepted VAT collection management method, most of the VAT is left in the final consumption region and collected during the final consumption. However, China's current mode of value-added taxation collection, which mainly collects VAT in production places, not only causes the central and western regions of the underdeveloped manufacturing industry to transfer tax burdens to the developed eastern regions but also encourages local governments to expand manufacturing investment and expand reproduction. Similar problems exist in resource taxation. At present, most of China's commodity prices are determined by market mechanisms, but a small number of primary product prices are still priced by the government. For a long time, the government has implemented lower prices for resource-based primary products (such as crude oil, natural gas, etc.), but when they, as raw materials, are processed into finished products then enter the consumption market, the price is determined by the market. The value of them will change dramatically, increasing by several times or even dozens of times. As a result, part of the tax benefit is transferred from the place of resource supply to the place of resource utilization. The resource development area lacks sufficient financial resources to make necessary compensation for resource consumption.

[Column 2-10]

Changes in the pattern of regional interest distribution caused by cross-regional resource allocation (taking the West-to-East Power Transmission Project as an example)

Although China has abundant resource types and luxuriant resources, the regional distribution of resources is seriously uneven. For example, 90% of China's hydropower resources are concentrated in the southwestern, central and southern regions, and parts of the northwest. Most of the coal resources are concentrated in Shanxi, Shaanxi, and western

Inner Mongolia, but electricity demand is concentrated in the economically developed eastern regions. Since the beginning of the twenty-first century, China has begun to implement a large-scale West-to-East Power Transmission Project, which has effectively changed the imbalance of China's resource spatial distribution, the irrational use of resources, and the dislocation of resource endowments and consumer demand. However, the trans-regional scale resource transfer will undoubtedly establish a new type of trading relationship between the resource output area and the resource input area, and on this basis, a complex and diverse regional interest relationship will be formed. Because the ecological compensation mechanism and resource taxation system are not perfect, the imbalance in the development of the eastern and western regions is increasing.

First of all, many costs of sending electricity from West to East have not been effectively reflected in the price of electricity. In addition to direct investment costs and various operating and maintenance costs in power development and production, there are many potential and related economic and ecological costs, such as the resettlement and subsequent development costs involved in the construction of hydropower stations in the western region, the ecological environment damage loss because of the long-term thermal power generation, as well as the market transaction costs caused by the western region government for limiting the power supply to the local enterprises to ensure the power supply to the east. Therefore, the rationality of the electricity price is affected.

Second, only a small portion of the economic benefits from the West-to-East Power Transmission Project has been directed to the resource output place. According to statistics, the distribution pattern of interest transmission from west to east is roughly as follows: the eastern power input area saves a large amount of electricity purchase costs, and the power development, power transmission and distribution enterprises obtain partial profits, but the resource output places only receive a small portion of benefits. Calculated by an annual transportation of 200 billion kWh, the eastern region can save electricity expenditures of 56 billion yuan, power companies profiting 14 billion yuan, but the tax revenues of resource output place and the central government can only profit less than10 billion yuan.

Finally, the delivery of cheap electricity has exacerbated the development gap between resource output areas and resource input areas. The resources and energy provided by the resource output region are of great significance to the industrial development in the eastern region. However, from a regional perspective, resource taxation is actually an origin tax, but not consumption tax. It has the problem of tax transfer between the place of origin and the place of consumption. That is, it is added to the price of the commodity to be borne by the consumer. Therefore, the resource input area enjoys the additional benefit brought by the resource, and the resource output place needs to pay for the additional cost of the resource and the energy product when purchasing the finished product.

Source The 2009 National Social Science Fund Project, *Coordination of Regional Interests between the East and the West and Accelerating the Economic and Social Development of Western Minorities: A Case Study of West-East Power Transmission*, 2009.

Fourth, regional tax policies are not uniform, and taxation is transferred from high-tax areas to low-tax areas. At present, there are many regional preferential policies in China, such as special economic zones, coastal economic open cities, high-tech industrial development zones, and economic and technological development zones, all of which stipulate some regional preferential policies. In addition, in order to attract investment, the local government has also issued a number of fiscal and taxation policies to support the development of enterprises. While attracting investors, these policies have also created vicious competition for taxation between regions. Some companies register companies in preferential areas of fiscal and taxation policies. Even if the main production bases are not there, they can make full use of various methods to transfer corporate profits and taxes from high-tax areas to low-tax areas, resulting in the separation of regional taxes and tax sources.

Although the above-mentioned types of taxation and tax source divergence are slightly different, they all suggest that taxation is transferred from underdeveloped regions (mainly the central and western regions) to economically developed regions. Not only has it caused financial constraints in underdeveloped regions and widened the interregional financial gap, it has also deviated from the national goal of promoting coordinated regional development, which has constrained the realization of coordinated regional development goals.

CHAPTER 3

New Trends of Regional Development Since the 18th CPC National Congress

Since the 18th CPC National Congress, the central government has attached great importance to the problems of regional development and put forward the new requirements—to coordinate the east, the middle and the west as a whole and the north and the south as a whole, and focus on implementing Three Strategies, including the Belt and Road Initiative, Coordinated Development of the Beijing-Tianjin-Hebei Region and the Yangtze River Economic Belt, while continuing to implement regional development strategies such as the Western Development Strategy, the Revitalization Plan of Old Industrial Bases Including Northeast Region and the Rise of Central China.

Coordinated implementation of the Four Regional Plans (East Taking the Lead, the Rise of Central China, the Revitalization of the Northeast Region and the Western Development Strategy) and Three Strategies (the Belt and Road Initiative, Coordinated Development of the Beijing-Tianjin-Hebei Region and the Yangtze River Economic Belt) is conducive to a better balance between the domestic and international markets and interconnected development of the eastern area and the central and western regions. In addition, it also helps foster new poles, belts and points of economic growth by connecting the dots, so as to build a new pattern of all-round opening up and cooperation in coastal, riverside, border and inland areas.

X. Song et al., *The Great Change in the Regional Economy of China under the New Normal*, The Great Transformation of China,
https://doi.org/10.1007/978-981-32-9475-2_3

1 Continue the Implementation of Strategies Including the Western Development Strategy, the Revitalization Plan of Old Industrial Bases Including Northeast Region, and the Rise of Central China

1.1 Make Extensive Efforts to Develop the Western Region

The western region has been given priority in China's regional development for more than 10 years, and the development of the western region has entered a new stage of comprehensive and in-depth progress. In the new era, we should adhere to the principle of "putting people's wealth and stability first", pay more attention to maintaining social stability, expanding employment opportunities and bringing real benefits to the people, and substantially improve the self-development ability and comprehensive competitiveness of the western region, to put the western region on the track of sustained, stable, rapid and sound development as soon as possible.

First, we should strengthen the top-level design of the Western Development Strategy, and draw up *The 13th Five-Year Plan for the Western Development Strategy* to promote more construction of the state key infrastructure to the western region.

Second, we should speed up infrastructure construction, continue to prioritize the construction of transportation, water conservancy and other facilities, and accelerate the establishment of a modern infrastructure system that is functionally supported, safe, efficient and moderately advanced.

Third, we need to strengthen ecological construction and environmental protection, promote the comprehensive management of the five major ecological zones such as the Northwest Grassland Desertification Control Zone, accelerate the promotion of key ecological projects such as returning farmland to forests and grazing to grass, and build a national ecological security barrier.

Fourth, we should support the development of industries with local advantages, build national energy bases, resource deep processing bases, equipment manufacturing bases and strategic emerging industrial bases, rationally arrange a number of major industrial projects, focus on the development of modern service industry, and orderly undertake domestic and international industrial transfer.

Fifth, we need to enhance the capacity of independent innovation, promote the construction of innovative regions and innovative cities, increase personnel training, continue to implement key talent development projects, and enhance the self-development capabilities of the western region.

Sixth, we should vigorously develop social undertakings, focus the support of the central government on improving the production and living conditions of the people of all ethnic groups in the west, and establish a public service system covering both urban and rural residents.

Seventh, we need to strengthen the development of key economic zones and promote the development of key economic zones with good economic foundation, strong resource and environmental carrying capacity and great development potential, such as Chengdu, Chongqing, Guangxi Beibu Gulf Economic Zone, Guanzhong-Tianshui Economic Zone and Hohhot-Baotou-Ordos-Yulin Region, so as to nurture new economic growth poles.

Eighth, we should adhere to the innovation of institutions and mechanisms, give full play to the basic role of market in allocating resources, and explore new modes of development and opening up in border areas.

1.2 Comprehensively Revitalize Old Industrial Bases Including Northeast China

Northeast China is an important industrial and agricultural base of the country. With the support of relevant state policies, the revitalization of the Northeast has seen initial success in recent years. However, in order to achieve the goal of comprehensive revitalization in the Northeast region, the task ahead will remain quite arduous. At present, the Northeast region is also faced with many problems such as heavy tasks of state-owned enterprise reform, weak industrial competitiveness, insufficient private economy, and backward development of the service industry. The next step is to pay more attention to structural optimization and institutional innovation, highlight industrial revitalization and key regional development, strengthen national strategic industrial bases and innovation capacity building, accelerate the implementation of a comprehensive opening strategy, and promote comprehensive revitalization in the Northeast.

First, we should issue *Several Opinions of the Central Committee of the Communist Party of China and the State Council on the Comprehensive*

Revitalization of the Old Industrial Bases Including Northeast China as soon as possible, and implement *Opinions of the State Council on Major Policy Measures for Supporting the Revival of Northeast China in the Near Future.*

Second, we should further clarify the regional layout of the strategy of the Revitalization of Northeast China, support the Northeast region to create new economic growth points, and, through adjusting to local conditions, transform the old industrial bases in the northeast to an important economic growth region in the country and realize the comprehensive, coordinated and sustainable development.

Third, we should improve the modern industrial system, enhance the core competitiveness of advantageous industries, support the development of strategic emerging industries and vigorously develop productive service industries as well as tourism and cultural industries. Efforts should also be made to accelerate the transformation of agricultural development mode, and build old industrial bases, such as the Northeast region, into stable national food strategic bases, important livestock and poultry aquatic product production and processing bases and agricultural modernization demonstration zones.

Fourth, we should strengthen ecological and environmental protection, promote comprehensive and sustainable development of forest areas, advance pollution control in Liao River and Songhua River basins, accelerate the control of Horqin Sandy Land, and strengthen the protection of black soil, important wetlands and three grasslands in Northeast China.

Fifth, we should accelerate the development of key areas, enhance the development of Liaoning Coastal Economic Belt, Shenyang Economic Zone, Changchun-Jilin-Tumen Economic Zone, and the Harbin-Daqing-Qiqihar area, and build pilot and demonstration zones for revitalization.

Sixth, we should strengthen the construction of social undertakings and people's livelihood projects, accelerate the transformation of shantytowns, promote the upgrading of urban central heating pipes, and further improve employment and social security.

Seventh, we should continue to deepen reform, strengthen the policy ideas of the reform of old industrial base enterprises, improve the collective reform policy of factories, promote the disposal of "debt-to-equity" assets as soon as possible, and actively and steadily promote the reform of state-owned forest areas, forest farms and agricultural land.

Eighth, we should further expand opening up to foreign countries, promote the process of regional cooperation in Northeast Asia, enhance cooperation with Russia, deepen economic cooperation with Japan and South Korea, pragmatically promote mutually beneficial cooperation with the Democratic People's Republic of Korea and Mongolia, building the Northeast China into an important hub in opening to and cooperation with Northeast Asia.

Ninth, we should promote the sustainable development of resource-based cities nationwide, perfect the long-term mechanism to improve the sustainable development of resource-based cities, and carry out corresponding pilot projects.

Tenth, we should coordinate and promote the adjustment and transformation of the old industrial bases, and to study and formulate policies and measures that support the transformation and development of the old industrial cities in line with reality and effectiveness.

1.3 Substantively Promote the Rise of the Central Region

The central region plays an important role in the development of the country for it links the east and west. At the same time, it has a large-capacity for resources and environment, a good foundation for economic development, and great potential for industrialization and urbanization. It is an important region for China to undertake the transfer of rural population and coastal industries in the future. In the very near future, importance should still be attached to the construction of the "Three Bases and One Hub" in the central region, to the development of key areas with urban agglomeration as the core, and to the process of industrialization and urbanization, so as to promote the key areas to rise first and then to drive the rise of the entire central region.

First, we should strengthen and consolidate the construction of important grain production bases across the country, actively develop modern agriculture, accelerate the adjustment of agricultural structure, and strengthen the construction of agricultural and rural infrastructure.

Second, we are going to consolidate and upgrade the status of energy and raw materials bases, promote the construction of national large-scale coal bases, strengthen the development and utilization of new energy sources and the construction of power bases, and promote the structural adjustment and optimization of advantageous industries such as steel, chemicals, nonferrous metals and building materials.

Third, we should cultivate and strengthen the modern equipment manufacturing and high-tech industries, vigorously develop equipment manufacturing industries such as machinery, automobiles, rail transit and ships, cultivate and expand strategic emerging industries, and transform traditional manufacturing industries with high-tech and advanced applicable technologies.

Fourth, we should strengthen the status of integrated transportation hub, implement the construction of railway passenger line, intercity railway and coal transportation channel, improve the trunk line network, accelerate the construction of major and feeder airports, improve the capacity of water transport and pipeline transportation, and strengthen the planning of national comprehensive transportation hub cities.

Fifth, we need to give full play to the leading role of key areas, guide the integrated development of the middle reaches of the Yangtze River, support Henan Province to accelerate the development of Central Plains Economic Region, guide the central and western regions to undertake industrial transfer in an orderly manner, and promote the construction of Anhui Wanjiang City Belt and industrial transfer demonstration zones such as Xiangnan in Hunan Province, Jingzhou in Hubei Province, Gannan in Jiangxi Province (the southern Jiangxi) and Shanxi-Shaanxi-Henan Golden Triangle Along the Yellow River, so as to form an economic belt along the Yangtze River, along the Lanzhou–Lianyungang Railway, along the Shanghai–Kunming High-speed Railway, along the Beijing–Guangzhou Railway, along the Beijing–Kowloon Railway and along the Jiaozuo–Liuzhou Railway, shortly for "Three Vertical and Three Horizontal Economic Belts".

Sixth, we will strengthen resource conservation and environmental protection, further improve the comprehensive management of large rivers and lakes, accelerate the construction of the South-to-North Water Diversion, and increase efforts in ecological construction and environmental protection.

Seventh, we are to vigorously develop various social undertakings, give priority to the development of education, prosper cultural and sports undertakings, enhance basic medical and public health service capabilities, do everything possible to expand employment, and improve the social security system.

Eighth, we should deepen institutional reform and mechanism innovation, and actively promote the construction of the "Two-Oriented" social comprehensive supporting reform pilot zone in Wuhan City Circle and Changsha-Zhuzhou-Xiangtan City Agglomeration, and promote the transformation of Shanxi's resource-based economy.

1.4 Continue to Encourage the Eastern Coastal Region to Take a Lead in Development Transformation

Since the Reform and Opening up, the economy of the eastern region has maintained a rapid growth trend. In particular, the Pearl River Delta and the Yangtze River Delta have become important growth poles and lead China's economic development. However, in recent years, with the overall rise in factor costs, the traditional development in the eastern region, which has been highly resource-consuming, highly dependent on the export market, at the low end of the industrial chain, and maintained industrial competitive advantages with low wages, low-cost and low prices, has been severely challenged. It can be said that the current economy of the eastern region has reached a new stage of comprehensive transformation and upgrading, and we should further support its transformation and development.

First, efforts should be made to improve scientific and technological innovation capabilities, to create a policy environment that encourages independent innovation, to promote innovation breakthroughs in key areas and core technologies, and to accelerate the construction of national innovative cities and regional innovation platforms to take the lead in building innovative regions.

Second, we are to focus on cultivating new advantages in industrial competition, using advanced technology to transform and upgrade traditional industries, actively developing strategic emerging industries, vigorously giving play to modern service industries and accelerating the pace of industrial transfer with weaker comparative advantages.

Third, we should promote institutional and mechanism innovation, promote relatively mature and effective reform policies on the basis of summarizing the comprehensive supporting reform pilots, and allow for pilot tests in some key reform areas related with financial innovation and opening up.

Fourth, efforts will be made to enhance the capacity for sustainable development, and to take the lead in the country in terms of energy conservation and emission reduction, ecological protection, environmental management, and green development, and to explore institutional mechanisms for effectively restoring ecology and protecting the environment.

Fifth, we will accelerate the process of regional integration, further break through the boundaries of administrative divisions, promote integration of planning, infrastructure, industrial development, environmental protection and public service in conditional urban agglomerations, support regional cooperation and coordinated development of the Bohai Rim, the Yangtze River Delta and the Pan-Pearl River Delta Region, and support the construction and development of emerging economic zones such as the Shandong Peninsula, the Western Taiwan Straits Economic Zone and the Guangxi Beibu Gulf Economic Zone.

Sixth, efforts will be made to improve the level of open economy, to actively participate in the international industrial division of labor, to improve the ability to gather elements of international resources, and to undertake the level of international industrial transfer.

1.5 Continue to Increase Support for Old Revolutionary Base Areas, Areas with Concentrations of Ethnic Minorities, Border Areas and Poor Areas, Reverse the Trend of Widening Gaps of Economy Development Between the Old, Poor and Border Areas and the National Average, and Narrow the Gap with the National Average Level of Basic Public Services

First, we should strengthen the construction of infrastructure including transportation, energy and water conservancy, especially to accelerate the improvement of the external development environment in contiguous poor areas, and to further improve the production and living conditions of old revolutionary base areas, areas with concentrations of ethnic minorities, border areas and poor areas.

Second, we should enhance public service capabilities, further improve the level of public services such as education, health, culture and social security, and focus on ensuring and improving people's livelihood.

Third, we should accelerate economic development, upgrade the development of featured industries, accelerate the development of industries with local advantages and tourism, vigorously develop the non-public economy and improve self-development capabilities.

Fourth, we should strengthen ecological environment protection and achieve sustainable development. We should attach great importance to ecological environmental protection and construction, increase protection and governance, and achieve harmonious development of economy, society, people and nature.

2 Draw Up a New Layout of Regional Development

We should promote the construction of the "Belt and Road" and promote the coordinated development of Beijing, Tianjin and Hebei. The construction of the Yangtze River Economic Belt is an important platform and a focus for promoting coordinated regional development in the new era.

2.1 The "Belt and Road" Leads the Development and Opening Up of Inland Areas

On September 7, 2013, General Secretary Xi Jinping, during his visit to Kazakhstan, said that in order to make our European and Asian countries closer to each other, to deepen mutual cooperation and to develop more space, we can use the innovative cooperation model to jointly build "The Silk Road Economic Belt". On October 3, President Xi, during his visit to Indonesia, put forward that Southeast Asia has been an important hub of the Maritime Silk Road since ancient times, and that China is willing to strengthen maritime cooperation with ASEAN countries, to develop a good maritime partnership, and jointly build a 21st Century "Marine Silk Road". In November 2013, *Decision of the CPPCC on Some Major Issues Concerning Comprehensively Deepening Reform*, adopted by the Third Plenary Session of the 18th CPC Central Committee, proposed to speed up the interconnection and construction of neighboring countries and regional infrastructure and to promote the construction of the Silk Road Economic Belt and the Maritime Silk Road so as to form a new pattern of all-round opening. In March 2015, the relevant state departments jointly issued *Vision and Actions on Jointly Building the Silk Road Economic Belt and the 21st-Century Maritime Silk Road.*

The Belt and Road Initiative has been raised at the right time. The Initiative is both a strategy for opening up to the outside world and one for promoting coordinated regional development. It focuses on gathering transportation channels, relies on the infrastructure and the central cities along the road, optimizes the domestic and foreign trade and production factors, and promotes regional economic integration.

First, it is in line with the development reality of strengthening regional economic cooperation between China and the surrounding areas. In the past 30 years, China's rapid economic development has produced centripetal force in many countries. Seeking cooperation and mutual benefit can provide a broader geographical space for the economic development of all countries, and also meet the strategic needs of China's deepening development and opening up. The "Belt and Road" is the point of convergence between China and other countries.

Second, it complies with the trend of regional economic integration. In recent years, although China has actively participated in regional economic and trade cooperation, the cooperation mechanism between ASEAN and China is still not close enough. The China-Japan-Korea Free Trade Area is making slow progress, the United States is actively building *Trans-Pacific Partnership Agreement*, and Russia has launched Eurasian Alliance Program. In this context, China urgently needs to strengthen regional economic cooperation organizations to enhance development space.

Third, it is the inherent requirement of coordinated regional development in China. The "Belt and Road" is expected to drive the development of the western region with weak economic strength and solve the problem of imbalance in the development of the eastern and western regions. The Belt and Road construction can promote the opening up of the western region and the level of economic development by developing an export-oriented economy oriented to Central Asia and neighboring countries, and promote the western region to become China's new economic growth pole and the coordinated development of the regional economy.

Fourth, it is a major shift in China's diplomatic strategic thinking. In recent years, efforts to ease the doubts of neighboring countries by economic appeal have not been enough, so China urgently needs to actively seek out the focus and breakthrough of future development This breakthrough is sub-regional cooperation, that is, to build an economy with Central Asia and neighboring countries, jointly respond to external threats, resolve security conflicts, prevent political interference from non-regional forces, and serve the Chinese dream of the great rejuvenation of the Chinese nation.

The Belt and Road run through the continents of Asia, Europe and Africa, connecting the vibrant East Asia economic circle at one end and developed European economic circle at the other, and encompassing countries with huge potential for economic development. The Silk Road Economic Belt focuses on bringing together China, Central Asia, Russia and Europe (the Baltic); linking China with the Persian Gulf and the Mediterranean Sea through Central Asia and West Asia; and connecting China with Southeast Asia, South Asia and the Indian Ocean. The 21st Century Maritime Silk Road is designed to go from China's coast to Europe through the South China Sea and the Indian Ocean in one route, and from China's coast through the South China Sea to the South Pacific in the other.[1] The Belt focuses on the Eurasian continent and speeds up its opening to the west, and the Road focuses on the ocean and raises the level of openness at sea.

The Belt and Road focuses on regional linkage and emphasizes the interaction between different sectors. In advancing the Belt and Road Initiative, China will fully leverage the comparative advantages of its various regions, adopt a proactive strategy of further opening up, strengthen interaction and cooperation among the eastern, western and central regions, and comprehensively improve the openness of the Chinese economy.

Northwestern and northeastern regions. We should make good use of Xinjiang's geographic advantages and its role as a window of westward opening up to deepen communication and cooperation with Central, South and West Asian countries, make it a key transportation, trade, logistics, culture, science and education center, and a core area on the Silk Road Economic Belt. We should give full scope to the economic and cultural strengths of Shaanxi and Gansu provinces and the ethnic and cultural advantages of the Ningxia Hui Autonomous Region and Qinghai Province, build Xi'an into a new focus of reform and opening up in China's interior, speed up the development and opening up of cities such as Lanzhou and Xining, and advance the building of the Ningxia Inland Opening-up Pilot Economic Zone with the goal of creating strategic channels, trade and logistics hubs and key bases for industrial and

[1] National Development and Reform Commission, Ministry of Foreign Affairs, and Ministry of Commerce of the People's Republic of China, *Visions and Actions on Jointly Building the Silk Road Economic Belt and the 21st-Century Maritime Silk Road*, March 8, 2015.

Quoted from: http://news.xinhuanet.com/gango/2015-06/08/c_127890670.htm.

English Translation from: https://www.fmprc.gov.cn/ce/cevn/chn/sghkt/t1251121.htm.

cultural exchanges opening to Central, South and West Asian countries. We should give full play to Inner Mongolia's proximity to Mongolia and Russia, improve the railway links connecting Heilongjiang Province with Russia and the regional railway network, strengthen cooperation between China's Heilongjiang, Jilin and Liaoning provinces and Russia's Far East region on sea-land multimodal transport, and advance the construction of a Eurasian high-speed transport corridor linking Beijing and Moscow with the goal of building key windows opening to the north.

Southwestern region. We should give full play to the unique advantage of Guangxi Zhuang Autonomous Region as a neighbor of ASEAN countries, speed up the opening up and development of the Beibu Gulf Economic Zone and the Pearl River-Xijiang Economic Zone, build an international corridor opening to the ASEAN region, create new strategic anchors for the opening up and development of the southwest and mid-south regions of China, and form an important gateway connecting the Silk Road Economic Belt and the 21st Century Maritime Silk Road. We should make good use of the geographic advantage of Yunnan Province, advance the construction of an international transport corridor connecting China with neighboring countries, develop a new highlight of economic cooperation in the Greater Mekong Sub-region, and make the region a pivot of China's opening up to South and Southeast Asia. We should promote the border trade and tourism and culture cooperation between Tibet Autonomous Region and neighboring countries such as Nepal.

Coastal regions, and Hong Kong, Macao and Taiwan. We should leverage the strengths of the Yangtze River Delta, Pearl River Delta, west coast of the Taiwan Straits, Bohai Rim and other areas with economic zones boasting a high level of openness, robust economic strengths and strong catalytic role, speed up the development of the China (Shanghai) Pilot Free Trade Zone and support Fujian Province in becoming a core area of the 21st Century Maritime Silk Road. We should give full scope to the role of Qianhai (Shenzhen), Nansha (Guangzhou), Hengqin (Zhuhai) and Pingtan (Fujian) in opening up and cooperation, deepen their cooperation with Hong Kong, Macao and Taiwan, and help to build the Guangdong-Hong Kong-Macao Big Bay Area. We should promote the development of the Zhejiang Marine Economy Development Demonstration Zone, Fujian Marine Economic Pilot Zone and Zhoushan Archipelago New Area, and further open Hainan Province as an international tourism island. We should strengthen the port construction of coastal cities such as Shanghai, Tianjin, Ningbo-Zhoushan, Guangzhou, Shenzhen, Zhanjiang, Shantou, Qingdao, Yantai, Dalian, Fuzhou, Xiamen, Quanzhou, Haikou and Sanya, and strengthen the functions of international hub airports such as Shanghai and Guangzhou. We should use opening up to motivate these areas to carry out deeper reform, create new systems and mechanisms of open economy, step up scientific and technological innovation, develop new advantages for participating in and leading international cooperation and competition, and become the pace-setter and main force in the Belt and Road Initiative, particularly the building of the 21st Century Maritime Silk Road. We should leverage the unique role of overseas Chinese and the Hong Kong and Macao Special Administrative Regions, and encourage them to participate in and contribute to the Belt and Road Initiative. We should also make proper arrangements for the Taiwan region to be part of this effort.

Inland regions. We should make use of the advantages of inland regions, including a vast landmass, rich human resources and a strong industrial foundation, focus on such key regions as the city clusters along the middle reaches of the Yangtze River, around Chengdu and Chongqing, in central Henan Province, around Hohhot, Baotou, Erdos and Yulin, and around Harbin and Changchun to propel regional interaction and cooperation and industrial concentration. We should build Chongqing into an important pivot for developing and opening up the western region, and make Chengdu, Zhengzhou, Wuhan, Changsha, Nanchang and Hefei leading areas of opening up in the inland regions. We should accelerate cooperation between regions on the upper and middle reaches of the Yangtze River and their counterparts along Russia's Volga River. We should set up coordination mechanisms in terms of railway transport and port customs clearance for the China-Europe corridor, cultivate the brand of "China-Europe freight trains", and construct a cross-border transport corridor connecting the eastern, central and western regions. We should support inland cities such as Zhengzhou and Xi'an in building airports and international land ports, strengthen customs clearance cooperation between inland ports and ports in the coastal and border regions, and launch pilot e-commerce services for cross-border trade. We should optimize the layout of special customs oversight areas, develop new models of processing trade and deepen industrial cooperation with countries along the Belt and Road.

Currently, the Chinese government has been actively promoting the building of the Belt and Road, enhancing communication and consultation and advancing practical cooperation with countries along the Belt and Road, and has introduced a series of policies and measures. As an important part of the Silk Road Economic Belt, the Northwest Region is strengthening cooperation with countries along the Silk Road Economic Belt for early outcomes.[2]

The first is to rely on humanistic advantages to create cultural and technological centers and hubs for exchange and cooperation. For example, ethnic minorities such as Uyghur and Kazakh in Xinjiang and Gansu share languages with Central Asian, and their customs are similar. Under this background, Xinjiang is expanding its exports of cultural tourism products and services to Central Asia and West Asia. Gansu is based on the Dunhuang International Cultural Tourism City as a platform to carry out cultural heritage protection cooperation and exchange with the theme of Silk Road culture.

The second is to rely on location advantages to create trade transportation channels and develop industries with transportation advantages. By improving the route network, we will accelerate the development of aviation service industry such as aviation logistics and aviation maintenance, and promote the construction of free trade parks for Central and Western Asia and Europe, build high-end manufacturing clusters associated with the aviation industry, and build comprehensive transportation system which links China and Central and Western Asia, South Asia, Europe and Africa, and build a modern domestic and international logistics network system with the help of transportation advantages.

The third is to build an industrial docking base based on industrial advantages. For example, Ningxia and the Middle East and other regions have strong complementarity of ethnic characteristics. With the help of the China-Arab States Expo, focusing on industries such as halal food and ethnic crafts, we will gradually establish important halal food,

[2] National Development and Reform Commission, Ministry of Foreign Affairs and Ministry of Commerce of the People's Republic of China, *Visions and Actions on Jointly Building the Silk Road Economic Belt and the 21st-Century Maritime Silk Road*, March 8, 2015.

Quoted from: http://news.xinhuanet.com/gango/2015-06/08/c_127890670.htm.

English Translation from: https://www.fmprc.gov.cn/ce/cevn/chn/sghkt/t1251121.htm.

Muslim products production and service bases for Arab countries and Muslim regions; In addition, we can jointly explore and develop oil and gas resources with Central Asia and other regions to cooperate in the construction of high-end oil and gas chemical projects.

The "Belt and Road" is a major benefit to the western region. In the future, with the construction of the "Belt and Road" and the advancement of urbanization, some important infrastructures, such as railways, will be built faster, and major water conservancy projects will be built and reconstructed. The transformation of the underground pipe network in some cities will also accelerate, and projects related to people's livelihood such as the construction of affordable housing will be further accelerated. For the western region, through the interconnection of infrastructure, the "Belt and Road" can change the local development conditions and environment through the construction of railways, highways, airports, pipelines and ports. In addition, the energy resources in the western region are enriched, and under the current situation of insufficient domestic demand and overcapacity, especially in the backward western regions, these resources can be revitalized through the "Belt and Road" construction. By opening to countries in the west, it is also possible to use local advantages to develop foreign processing trade and change the path dependence of economic development on resources. Under the "Belt and Road" initiative, China's advantageous resources can be transported outwards, and the industry will also accelerate its transfer to the west. Now, the electronics processing industry has begun to shift westward. The middle and west region can seize the favorable opportunity and form a new driving force for development. As the opening up to the west strengthens, and China's advantageous industries and advanced technologies "go out", the industries in the eastern region will also accelerate their transformation.

The implementation of the "Belt and Road" cannot be achieved within one day, and it is necessary to fully exchange and cooperate with countries along the line to balance the relationship between the major powers. We should do basic research work, formulate development plans for different periods, strengthen humanities exchanges, care about people's livelihood projects, and provide backup and support for cooperation in various fields. Through the construction of the "Belt and Road", we will support the development and opening up of inland areas and promote coordinated regional development.

2.2 *Promote Economic Cooperation Between the Bohai Rim and the North Region Through Coordinated Development of Beijing, Tianjin and Hebei*

Located right in and near China's capital, Beijing-Tianjin-Hebei region is an economic center in the Bohai Rim and northern China. Its strategic position is very important. With a regional area of 216,000 square kilometers, the resident population at the end of 2013 was 109 million, and the regional GDP was 6.22 trillion yuan. It carried the population of 8.02% of the country with a regional area of 2.25%, creating a total economic output of 10.93%; The annual per capita GDP in 2013 was 57,000 yuan, which was 1.36 times the national average. The Beijing-Tianjin-Hebei region is dominated by the automobile industry, electronics industry, machinery industry and metallurgical steel industry. It is the country's major high-tech and heavy industry base, and is the largest and most dynamic region in the north of China. The Beijing-Tianjin-Hebei region stands shoulder to shoulder with the Yangtze River Delta region and the Pearl River Delta region as a region with the most vitality, the highest degree of openness, the strongest innovation capability, and the largest population in China, and also an important engine for stimulating China's economic development. However, at present, there are some outstanding problems in the Beijing-Tianjin-Hebei region.

First, the problem of "big city disease" in Beijing is highlighted. By the end of 2013, the resident population of Beijing reached 21.148 million. The excessive population expansion led to traffic congestion, rising housing prices, serious air pollution and a series of economic and social problems. Social management was difficult, which brought tremendous pressure on urban management.

Second, the resource and environment are overloaded, and the natural ecosystem is degraded. Beijing, Tianjin and Hebei have a serious shortage of water resources, and the per capita water resources are only 1/9 of the national average. Soil and water loss is severe, sand and dust weather has appeared, and the ecology is overwhelmed. It has become the region with the most intense relationship between people and nature in the eastern part of China and the most contradictory one between resources and environment.

Third, the regional development gap is wide, and it is further expanding. The gap in economic development level is large. In 2013, Hebei's per capita GDP was less than 50% of Beijing and Tianjin, and its per capita fiscal revenue was only 1/6 and 1/5 of Beijing and Tianjin respectively. The per capita disposable income of urban residents and per capita net income of farmers was half of that in Beijing, about 70 and 60% of Tianjin (see Fig. 1); the urbanization rate of Hebei was about 38 percentage points and 35 percentage points lower than that of Beijing and Tianjin respectively.

Fourth, the gap in public service levels is obvious. In 2013, Hebei's per capita fiscal expenditure was only 30 and 35% of Beijing and Tianjin respectively. The problem of the poverty belt around Beijing and Tianjin is outstanding. At present, there are still 3.66 million poor people in Hebei and 39 national-level poverty-stricken counties, including 9 poverty-stricken counties around the capital.

Fifth, the administrative color of resource allocation is strong, and the role of market mechanisms is not sufficient. With its superior administrative conditions, Beijing has gathered a large number of high-quality resources such as central enterprise headquarters, well-known colleges, and 3A hospitals. A large number of high-quality resources such as capital, talents and technology have gathered in Beijing and Tianjin, and the "siphon effect" of surrounding areas is obvious (see Fig. 2). In order to attract the superior resources of Beijing and Tianjin, some cities and counties in Hebei have adopted competitive means, including lowering land prices, to attract investment, aggravating vicious competitions and having paid high costs.

On February 26, 2014, General Secretary Xi Jinping delivered an important speech during his inspection tour in Beijing, which comprehensively and profoundly expounded the basic ideas and work priorities of the coordinated development of Beijing-Tianjin-Hebei and put forward seven requirements. The Beijing-Tianjin-Hebei coordinated development bid farewell to the "paper talks" and entered the stage of substantial speed up. In response to the problems in the development of Beijing-Tianjin-Hebei, General Secretary Xi Jinping pointed out that there are more than 100 million people in this region of which the land area is 216,000 square kilometers, and that the three places are geographically connected and share the same culture, whose history is profound and radius of communication is appropriate, thus making it possible to fully integrate and develop synergistically.

The first is to strengthen the top-level design, clarify major issues such as functional positioning, industrial division of labor, urban layout,

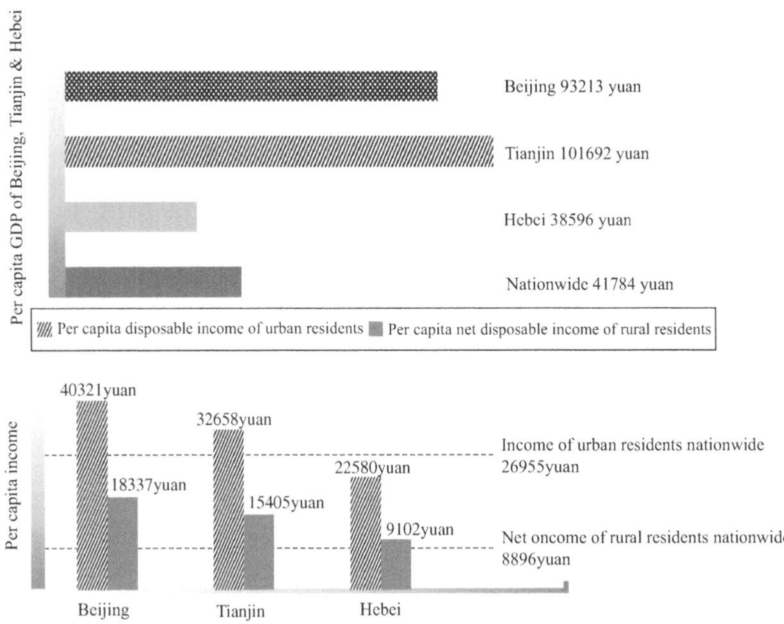

Fig. 1 京津冀人均 GDP 和人均收入对比 (2013年) (Comparison of per capita GDP and per capita income of Beijing, Tianjin and Hebei [2013])

- 京津冀人均 GDP: Per capita GDP of Beijing, Tianjin and Hebei
- 北京: Beijing
- 天津: Tianjin
- 河北: Hebei
- 全国: Nationwide
- 元: yuan
- 城镇居民人均可支配收入: Per capita disposable income of urban residents
- 农村居民人均纯收入: Per capita net disposable income of rural residents
- 人均收入: Per capita income
- 全国城镇居民收入: Income of urban residents nationwide
- 全国农民纯收入: Net oncome of rural residents nationwide
- 资料来源: 中国经济网新闻部: http://www.cet.com.cn (*Source* News Office of China Economic Times: http://www.cet.com.cn)

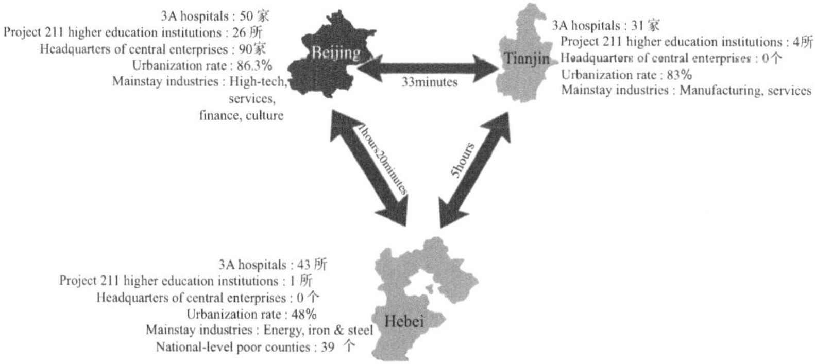

Fig. 2 京津冀基本公共服务和产业对比 (2013年) (Comparison of basic public services and industries in Beijing, Tianjin and Hebei [2013])

- 北京: Beijing
- 天津: Tianjin
- 河北: Hebei
- 分钟: minutes
- 小时: hours
- 三甲医院: 3A hospitals
- 211高校: Project 211 higher education institutions
- 央企总部: Headquarters of central enterprises
- 城镇化率: Urbanization rate
- 支柱产业: Mainstay industries
- 国家级贫困县: National-level poor counties
- 高科技、服务业、金融、文化: High-tech, services, finance, culture
- 制造业、服务业: Manufacturing, services
- 能源、钢铁: Energy, iron and steel
- 资料来源: 中国经济网新闻部: http://www.cet.com.cn (*Source* News Office of China Economic Times: http://www.cet.com.cn)

facilities and comprehensive transportation systems, and to form specific measures in fiscal policy, investment policy, and project arrangement.

The second is to increase the promotion of coordinated development, consciously break the mindset of merely looking after their own interests, work together to achieve the goal of top-level design, and give full play to the role of the economic cooperation and development coordination mechanism in the Bohai Rim.

The third is to accelerate the promotion of industrial docking cooperation, rationalize the industrial development chain of the three places, form a rational distribution of industries between the regions and an upstream and downstream linkage mechanism, dock industrial planning, and ensure not to engage in isomorphic and homogenous development.

The fourth is to adjust and optimize urban layout and spatial structure, promote urban division of labor and cooperation, improve the level of urban agglomeration integration, and improve its comprehensive carrying capacity and intension development level.

The fifth is to expand the ecological capacity and environment, strengthen cooperation in ecological environmental protection and improve cooperation mechanisms in the areas of shelterbelt construction, water resources protection, water environment management, and clean energy use on the basis of the cooperation mechanism for air pollution prevention and control.

The sixth is to focus on building a modern transportation network system, take traffic integration as a pioneering field, and accelerate the construction of an integrated transportation network that is fast, convenient, efficient, secure, with large-capacity and low-cost.

The seventh is to accelerate the process of market integration, resolve to remove various institutional obstacles that restrict the free flow and optimal allocation of production factors such as capital, technology, property rights, talents, and labor force, and promote the free flow and optimized configuration of various elements in the region according to market rules.

These arrangements for the development of Beijing-Tianjin-Hebei include three important implications: first, coordinate the development of Beijing-Tianjin-Hebei region, eliminate environmental pollution sources and promote economic growth; second, solve Beijing's "big city disease" and rid Beijing of such a heavy burden; third, speed up the development of Hebei and get rid of the backward situation as soon as possible. Promoting the coordinated development of

Beijing-Tianjin-Hebei is to create a new capital economic circle for the future, promote the innovation of regional development systems and mechanisms, explore effective ways to build ecological civilization, and promote the coordination of population, economy, resources and environment, to further advance the development of the Bohai Rim, the development of the entire hinterland in the North and the coordinated development of the North and the South.

In the process of promoting the coordinated development of Beijing-Tianjin-Hebei, the top priority is to make initial breakthroughs in the three key areas of ecology, transportation and industry.

First, we should accelerate industrial coordination. General Secretary Xi Jinping pointed out at the Beijing-Tianjin-Hebei Collaborative Development Symposium that we will focus on accelerating industrial docking cooperation, rationalizing the industrial development chain of the three regions, forming a rational distribution of industries between the regions and an upstream and downstream linkage mechanism, docking industrial planning and ensuring not to engage in isomorphic and homogenous development. The core contents of the coordinated development strategy of Beijing-Tianjin-Hebei are relieving the non-core function of the capital and promoting migration of some industries. In fact, due to historical and political reasons, the industrial development of the three places has been different from the beginning, and the differences have gradually increased with the development of the economy. At the same time, the differences between the three places provide a complementary development opportunity for the Beijing-Tianjin-Hebei region. The industrial map of Beijing-Tianjin-Hebei is undergoing reconstruction: Beijing must get rid of non-core functions and build a high-tech and sophisticated industrial system; Tianjin should work hard to strengthen coordination and strive for the real northern economic center; Hebei should, at any cost, fight against the overcapacity and leverage the green rise of Beijing and Tianjin.

Second, we should accelerate ecological cooperation. General Secretary Xi Jinping pointed out at the Beijing-Tianjin-Hebei Collaborative Development Symposium that we should focus on expanding environmental capacity and ecological space, strengthen cooperation on ecological environmental protection, and improve shelterbelt construction, water resources protection, and water environmental governance and clean energy use on the basis of the cooperation mechanism for air pollution prevention and control. The air and water pollution in

Beijing-Tianjin-Hebei is an urgent problem facing regional development. It can be said that the ecological environment problem of Beijing-Tianjin-Hebei has become a pain shared by all. In order to improve the ecological environment, the three places must jointly control and realize the integration of ecological protection. Considering the overall environmental carrying capacity of the three places, we should focus on expanding the overall environmental capacity and ecological space, actively establish the Beijing-Tianjin-Hebei environmental protection and ecological construction cooperation mechanisms, and accelerate the implementation of *Ten Air Pollution and Control Measures.*

Third, we should speed up traffic coordination. General Secretary Xi Jinping pointed out at the Beijing-Tianjin-Hebei Collaborative Development Symposium that we should focus on building a modern transportation network system, take traffic integration as a pioneering field, and accelerate the construction of a fast, convenient, efficient, secure, large-capacity, low-cost, interconnected and integrated traffic network. The troubles of "big city disease" in Beijing, the problems of traffic integration, the construction of market integration, and how to solve these problems are the difficulties in the coordinated development of the three places. The coordinated development of Beijing-Tianjin-Hebei is like a huge network, and the integrated thinking connects the urban agglomerations, transportation and markets of the three places. "Only with access to roads can talents and capitals flow freely". That traffic problems should be given priority to has become a consensus in Beijing-Tianjin-Hebei coordinated development, and the transportation infrastructure construction of the three places must be considered within a same picture. The first need is the top-level design and integrated planning, and the resulting institutional innovation. The Beijing Outer Ring will be opened to traffic in 2016, and the relevant departments are promoting the development of new rail-oriented towns, with the focus on the Beijing-Tianjin-Hebei region.

In the coordinated development of Beijing-Tianjin-Hebei, it is necessary to do a good job in top-level design and strengthen cooperation among the three places; to adjust the industrial layout and promote the integration of transportation; to optimize the urban layout and expand the ecological space; it is up to the market to decide and the government to do the right thing. Beijing-Tianjin-Hebei coordinated development is not only a major change in the reconstruction of regional development pattern, but also a major experiment in the innovation of coordinated regional development mechanisms.

2.3 Promote the Coordinated Development of the East, Central and West with the Yangtze River Economic Belt

The Yangtze River Economic Belt starts from Shanghai in the east and Yunnan to the west, involving two municipalities, i.e. Shanghai, Chongqing and nine provinces, i.e. Jiangsu, Zhejiang, Anhui, Hubei, Jiangxi, Hunan, Sichuan, Yunnan, Guizhou. The Yangtze River is China's first and the world's third largest river. At present, the cargo volume carried by trunk and branch streams is about 2.3 billion tons, ranking first in the world's inland waterways. 11 provinces and cities are included in the Yangtze River Economic Belt, covering an area of 2.051 million square kilometers, accounting for 21.4% of China. In 2012, it had a population of 580 million people, 42.9% of China, and GDP reached 23.6 trillion yuan, 40.9% of the country. The Yangtze River Economic Belt spans the East, Central and West, with huge potential for development and leeway.

The Yangtze River Economic Belt has a unique development base and comprehensive advantages.

The first is the convenient traffic. It has obvious location advantages. The Yangtze River Economic Belt traverses the heartland of China, and the economic hinterland is vast. It not only connects the East, Central and West, but also meets the northern and southern railways such as the Beijing–Shanghai, Beijing–Kowloon, Beijing–Guangzhou, Anhui–Jiangxi and Jiaozuo–Liuzhou railways.

The second is its resource advantage. First of all, it has extremely abundant fresh water resources, and then the mineral resources with large reserves and various types. In addition, it has many famous tourism resources and abundant agricultural and biological resources. In conclusion, it has great development potential.

The third is the industrial advantage. It has always been one of the most important industrial corridors in China. Most modern industries such as steel, automobiles, electronics and petrochemicals in China gather here, nurturing a large number of high-energy, high-capacity, high-tech industries and extra-large enterprises. In addition, the basic status of its large-scale agriculture ranks first in the country, and the output of grain, cotton and oil in 9 provinces and cities along the Yangtze River accounts for more than 40% of the country.

The fourth is the advantage of human resources. The Yangtze River Basin is one of the cultural cradle of the Chinese nation. It has a talent pool, developed science and education, and advanced technology and management.

The fifth are the densely-urbanized cities and vast markets. There are 216 large and small cities in 9 provinces and direct-controlled municipalities along the Yangtze River, accounting for 33.8% of the national cities; the urban density is 2.16 times the national average. Moreover, the region is densely populated, the income level of residents is relatively high, and various consumer demands are also considerable, which is very attractive to domestic and foreign investors.

It can be seen that the Yangtze River Economic Belt is the economic zone with the highest economic density except for the coastal open areas. Its strategic significance for China's economic development is unparalleled with other economic belts. Compared with China's coastal and other economic belts, the Yangtze River Economic Belt has the vastest hinterland and development space, and is the region with the greatest economic growth potential. It should become an inland river economic belt with the largest development scale and the widest impact in the world.

Combined with the realistic conditions of the Yangtze River Economic Belt, the State Council proposed that the key tasks for the construction of the Yangtze River Economic Belt include the following seven aspects.

The first is to enhance the function of the Yangtze River as "golden waterway". We should enhance trunk shipping capacity, improve distribution and navigation conditions of branch streams, optimize port functional layouts, strengthen the collection and distribution systems, accelerate the implementation of inland river ship standardization, and expand the capacity of the Three Gorges Hub.

The second is to build a comprehensive three-dimensional traffic corridor. We should form a fast and large-capacity railway channel, build a high level and wide-cover road network, promote the construction of aviation networks, improve the layout of oil and gas pipelines, accelerate the development of multimodal transport, and build integrated transportation hubs.

The third is to drive industrial transformation and upgrading through innovation. We should enhance the ability of independent innovation of industries, advance the development of world-class industrial clusters, accelerate the development of modern service industries, build a green energy industry belt along the Yangtze River, improve the development level of modern and characteristic agriculture, and guide the orderly transfer of industries and division of labor.

The fourth is to comprehensively promote new urbanization. We should enhance the international competitiveness of the Yangtze River Delta urban agglomeration, foster the development of the middle reaches of the Yangtze River, promote the integration of the development of Chengdu-Chongqing Urban Agglomeration, advance the development of regional urban agglomerations, reasonably guide the development of cities along the Yangtze River, and strengthen the construction of urban agglomeration transportation networks.

[Column 3-1]
Summary of the *Urban Agglomeration Development Plan for the Middle Reaches of the Yangtze River*
On March 26, 2015, the State Council officially approved the *Urban Agglomeration Development Plan for the Middle Reaches of the Yangtze River* (hereinafter referred to as the "Plan") in Letter No. 62[2015]. This was an important measure to implement the major national strategy of the Yangtze River Economic Belt and the first cross-regional urban agglomeration plan approved by the state after the publishment of the *National Plan on New Urbanization (2014–2020).*

The Middle Reaches of the Yangtze River is a large-scale urban agglomeration with Wuhan City Circle, the Changsha-Zhuzhou-Xiangtan City Group and the Poyang Lake City Group as the main body. The planning scope includes: Wuhan, Huangshi, Ezhou, Huanggang, Xiaogan, Xianning, Xiantao, Qianjiang, Tianmen, Xiangyang, Yichang, Jingzhou and Jingmen in Hubei Province, Changsha, Zhuzhou, Xiangtan, Yueyang, Yiyang, Changde, Hengyang and Loudi in Hunan Province, Nanchang, Jiujiang, Jingdezhen, Yingtan, Xinyu, Yichun, Pingxiang, Shangrao, Fuzhou and some counties and districts of Ji'an in Jiangxi Province. The total area is about 317,000 square kilometers, accounting for 3.3% of China. In 2014, the regional GDP was 6 trillion yuan, and the population at the end of the year was 121 million, both accounting for 8.8% of the national total. The middle reaches of the Yangtze River are an important part of the Yangtze River Economic Belt and links the East with the West, the South with the North. It is also a key area for implementing the strategy of promoting the rise of the central region, deepening Reform and Opening up, and promoting new urbanization, and has a significant position in China's regional development.

The Plan defined the four strategic positions of the middle reaches of the Yangtze River: First, it is China's new economic growth pole. By accelerating the transformation of economic development mode and implementing the innovation-driven development strategy, the urban agglomeration of the middle reaches of the Yangtze River will be built into a modern industrial base and an important national innovation base with global influence, with its comprehensive strength and competitiveness enhanced. We should build an important support for the development of the Yangtze River Economic Belt and make it a new growth pole for the Chinese economy; Second, it is a pilot area of urbanization in the central and western regions. We need to improve the institutional mechanisms of urban agglomeration development, optimize urban spatial form and spatial layout, improve urban comprehensive carrying capacity, promote coordination of urban development and industrial support, transfer employment and population agglomeration, and build livable and suitable cities that suit their local environment; Third, it is an inland open cooperation demonstration zone. With the Yangtze River's waterway and other important traffic passages as the link, the internal and external links will be unblocked, a unified and open market system and a high-level open platform will be built to deepen global cooperation and international exchanges, to create a demonstration of all-round and multi-level open cooperation in inland areas; Fourth, it is a leading area in "two-oriented" society construction. We should accelerate the construction of a resource-saving and environment-friendly society, establish a linkage mechanism for cross-regional ecological construction and environmental protection, build an ecological city agglomeration with important influence, and accumulate new experience and provide new examples of national "two-oriented" social and ecological civilization construction.

The Plan clarified the key tasks of promoting "five coordinated development" in urban and rural areas, industries, infrastructure, ecological civilization and public services. In terms of coordinated urban and rural development, the Plan proposed to adhere to the new urbanization road, strengthen the status of central cities (Wuhan, Changsha and Nanchang), and build multi-centers based and gridding development pattern along the Yangtze River, Shanghai–Kunming, Beijing–Guangzhou, Beijing–Kowloon Railways and Erenhot–Guangzhou Expressway, which supports the cooperative development of inter-provincial neighboring cities and promotes the construction of beautiful homes and the integration of urban and rural development. In terms of infrastructure interconnection, the Plan focused on improving comprehensive support and support capabilities, and comprehensively promoted the construction of major infrastructure such as integrated transportation networks, water infrastructure systems, energy security systems and information infrastructure to enhance the level of interconnection and modernization. In terms of industrial synergy development, the Plan emphasized the importance of relying on the industrial base and comparative advantages of urban agglomerations to establish an industrial synergy development mechanism, to jointly build advantageous industrial clusters, to build modern service industry clusters, to develop and expand modern agricultural bases, to orderly promote cross-regional industrial transfer and acceptance, to accelerate industrial transformation and upgrading, and to build a modern industrial system with regional characteristics. In the aspect of joint ecological civilization construction, we will promote the construction of ecological civilization and enhance the capacity for sustainable development, establish and improve the inter-regional ecological environmental protection linkage mechanism, strengthen the comprehensive management of the ecological environment, and jointly build an ecological barrier to form a harmonious development pattern between people and nature. In terms of public service sharing, the Plan focused on promoting the equalization of basic public services, comprehensively strengthening exchanges and cooperation in education, science and technology, health care and public services, jointly promoting cultural prosperity, working together to develop human resources, innovating social governance systems, improving public services and raising the level of joint contribution and sharing of public services.

The Plan took reform, innovation and pilot establishment as the support and driving force for the development of urban agglomerations. These were placed in a prominent position and ran through the full text of the plan, mainly reflected in the following aspects: First, innovating urban linkage and the urban and rural development mechanism. We should promote urban agglomeration planning, information exchange and resource sharing, jointly explore ways to solve "city diseases" and to establish an urban agglomeration management coordination mechanism, innovate urban agglomeration factor market management, and promote the free flow of production factors and optimize allocation. We will promote the construction of urban and rural unified factor markets and the integration of urban and rural planning, infrastructure, and public services, accelerate the improvement of the urban-rural integration development system and mechanism, and promote the coordinated promotion of new urbanization and new rural construction.

Second, we should promote the reform and innovation of integrated transportation and urban traffic development. We are to establish a management system and coordination mechanism to adapt to the development of integrated transportation, explore efficient and unified planning and management of various modes of transportation, and promote the sharing of urban agglomerations; explore the reform of logistics management system, and break the segmentation and regional blockade of logistics business in the middle reaches of the Yangtze River, reduce the cost of logistics enterprises; carry out railway, highway and port investment and financing and toll price reform, and establish a joint investment construction and management model that crosses three provinces' regional railway and highway, to attract social capital to participate in the construction.

Third, we should promote the reform and innovation of the water conservancy construction management system. We need to improve the cooperation mechanism of regional water conservancy projects, explore the construction of an integrated platform for water resources, and plan the construction of major water conservancy projects in a coordinated way; establish a mechanism for organic integration of the government and the market, and further improve the water supply price, on-grid price and fiscal, finance and land support for water conservancy projects; strengthen integrated management of watersheds and urban and rural water resources, improve the management system which combines river basin management and administrative regional management, and promote the balance between economic and social development and water resources and water environment carrying capacity.

Fourth, we should establish a mechanism for industrial synergy development. We are to strengthen industrial policy docking, establish and improve industrial transfer promotion mechanism and interest coordination mechanism, and gradually unify policies for land and environmental protection within urban agglomerations; give full play to the role of industry associations and chambers of commerce as bridges, to build an industrial cooperation platform for urban agglomerations; carry out a unified admittance system, and explore to establish a credit information exchange and sharing mechanism of urban agglomeration enterprises; strengthen the main position of enterprises in technological innovation, face market demands and accelerate the innovation of key common technologies in industries.

Fifth, we should build a cross-regional environmental protection mechanism. We need to strengthen environmental pollution joint prevention and control, and gradually unify environmental access and major pollutant discharge standards for urban agglomeration industrial projects and construction projects; strengthen emergency linkage mechanism cooperation, establish a rapid notification mechanism for sudden environmental incidents, and jointly address regional emergent ecological environmental problems; jointly implement the water environmental protection strategic action plan, promote the prevention and control of transboundary water pollution, and work together to prevent air pollution and heavy metal pollution; improve the ecological compensation mechanism, implement environmental supervision and law enforcement linkage, establish and improve the environmental governance tracking mechanism, negotiation mechanism and arbitration mechanism across administrative regions.

Sixth, we should innovate the social governance system. We need to give play to the leading role of the government, encourage and support all sectors of society to participate, and achieve an integration of government governance, social self-regulation and residents autonomy; promote social governance to the front end and to the grassroots level, improve the grassroots integrated service management platform, and gradually implement grid management; support all city industry associations to form alliances, actively carry out cross-regional cooperation and jointly maintain regional industry development order; carry out public service quality assessment of urban agglomerations in the middle reaches of the Yangtze River, and promote sharing of inter-regional inspection and testing resources; innovate and improve population service and management systems, and promote orderly flow of population, rational distribution and social integration; and improve the public safety system, and strengthen cross-regional joint law enforcement, police cooperation and coordinated disposal.

Source The website of the Central People's Government of the People's Republic of China, Interpretation of the *Urban Agglomeration Development Plan for the Middle Reaches of the Yangtze River* by the Head of the Regional Economic Department of the National Development and Reform Commission, April 2015, http://www.gov.cn.

The fifth is to cultivate new advantages in opening up to the outside world. We should give play to the leading role of the opening up of the Yangtze River Delta region, expand the demonstration effect of the China (Shanghai) Pilot Free Trade Zone, enhance the leading function of Yunnan in opening to the southwest, strengthen strategic interaction with the Silk Road Economic Belt and build a Yangtze River customs clearance system.

The sixth is to build a green ecological corridor. We should effectively protect and utilize the Yangtze River water resources, strengthen the comprehensive management of the river basin environment, implement the full collection and treatment of urban sewage waste along the Yangtze River trunks and tributaries, strengthen the ecological protection and restoration along the Yangtze River and implement the strategy that requires returning farmland to forests and grasslands in the upstream, and returning farmland to lakes and wetlands in the middle and lower reaches.

The seventh is to innovate regional coordination and development of institutional mechanisms. We are to establish a regional interaction and cooperation mechanism, promote the construction of an integrated market system, increase the intensity of financial cooperation and innovation, strengthen the coordinated protection of ecological environment, and improve the level of public service and social governance cooperation.

In the process of building the Yangtze River Economic Belt, the most important thing is to accelerate the construction of a modern integrated transportation system. At present, the Yangtze River Economic Belt has initially formed a transportation network, consisting of waterways, railways, highways, civil aviation and pipelines, with the golden waterway of the Yangtze River as the main body. However, it should be noted that the potential of the Yangtze River shipping has not been fully utilized, the capacity of east-west railways and highways is insufficient, the capacity of the north-south channel is tight, the construction of integrated transportation hubs is lagging, and the intercity railways are not compatible with the spatial layout of urban agglomerations. Therefore, the state has clearly stated that it is necessary to speed up the construction of the transportation network of the Yangtze River Economic Belt and that by 2020, it will take the lead in building an integrated three-dimensional traffic corridor to achieve "four completions".

The first is to build a smooth golden waterway. We are to form the Yangtze River Golden Waterway with the Shanghai International Shipping Center as the leader and the Yangtze River trunk as the backbone, in which the tributaries are connected, and the collection and distribution systems are improved. The mileage of the high-grade navigation channel will be increased from the current 6700 to 12,000 kilometers.

The second is to build an efficient railway network. We will form a rapid railway network with Shanghai–Wuhan–Chengdu and Shanghai–Kunming high-speed railways as the main body and an ordinary railway network with the Quzhou–Lijiang Railway, the Shanghai–Kunming Railway and railways along the Yangtze River as the backbone. The operating mileage will be increased from the current 29,600 to 40,000 kilometers, among which the high-speed railway will be raised from 4000 to 9000 kilometers.

The third is to build a convenient expressway network. We are to form a national expressway network with Shanghai–Chengdu, Shanghai–Chongqing, Shanghai–Kunming and Hangzhou–Ruili Expressways as the main body, covering the ordinary national highway network of all counties. The mileage of traffic will be increased from the current 1.89 million kilometers to 2 million kilometers, of which the national expressway will be improved from the current 32,000 to 42,000 kilometers.

The fourth is to build a developed aviation network. We will form a civil aviation network with Shanghai International Aviation Hub and regional aviation hubs in Chongqing, Chengdu, Kunming, Guiyang, Changsha, Wuhan, Nanjing and Hangzhou at its core, and the number of civil airports will be increased from the current 74 to 100.

CHAPTER 4

New Ideas for Regional Development Under the New Normal of Economic Development

Since our economic development has entered the new normal, and regional development is faced with a new situation, it is necessary for us to clarify new goals, new connotations and new ideas. On the basis of past experiences, with the equalization of basic public services among regions as our main aim, it is proposed that we should focus on narrowing the gap in basic public services and living standards among different regions, guide all regions to give full play to comparative advantages so as to make economic development coordinated with population and ecology. It's suggested that one important task for promoting coordinated regional development is to build a unified national market, reasonably define the relationship of administrative powers and fiscal powers between the central and local governments, and reform the relevant fiscal and taxation policies, so as to improve the long-term mechanism for promoting coordinated regional development. On the basis of giving full play to respective advantages of the "Four Major Regions", we should promote the development of the Belt and Road Initiative, the coordinated development in Beijing-Tianjin-Hebei region and the development of Yangtze River Economic Belt. Therefore, forming a new situation of regional development that organically combines the major regions and axis belts, administrative areas and type areas, China and the world, and regional strategies and regional policies.

X. Song et al., *The Great Change in the Regional Economy of China under the New Normal*, The Great Transformation of China,
https://doi.org/10.1007/978-981-32-9475-2_4

1 New Situation for Regional Development

1.1 New Requirements for the New Normal of Economy

In 2014, the Central Economic Work Conference put forward that China's economic development has entered the new normal.[1] The conference called for us to have a scientific understanding of the current situation and an accurate analysis of future development trends, view the stage characteristics of China's economic development historically and dialectically, and accurately grasp the new normal of economic development. At present and in the future, the big logic of China's economic development is to understand, adapt to and lead the new normal. It can be seen that the basic characteristics of the new normal are the medium- and high-speed growth, the change of development mode, the deep adjustment of economic structure, and the shift of development power.[2] On the basis of the above, regional development under the new normal has also shown new characteristics.[3]

First, we should create new advantages in exports. At present, global total demand is sluggish, and China's low-cost comparative advantage has also changed, while China's export competitive advantage still exists. High-level "bringing in" and large-scale "going global" are taking place simultaneously. It is necessary for us to step up in fostering new comparative advantages and make exports continue to support economic development. The traditional low-cost advantage of China's exports has changed. On the one hand, in the international market, the world economy is developing unstably and in slow recovery. On the other hand, China's own comparative advantage has also changed. Therefore, China needs to change its development mode of foreign trade, find new advantages, and change the traditional method of focusing on low price. More importantly, we should improve product quality, increase technical content in products, carry out brand strategy, and build a service network.

[1] Xinhua News Agency: *Central Economic Work Conference Held in Beijing*, December 11, 2014, quoted from the website: http://news.xinhuanet.com/2014/12/11/c_113611795_2.htm.

[2] People's Daily commentator: "Actively Adapt to the New Normal of Economic Development—The Second Comment on Implementing the Spirit of the Central Economic Work Conference," *People's Daily*, 1st edition, December 14, 2014.

[3] National Information Center: *Positioning the New Normal with Nine Trends, National Information Center Decisions Reference*, No. 47, 2014.

The Silk Road Economic Belt, the twenty-first century Maritime Silk Road, the Yangtze River Economic Belt and the Shanghai Free Trade Zone will create China's new advantages in foreign trade.

Second, innovation should become the new engine. From the perspective of the relative advantage of production factors, economic growth will rely more on the quality of human capital and technological progress, so innovation must become a new engine for economic development. Over the past 30 years of reform and opening up, China has maintained rapid economic growth, mainly relying on the expansion of quantity and scale, and the extensive investment in low-cost factors such as labor costs and land costs. However, the current economic situation has undergone great changes, one of which is that the economy has turned from high growth to medium-high growth. This economic growth of new normal may last for a long time, which means to enter into the connotative economy that we are talking about. This kind of innovation-driven economic development mode that relies on technological progress also represents a higher level of development model and level, which is a far-sighted new thinking put forward by the central government. The aims of transforming the economic development mode lie in improving the quality of economic development and encouraging innovation, which includes product, technology, as well as model and system innovation.

Third, we should create a low-carbon environment. From the perspective of resource and environment constraints, energy, resources and ecological environment used to be relatively large, but now the environmental carrying capacity has reached or approached the upper limit, so we must conform to people's expectations of a good ecological environment and promote a new cycle development mode that is green and low-carbon. First, China's economy has developed to such a stage that the carrying capacity of resources and environment has reached a limit, so we have to abandon the development mode of high pollution, energy consumption and emissions. Second, in accordance with the laws of economic development, it's also necessary for China's economy to upgrade itself and walk toward the high-end of the industrial chain featuring low pollution, low energy and high added value. We can say that under the joint effect of economic laws and natural laws, economic development under the new normal will no longer focus on boring GDP figures, but rather, pay more attention to people's life, health, quality of life and living environment.

Fourth, investment should shift to new industries. From the perspective of investment demand, after more than 30 years of high-intensity and large-scale development and construction, traditional industries have become relatively saturated, but infrastructure connectivity and investment opportunities for new technologies, products, formats and business models have been increasing, which raised new requirements for us to innovate investment and financing methods. We should eliminate investment barriers, and make investment continue to play a key role in economic development. At present, under the context of large economic downward pressure, serious overcapacity, and emerging deflation risks, steady growth should still be our priority. Achieving steady growth requires stable investment and more importantly, connectivity, which is the infrastructure construction derived from the connection among road networks and railway networks of every corner of China, as well as the new investment opportunities from the Internet, e-commerce, information consumption and creative culture industries. Connectivity makes regional economic development integrated, reduce the logistics cost and cost of commodities for enterprises, and also generate investment and construction opportunities such as roads, docks, ports, logistics and industrial park construction. All of this will produce a "multiplier effect" on economic growth. Different from the past, the investment under the new normal is no longer blind. Rather, it focuses on promoting economic restructuring, optimizing industrial structure, guiding the orderly flow of private capital, spending money at where they can be put to best use, improving the efficiency of resource allocation, restructuring the economy, making up the shortcomings of economic development, improving people's livelihood, and finally guiding the economy to grow steadily.

Fifth, industries should develop in new ways. Given that our economic structure will further upgrade, business merger and reorganization and the relative concentration of production will be inevitable and the role of emerging industries, service industries, small and micro enterprises will become more prominent. Therefore, miniaturization, intelligence and specialization of production will become new features of industrial organizations. In terms of entrepreneurship, the government should take the initiative to lower the threshold, support the development of small and micro enterprises, lift the control over investment in some monopoly areas, establish a negative list system; as for industrial innovation, the government should vigorously develop the modern service industry. At the same time, we should encourage innovation, including mass innovation and entrepreneurship and stimulate the innovation potential of all the people. This is not only the need to maintain steady growth, but also a necessary step we should take in the new normal to upgrade and improve the efficiency of industries.

Sixth, competition should focus on differentiation. From the perspective of the characteristics of market competition, it used to mainly rely on quantitative expansion and price competition, but now it is gradually turning into quality-based, differentiated competition. Unifying the national market and improving the efficiency of resource allocation are internal requirements of economic development, so we must deepen reform and opening up, and step up the building of a unified, transparent, orderly and standardized market environment. What lies under differentiated competition is to change our economic model, especially to adjust the interest relationship between the central and local governments. Over the past 30 years of reform and opening up, the most fundamental driving force of economic growth comes from the so-called GDP competition among local governments. Local governments have a strong desire toward greater GDP, which has led to market segmentation and industry homogenization, overcapacity and resource mismatch in the entire country, and has hindered the formation of a unified national production factor market. Now if we want to turn to quality-oriented and differentiated competition, we must fundamentally break the pattern of driving the economy by local governments, re-adjust the relationship of administrative and financial power between central and local governments and turn local governments from economic-oriented into services-oriented, which means that the administrative power of local governments should be redefined. Their functions on economic development should be gradually weakened and they should provide more products and services on social security, people's livelihood and public services. When the administrative power and financial power are clearly defined, it's inevitable to adjust the functions of local governments, including reform on land transfer and household registration.

Seventh, regulation should focus on total supply and demand. From the perspective of resource allocation mode and macro-control mode, the marginal effect of the policy of comprehensively stimulating the economy is obviously diminishing. We should not only resolve overcapacity, but also explore the future development direction of industries through market mechanism. It is necessary to comprehensively grasp the new changes in the relationship between supply and demand and scientifically carry out macroeconomic regulation. In the past, our resource allocation was up to the "mayor" rather than the "market". Such mayor-decided system makes it difficult to eradicate "problem officials" and "problem magnates". The Third Plenary Session of the 18th CPC Central Committee proposed that the market should play a "decisive" role. The biggest "difference" of the new normal is to conduct scientific regulation with a mark-based mechanism.

1.2 New Trends Emerged in the Development Stages and Development Potential of Various Regions

First, inland areas such as the central and western regions have accumulated a strong material foundation, which means that they have enormous potential for future development. Over the past 10 years, in response to economic globalization and regional integration, the adjustment of international and domestic industrial structure has been accelerated. For the eastern region, this process is conducive to optimizing its industrial structure and improving the overall quality and international competitiveness of its economy. For the central and western regions, this process provides conditions for them to accept industrial transfer, as a result, the regions have undertaken a large number of industrial transfers, which has promoted the transformation of economic growth power, and significantly improved the development speed and sustainability of these regions. At present, the investment environment and development conditions in the central and western regions have been continuously improving, their independent development capabilities have been enhancing, and their ideas for further development have become clearer, laying a good foundation for better and faster development. In particular, the construction of major infrastructure in the central and western regions has been accelerated, creating a sound foundation for promoting balanced economic development among regions. For example, in 2014, the national railways completed a total investment of 808.8 billion yuan in fixed assets, the investment scale reaching the second highest in history.[4] Among them, railway investment in the central and western regions accounted for 78%; the new lines put into production in the central and western regions totaled 6747 kilometers, accounting

[4]Bai Tianliang: *Coordinated Regional Development a New Economic Highlight*, People's Daily, 6th edition, March 3, 2015.

for 80%. With the operation of 18 railway projects in the central and western regions such as Lanzhou-Xinjiang High-speed Railway and Lhasa-Shigatse Railway, the mileage of the Midwest railway reached 70,000 kilometers, accounting for 62.3% of China, significantly increasing the high-speed railway accessibility rate in central-western China. In the future, in response to the profound changes of world economic structure, China should remain committed to the basic policy of expanding domestic demand. The central and western regions are endowed with huge market potential and rich strategic resources, which will be further highlighted, creating favorable conditions for accelerating the development of the central and western regions.

Second, the problems of special types of areas have become increasingly prominent. Poverty-stricken areas and some minority areas are still faced with problems such as backward infrastructure, a fragile ecological environment, irrational industrial structure, an underdeveloped market system, and weak self-development ability, so we are still burdened with the heavy tasks of supporting poor areas in building a well-off society in an all-round way and maintaining the stability in border areas.

Areas with single economic structure such as old industrial cities and resource-based cities are at the low end of the industrial chain, since their industries mainly rely on energy and chemical industry and resource processing. These regions are faced with dual pressures of both accelerating development and transforming the economy. With greater pressure to change the development mode, they have more problems to solve. Moreover, these regions cover a number of provincial administrative regions, but at present there are some shortcomings in using administrative region-based regional policy systems to solve these problems.

Third, the regional policy system has continued to improve, but there is still a huge room for further improvement. With the enhancement of China's comprehensive strength, its policy systems have been continuously improved, the ability to coordinate regional development has been significantly improved, and the support for the development of the central and western regions has been significantly increased, which have been conducive to the formation of a new situation of positive interaction between the East and the West. However, there are many restrictions. For example, coordinated regional development is still constrained by institutional barriers, industrial transfer and optimized productivity distribution are restricted by administrative divisions, the population and labor mobility are limited by the household registration system and the coordinated development, and interests coordination between underdeveloped regions and economically developed regions are constrained by the fiscal and taxation systems. There are many things we can do to improve regional policies and systems.

1.3 New Changes in the Connotation of Coordinated Regional Development

The connotations of coordinated regional development are rich and keep deepening and developing. In general, coordinated regional development should meet the needs of socio-economic development and be in line with the goals of China's socialist modernization drive, which are dialectical and inseparable. In recent years, with the deepening of regional development practices, people from all walks of life have become increasingly aware of the new connotation of coordinated regional development in the new era. Specifically, it may be divided into two aspects.

First, we should attach more importance to the equalization of basic public services and make it as the main goal of coordinated regional development. Initially, most studies often view coordinated regional development from the perspective of balanced development or spatial equilibrium. The problems such as balanced layout of projects, balanced economic growth and economic disparities among regions, especially the narrowing of the per capita GDP gap, have been a great concern to the academic and government departments. However, at present, such investigation from the perspective of production or output has certain limitations, since in the market economy, economic production and industrial activities are unevenly distributed, and market factors tend to concentrate in places with prominent comparative advantages. In view of this, in the future we should extend our study from coordinated regional development to social development, ecological environment and people's all-round development, emphasizing on narrowing the gap in personal income, consumption level, basic public services and quality of life, stressing on improving people's livelihood and their own development, and promoting the free flow of production factors.

Second, more emphasis will be placed on improving institutions and mechanisms and taking them as the main means to promote coordinated regional development. First, clarify the relationship between the government and the market in promoting coordinated regional development, which has a new expression on the Third Plenary Session of the

18th CPC Central Committee. We should further improve institutions and mechanisms, combine the decisive role of the market with a better role of the government, making the "invisible hand" and the "visible hand" bring out the best in each other. Under the conditions of market economy, the optimal allocation of resources in space is mainly realized by the market, but the role of the government is not dispensable. Rather, it's irreplaceable. First of all, we need to study how to transform regional plans and change the role of regional policies in regional strategies, gradually change the model of guiding regional development mainly by major government-invested projects, shift government functions to build a unified national market, strengthen policy coordination, enhance control over national land and spatial planning, and guide industries, products and elements to flow freely among regions following the signals of the market. Secondly, we should clarify the positions of the central government and local governments in promoting coordinated regional development and further improve relevant systems and mechanisms, therefore, achieving a clear division of fiscal and administrative powers among the central and local governments, fully utilizing the enthusiasm of the central and local governments, guiding and ensuring that the priority of local governments shifts from striving for investment and preferential policies to creating a good development environment and providing public services. Finally, we should let finance, taxation, industries, investment and other policies play a bigger role in promoting coordinated regional development. Besides, we should give full play to the unique role of different policies in promoting coordinated regional development and rely on policy guidance to form a mechanism that each region voluntarily pursues new development models.

2 New Goals of Promoting Coordinated Regional Development

2.1 Promoting the Equalization of Basic Public Services and Narrowing the Gap in Regional Living Conditions

Today, some scholars still suggest that we should take a roughly equal GDP or per capita GDP among regions as the first or main measurement for the coordinated development of regions. But if we take GDP as the main measurement for coordinated regional development, it will inevitably make GDP growth rate the most realistic goal of regional development. Under the current mode, economic growth is driven more by investment, making comparing investment growth the most direct target of all regions. Under the conditions of market economy, all kinds of factor investment always gather in places with high rate of return. Therefore, if a roughly equal GDP or per capita GDP among regions is the main measurement of coordinated regional development, it will be rather tough and far away to achieve coordinated regional development. We suggest governments to take the equalization of basic public services and the completeness of public facilities as the main measurements of coordinated regional development. In other words, if education, medical care, social security, housing and other indicators concerning people's livelihood are generally equal among regions; water, gas, power and heating supply are generally balanced; and railway, roads, civil aviation and other transportation facilities are basically in place, then we can conclude that the development levels in the regions are roughly coordinated.

First, it is the essential requirement of socialism to take the equalization of basic public services as the main goal of coordinated regional development. It is the essential requirement of socialism to promote the equalization of basic public services nationwide, so that residents in cities and villages, in the east or west of China, can enjoy universal compulsory education, basic medical and health services, social security and safety. Moreover, in the long run, only by achieving a roughly consistent quality of life for urban and rural residents and residents in all regions can we truly share the fruits of reform, opening up and development with the general mass and achieve shared development.

Second, it is the objective need of stepping up the building of a unified socialist market economy to take the equalization of basic public services as the main goal of coordinated regional development. Only by taking the equalization of basic public services and basic public facilities as the main measurement for coordinated regional development can we weaken or even cancel performance indicators such as GDP and investment, and no longer use such indicators to evaluate the performance of local governments, so as to ensure the unification of national decrees and markets.[5] Only by doing these can it be possible for us to step up in building a national social security system, make the establishment of inclusive, equal and integrated basic public services as priority areas of regional policies and create necessary conditions for the adjustment of productivity layout.

[5]Song Xiaotong: "'Three-dimensional Market Economy' and the Definition of the Functions of Local Governments," *Xinhua Digest*, No. 6, 2014.

2.2 *Guiding the Full Utilization of Each Region's Comparative Advantages*

Given the differences of development stages, resource endowments and socio-economic characteristics, each region has its own advantages and disadvantages. There are two main sources of comparative advantages of regions. One is exogenous, that is, factor endowments and disparities in production technology level, which exist innately and remain unchanged in the short-term, such as resource advantages of resource-based regions, and maritime advantages of eastern coastal regions. The other is endogenous, which is gradually formed in the process of economic development, such as scale economy, technological progress and institutional changes. In addition, spatial distance and transportation costs also have a certain impact on regional comparative advantages. In recent years, more and more scholars have proposed that factor endowments and scale economy jointly determine the trade pattern and industrial space layout.[6] Generally speaking, with the deepening of reform and opening up, the decisive role of market mechanism has been strengthened, and the regional division of labor will be significantly strengthened. Therefore, giving full play to the comparative advantages of each region is an important connotation of regional development. Only when the comparative advantages of different regions are fully exerted can we maximize the overall benefits. And an important goal for achieving coordinated regional development will be to give full play to advantages, make the best use of advantages and bypassing (or making up) disadvantages, and gradually form a coordinated industrial development pattern with complementary advantages and rational division of labor. Therefore, whether regions are divided according to the four major regional sectors (developing the Western China, revitalizing the Northeastern China, rising the Central China, letting the Eastern China lead the development), or according to the main functional areas (optimized development areas, key development areas, restricted development areas, prohibited development areas), or according to the development of axis belts or type zones, we must carefully analyze the comparative advantages and development potential of each region, and promote the rational division of labor and misplaced development in regions. At the same time, we should speed up the building of a cross-regional interest sharing and interest

[6]Chen Xiushan et al.: *Coordinated Regional Development: Goals, Paths, Evaluations*, Commercial Press, 2013, p. 315.

compensation mechanism and effectively coordinate various interests in regional development and competition, ultimately achieving interregional complementary advantages and mutual benefits.

2.3 Realizing the Coordination of Population Distribution, Economic Layout and Ecological Environment

It is an important content and basic concept of national development strategy to keep economic and population layout coordinated. In the process of formulating regional major strategies, plans and development policies, it is suggested to study and evaluate their impact on economy and population layout, from the aspects of resources, environment, economics and population, and examine and grasp the relationship among major national industries, infrastructure and resource allocation. We should adopt more active and effective measures to reverse the imbalance in economy and population distribution, and gradually reduce regional disparities, ensuring interregional balance between economy and population development and promoting coordinated and scientific regional development. This goal includes two aspects, which are also important goals for coordinated regional development. On the one hand, it is necessary to keep regional population distribution and economic layout coordinated and promote the coordinated agglomeration of population and industries; on the other hand, it is necessary to keep regional population and economy coordinated with its resources and environment, keep regional population and economy compatible with resources and environmental carrying capacity, thereby forming a land-based development pattern with clear functional positioning. In particular, from the perspective of a large region, it is necessary to maintain a moderate spatial balance of the national economy, prevent the economy to become too concentrated or too sparse, and avoid the decline and marginalization of some large regions.

To achieve the coordination of population distribution, economic layout and ecological environment, it objectively requires the functional orientation of each region with clear development ideas and priorities in different areas. For example, for key urbanization areas such as Beijing-Tianjin-Hebei, the Yangtze River Delta and Pearl River Delta in eastern China, we suggest that their main goal should be promoting transformation and upgrading, building themselves into a pioneer in leading China's socio-economic development, an important innovation area of China, and an economic zone with global influence and China's largest area with intensive population and economy. For key development areas in the central and western regions, such as the middle reaches of the Yangtze River, Central China, Chengdu and Chongqing of Southeastern China, Harbin and Changchun of Northeastern China, their main objectives should be to vigorously promote new industrialization and urbanization, improve their capacity of agglomerating industries and population, form a relatively complete modern industry system based on the division of work, and become an important growth pole that supports the sustainable economic growth in China in the future. For the agricultural and ecological function areas in the central and western regions, we propose that their main objective should be to build their agricultural areas into important areas that ensure the supply of agricultural products, and to build their ecological areas into the main areas for national ecological security, China's important ecological functional areas, and demonstration areas where human and nature coexist in harmony. In accordance with these goals, we will formulate appropriate fiscal and social security policies, guide population and industrial activities to transfer orderly, and effectively protect the green mountains and waters.

3 New Ideas on Promoting Coordinated Regional Development

3.1 *From Solving Specific Regional Problems to Accelerating the Construction of a United National Market*

To promote coordinated regional development in the new era, we need to put regional development in the overall interest of China's development and formulate regional development strategies based on the problem in specific regions and on overall, global and long-term goals. In accordance with the "Four-Pronged Comprehensive Strategy", we should pay more attention to the overall goal of comprehensively deepening reform and building a moderately prosperous society, facilitate the formation of a unified national market and the free flow of market elements, stimulate the vigor and potential of regional development, promote rational division of labor in all regions, straighten out institutions and mechanisms which block coordinated regional development and break all kinds of restricted factors of production, especially the barrier to the free flow of labor force.

First, the legal system of territory development in national level should be formulated. We should achieve the full coverage of territory, establish a spatial planning system, optimize the territorial development pattern, promote effective protection, rational distribution and optimal utilization of national territory, and strengthen constraints on regional and spatial planning, thus connecting territory and regional development with the development plans of national economy, society, industries and regions. Policy systems of territory development and regulation at central government level should be improved and a coordination mechanism of cross-regional spatial planning should be established.

Second, the central government should shoulder the main expenditure responsibility on basic public services such as education, healthcare and social insurance. Firstly, the government should define the scope of basic public services and do some adjustment according to the increasingly higher economic and social development level. Secondly, the standards of the equalization of basic public services should be defined and a scientific evaluation index system should be established. The government should strengthen the collection and monitoring of statistical data on basic public services and build a performance appraisal mechanism on basic public services. Thirdly, the government should define the rights and responsibilities of providing basic public services in all levels of government and ensure clear and rational attribution of responsibility by evaluating financial investment, outputs and results of basic public services and improving the use efficiency of the financial fund and the quality and efficiency of basic public services.

Third, we should deepen reform and promote the free flow of labor elements across regions. Firstly, we should accelerate the reform of the household registration system, relax restriction on population mobility and establish a fair and uniform labor market, thus ensuring equal employment rights among different groups and orderly transferring population to areas with relatively developed economy, more jobs and higher income. Secondly, we should promote the reform of the income distribution system, raise the proportion of labor remuneration in national income and increase the income of labors. Thirdly, we should intensify the reform of the social security system, strengthen security responsibility of labor use land and focus on trans-regional transfer and linkage of social security, especially in the eastern coastal areas which should intensify social security for migrant workers from other provinces. Fourthly, we should improve the fiscal and taxation systems, rationally adjust the allocation of fiscal power among governments, and expand the sources of local tax revenue. Fifthly, we should improve the transfer payment system. For the policy of financial transfer payment, the central government gives proper encouragement to areas that actively absorb foreign population, encourages developed areas to absorb the population of less developed areas, and urges them to integrate into local communities and become stable migrants. Financial transfer system should be formulated based on permanent population rather than registered population while the local government is encouraged to implement plans and policies to attract foreign population. Sixthly, we should establish a trans-regional ecological compensation system, and support local governments to establish and improve mechanisms for joint monitoring and warning of transboundary pollution, and for emergency processing and management.

3.2 From Relying on the Major Regions to the Combination of the Major Regions, Points, Axes and Belts

Regional economic policy based on the "Four Major Regions" makes a general division of our country from geographical location and administrative divisions. The policy has been implemented for over a decade, during which, the self-development ability of Midwest and Northeast China has greatly improved and positive changes have been made in our regional economic territory. It's worth noting that the four major regions separate the economic relation among regions and result in the comparison of policies among regions, leading to the mismatching between development and supporting conditions. From the data in the past decade, we can see, for the vast West and Northeast region which has a big gap in natural conditions, historical basis and economic development level among areas, the division of the four major regions may seems too large from spatial scale, thus covering problems during the development of some difficult areas. It also leads to the increasingly-big internal discrepancy in regions and less targeted regional policies.

We should give full play to the important axis belts that cross East, Center and West China and connect South and North China and strengthen their role in leading and driving coordinated regional development. Along big rivers such as the Yangtze River, the Pearl River and the Yellow River and key traffic trunks such as Beijing–Guangzhou, Beijing–Harbin and Beijing–Shanghai Railway, we can promote the agglomeration and diffusion of production factors, optimize the layout of regional population, industries and cities and form economic development axis belts. The first-level axis belt should play its core role and drive the surrounding areas to form second-level development axis belts and compound development axis belts. For example, the Yangtze River Economic Zone should play a leading role and stretch to form second-level development axis belts like the Hanjiang River, the Xiangjiang River and the Ganjiang River economic belts, forming a main axis belt in the development of East, Center and West China. The Beijing–Guangzhou first-level axis belt stretches to the east and the west to form the main axis belt of North–south compound development among Beijing–Kowloon, Beijing–Guangzhou and Jiaozhou–Liuzhou, which is about 300 kilometers wide and 2000 kilometers long.

The coastal axis has strong economic foundation, reasonable industrial structure, complete infrastructure, high degree of internationalization and dense urban agglomeration. It is not only the most developed area in China, but also a key area of China's section of the Maritime Silk Road. We should accelerate the internal integration of urban agglomerations in coastal areas and enhance the competitiveness of urban agglomerations. On this basis, under the guidance of the idea of "grasping both ends and leading the middle", we should further enhance the leading role of the Yangtze River Delta, the Pearl River Delta and Beijing-Tianjin-Hebei Region and build world-class city clusters. On the other hand, we should focus on increasing the economic development level of the northwest Liaoning and coastal areas in northern Jiangsu, southwest Guangdong and Guangxi, and gradually narrow the gap within coastal areas.

Connecting city clusters of the Yangtze River Delta, middle reaches of Yangtze River and Sichuan-Chongqing, the Yangtze River axis has strong carrying capacity of resources and environment and the largest development potential. At the same time, linking the Bangladesh-China-India-Myanmar (BCIM) economic corridor, the axis has formed a new pattern of opening up to both land and sea. On the basis of navigation function of the golden waterway of Yangtze River, we should promote the construction of expressways and high-speed railways along the Yangtze River, take multi-channel linkage as breakthrough, and strengthen the ability to gather population and production factors in areas along the Yangtze River, forming an important development axis belt across East, Center and West China. Also, we should rely on important tributaries along the Yangtze River, such as the Hanjiang River, Ganjiang River, Xiangjiang River, Jialing River and Wujiang River, to build compound development axis belts.

The Beijing–Guangzhou axis, an important bridge between Bohai Rim and Pearl River Delta, connects metropolitan groups of the Pearl River Delta, middle reaches of Yangtze River, Central Plains and Beijing-Tianjin-Hebei region from the South to the North and covers the central part of China. We should regard the areas where Beijing–Guangzhou railway, Beijing–Kowloon railway and Taijiao–Jiaoliu railway pass as a whole and build a network system of compound regional development, thus greatly enhancing the vitality of the development of the Beijing–Guangzhou axis.

With a long history, Longhai–Lanxin railway, as an important part of the Eurasia Land Bridge, connects Jiangsu coastal area and urban agglomeration in the Central Plains, the Central Shaanxi Plain and the northern slope of the Tianshan Mountains. However, as horizontal ties and responsibility division is not close among the cities along the axis, we should take Eurasia Land Bridge as the starting point to strengthen the linkage of East, Center and West China, enhance cooperation among cities and accelerate the aggregation of industries along the two sides of the axis.

Beijing-Shenyang-Harbin-Dalian axis, a main economic belt connecting Beijing-Tianjin-Hebei region and Northeast China, connects Russia, Mongolia and North Korea through the border ports in the north and connects Japan, South Korea, Europe and the Americas through coastal ports in Liaoning in the south. We should ensure the interaction between coastal areas and the hinterland through Harbin-Dalian Economic Zone, focus on opening-up along the border, promote economic integration in Northeast China, strengthen coordinated development between the Northeast and Beijing-Tianjin-Hebei region through Beijing–Shenyang axis and further unleash the development potential of Northeast China.

The Pearl River-Xijiang River axis is an important economic belt linking Pearl River Delta and the hinterland in the Southwest and Central South. In the east, it contacts foreign countries through Pearl River Delta port group and in the West, Pearl River Delta leads gradient development from the east to the west. Surrounding the Pearl River Delta-Guangxi-ASEAN Opening-up Economic Belt, we should raise the class of Pearl River and Xijiang River waterway and lay out more convenient railways and highways, building multimodal-transport collecting and distributing system of seaway, highway, railway and pipeline and supporting the open development of Southwest and Central South China.

While developing the axis belts, we should further detail the four major regions and rely on the existing urban agglomeration and economic regions, to gradually form the eight regional economic plates of the Northeast, Beijing-Tianjin-Hebei Region, Pan-Yangtze River Delta, Pan-Pearl River Delta, middle reaches of Yangtze River, the Southwest, the Northwest and the west coast of the Taiwan Straits.[7] We should combine axis belts and the major regions and focus on the capacity of axis belts to coordinate regional development and on the aggregation and rational work division of production factors within the major regions, forming a new pattern of grid regional development and multiple supports.

3.3 Formulate Regional Policy from on the Basis of Administrative Region to Type Region and Functional Zone

At present, in western developed countries, regional policies are divided by problem-oriented type regions, rather than administrative divisions. For example, the European Union (EU) has established the Nomenclature of Territorial Units for Statistics (NUTS), and has taken it as the identification criteria for regional policies,[8] NUTS mainly includes two parts. One is the undeveloped and underdeveloped regions with poor economic base. For these areas, their main task is to quicken the economic growth and solve problems in economic development such as insufficient funds and the quality of the labor force. The other is areas with a vicious circle of few jobs, more unemployment and low benefit level because of institutional or structural problems in the process of industrial structure upgrading or the urbanization. For such areas, their main task is to adjust and improve the economic structure and stabilize employment.

In our current regional policies, supporting regions and policies are mainly divided by administrative divisions. It's suggested that we

[7] Project office of basic information base of national natural resources and geographic space: *Analysis Report of China Regional Planning and Sustainable Development*, 2013, April.

[8] See "5.2 Experiences of the European Union" in Chapter 5.

should base on this and divide the coverage of regional assistance policies according to the evaluation of territorial space development and problems. We should draw on NUTS to narrow the coverage of our regional policies and move the regional policies to a lower level, to prefecture-level city and county. According to a series of indexes, we should recognize areas that need assistance from the central government, including poverty-stricken areas, resources-exhausted cities, major grain producing areas, border areas, minority areas and old revolutionary base areas, and areas that need guidance on quickening development, such as metropolitan areas and reform pilot areas. For these areas, targeted regional policies should be formulated. We should strengthen support for special type regions and build a national regional aid policy system.[9]

For poor areas, we should remain committed to development-orientated poverty reduction, highlight targeted poverty alleviation, do a real poverty alleviation job, help people who are really poor, focus on the comprehensive management of contiguous poor areas and improve the self-development ability of rural poor population.

For old industrial cities, we should focus on combatting industry recession in the chemical engineering industry and raw material industry, restore the competitiveness of traditional industries through innovation and develop new leading industries. We should give priority to the historical burden of state-owned enterprises and dissolve social contradictions, creating necessary basic conditions for the innovation of enterprises.

For resource-exhausted cities, we should pay more attention to employment and their simple economic structure after resource exhaustion, focus on fostering continuous industries and upgrading industrial structure. At the same time, we should accelerate city transformation and develop cities from single production bases of mineral resources to comprehensive cities.

For major grain producing areas, we should focus on the problem of increasing grain yield without increasing income and strive to achieve increase in grain yield, farmers' income and financial resources. We should study the coordination mechanism between the main demand region of grain and the major grain producing areas, and the main sales areas should help the main producing areas build all kinds of grain storage bases, grain wholesale markets and deep processing projects of agricultural by products.

[9]Wei Houkai: *China's Regional Policies—Evaluation and Prospect*, Economy & Management Publishing House, 2011, pp. 38–44.

For border areas, we should emphasize expanding infrastructure connectivity and open wider to the outside world and enhance the self-development ability of the border areas, realizing the comprehensive development of its economy and society.

For over-expanded metropolitan areas, we should further strengthen spatial regulation of planning, define the urban expansion border and the red line of city construction, rely on strict and scientific city planning and good urban governance, enhance the comprehensive treatment of the over-expansion of metropolitan area and solve the dual structure problem.

For minority areas and old revolutionary areas, we should combine poverty relief policies and policies supporting the development of border areas and implement targeted assistance policies. Construction of infrastructure and industrial projects should be focused on.

Meanwhile, we should choose proper areas, target at specific problems, support the pilot of free economic zones, national new areas and comprehensive reform pilot areas in these areas, thereby accumulating development experiences and enhancing its driving effect of regional development.

While detailing regional policies, we should shift the priority of regional planning to the development of urban agglomeration. China's cities undertake over 50% population and 80% economic activities.[10] The proportion of urban population is increasing and cities play an important role in coordinating regional development and optimizing the distribution of productivity. The key of regional planning in the next stage is to adjust the function layout of administrative division to the rational planning of cross-district space relation between industries and cities, matching the choice and development of city industry with the scale and function of the city. We should improve city infrastructure and public service facility, build intercity modern infrastructure network, achieve overall coordinated development of industries, form good division of work and connection between cities, between urban and rural areas and between urban agglomerations, strengthen regional cooperation, encourage the strong to help the weak and promote mutual benefit and win-win outcome. We should take urban agglomerations made of several

[10] "Coordinate Regional Development and Optimize the Distribution of National Productive Forces" Research Group of the Development Research Center of the State Council: Ideas and Measures to Optimize Distribution of Productive Forces under Market Conditions, *Inside Information on Economic Reform*, No. 45, 2014.

cities as the main object of regional planning, strengthen fast traffic infrastructure construction such as the high-speed train, enhance physical connectivity and economic relation among cities and improve the overall ability of carrying population and economic activities in the city system.

3.4 *Turning from Relying on Investment Policies and Industry Policies to Financial Policies as the Main Means*

In recent years, we have increased our investment in promoting coordinated regional development, but we still mainly rely on investment from the central government and distribution of major industry projects, which leads to the intense competition of GDP among regions and heavy reliance on major projects. For the amount of transfer payment of the central government and the difference of financial capacity before and after the implementation of transfer payment, the current transfer payment system plays an important role in narrowing interregional disparity in financial capacity and contributes to the balance of basic finance in regions. But the current financial policy is mainly general transfer payment and does not serve regional development. In China, under the context of great disparities in regional economic development, natural ecology and population distribution, financial policy can perform much better in promoting regional development. From the perspective of international experiences, during the period when economy shifts from rapid growth to medium-to-high speed of growth, financial policy plays a leading role in regional development.[11]

Without the change of the available fund and investment channel in a short time, we should classify the related financial funds and establish the financial capital concept of regional coordination or regional development, which contribute to the coordinated implementation, analysis and research and policy support. The current regional fiscal policies should be divided into two types. One is the fiscal policies arranged under the strategy of coordinated regional development, corresponding to coordinated regional development strategy. Its main performance is policy support for three major regions, that is, fiscal policy of China Western Development, of revitalizing the northeast old industrial bases and of supporting old revolutionary base areas. The other is fiscal policies targeted at resources and environment under the strategy of sustainable

[11] See Chapter 5.

development, adapting to the national sustainable development strategy.[12] In the long run, we should learn from Canada, Germany and Japan.[13] Financial fund management and distribution mechanism under the concept of regional coordination and development in national level should be formed and implemented gradually. We should innovate and revolutionize financial policies, whose aims should be consistent with the aims of regional policies, playing its leading role in regional development.

First, through inter-governmental transfer payment system, we should reassign national land space and functional zone and improve the transfer payment system related with permanent population. We should ensure that the financial resources of all areas can support the provision of basically identical basic public services and all regions can enjoy equal access to basic public services.

Second, for the flow of resources elements, we should take leading finance and taxation discounts and support as the principal, properly compensate the short-term loss due to the flow and guide resources elements to flow to target functional zones. The concrete reflection is to guide funds, labor and technology to flow to key areas of urbanization, guide the orderly outflow of population from ecological areas and major grain production regions, and promote the reasonable domestic transfer of industries.

Third, misbehavior of resource waste and environment pollution should pay necessary finance and taxation cost, which can influence the behavior of market subjects and citizens. We should support enterprises that adopt resource conservation and environment protection technology in increasing their competitiveness and gradually establish a trans-regional compensation mechanism in the ecological environment.

3.5 *From Coordinating Domestic Regional Development to Opening-Up Both Externally and Internally*

Since the 1990s, economic globalization and regional economic integration have become two trends in the development of world economy.

[12] "Coordinate Regional Development and Optimize the Distribution of National Productive Forces" Research Group of the Development Research Center of the State Council: Ideas and Measures to Optimize Distribution of Productive Forces under Market Conditions, *Inside Information on Economic Reform*, No. 45, 2014.

[13] See the Experiences of Canada (5.3) and Japan (5.5) in Chapter 5.

According to incomplete statistics, about 80% of countries in the world have attended regional cooperation organizations of different levels. Major regional group organizations, which have been established or is being established, include the EU, NAFTA (North American Free Trade Area), APEC (Asia-Pacific Economic Cooperation), ASEAN (Association of Southeast Asian Nations), China-ASEAN Free Trade Area, CIS (Commonwealth of Independent States), Caribbean Community and Andean Group. Regional economic integration has been an important strategy and means for many countries to deal with globalization and integrate into the world economy. At present, China has joined many substantive international regional cooperation and sub-region cooperation, including APEC, SCO (Shanghai Cooperation Organization), China-ASEAN Free Trade Area, China-Switzerland Free Trade Agreement, Bangkok Agreement, Lancang-Mekong International Sub-Regional Cooperation, China-Central Asia Sub-Region Cooperation and Tumen River Sub-Regional Cooperation. But on the whole, China's participation in international regional and sub-regional cooperation is not deep and wide enough. We should strengthen international regional and sub-regional cooperation, and now is the right time to promote regional development with the "Belt and Road Initiative". The new trend of domestic regional development in the future is to promote reform, cooperation and development through opening up. We should base on the "Belt and Road Initiative" and support regions to find effective ways to promote development through opening up and promote cooperation through opening up.

First, for Southwest China, we should, though the Pearl River-Xijiang River Economic Belt, make full use of the China-ASEAN cooperation platform, deepen cooperation between the Pearl River Delta and Beibu Gulf, build Guangdong and Guangxi into the core area in China-Southeast Asia cooperation and build Yunnan and Sichuan into the "bridgehead" of opening up to South Asia.

Second, for Northwest China, we should strengthen cooperation with Central Asian and West Asian countries, build Xinjiang into the core area of the Silk Road and combine the development of the Northwest area with their opening up to the West.

Third, for Northeast China, we should enhance cooperation of China-Russia-Mongolia, China-Japan-South Korea and China-North Korea and build Heilongjiang, Jilin, Liaoning and Inner Mongolia into important hubs opening up to Northeast Asia. International regional cooperation in Northeast Asia can drive domestic regional cooperation and development.

Fourth, for eastern coastal areas, we should support them to continue to take the lead in opening development and restructuring, accelerate "bringing in" and "going out" in the context of deepening economic globalization, quicken the development of the twenty-first century Maritime Silk Road Economic Belt and develop a model of regional economic development that relies more on innovation and transformation.

4 Specific Measures and Suggestions for Promoting Coordinated Regional Development in the Near Future

According to the above goals and thoughts in promoting coordinated regional development, it's suggested that the following measures should be thoroughly studied and implemented as soon as possible in the near future.

4.1 Improve the Main Index and Assessment Mechanism of Evaluating Coordinated Regional Development

The local government is an important main body of regional economic development, whose reasonable behavior is a premise of coordinated regional development and optimized layout of productivity. A key point in promoting coordinated regional development is to change the thinking of local governments on regional development, that is, to change the incentive and restraint mechanisms of local governments in the short run. The most important manifestation of the incentive and restraint mechanisms of local governments is the assessment, appointment and dismissal mechanism of local government officials. Assessing local government officials mainly by economic indicators and economic growth is bound to make local governments pay more attention to economic growth while ignoring the investment in public products, guiding local governments to focus on directly boosting economic growth while neglecting social development and the coordination of resource and environment. Therefore, we should revolutionize the assessment mechanism and appointment and dismissal system of local governmental officials as well as the evaluation mode of local governments. According to the functional orientation of different areas, we should set assessment indicators with its own features and emphasis and substitute comprehensive assessment indicators for pure economic indicator.[14] The assessment can focus on three aspects.

First, we should comprehensively assess the development level of economic, social and ecological construction in areas under administration. We should take economic development, people's livelihood improvement, social harmony and ecological civilization construction as the main contents of assessment and evaluation to innovate the government's performance evaluation model, weaken the assessment of "fast" and highlight the assessment of "good". That is, while assessing the development speed, we should strengthen the assessment of development quality; while assessing the economic development, we should also assess the harmonious development of economy and society, and of human and nature. More attention should be paid to the assessment of indicators such as science and technology innovation, education, culture, labor employment, citizen income, social security and people's health, and more weight should be given to indicators such as resource consumption, environment protection, closing down outdated production facilities and resolving excess capacity.

Second, we should put the cooperation and coordinated development with other regions into the contents of assessment. For relatively developed areas with obvious integration of economic development, such as the Beijing-Tianjin-Hebei Region, Yangtze River delta and Pearl River Delta, we can emphasize trans-regional cooperation and coordinated development in the assessment, thus promoting trans-regional cooperation and horizontal interest compensation and resolving conflicts between local interests. We should encourage regions to make planning, share industries, build traffic network and control pollution together and support the rational division of labor in industries and benefit-sharing in regional development.

Third, for areas with different development levels, we should make different performance evaluation systems and implement different political achievement evaluation indexes in industry transfer. For industry outflow regions such as the eastern coastal areas, we should implement the performance evaluation of prioritizing change of the economic development mode, that is, strengthen the assessment indexes of economic structure, environment protection and independent innovation and weaken or cancel the assessment indexes of economic growth rate, investment promotion and export. For Central and Western China that accepts industry

[14] Zheng Zhiguo: *The Historical Evolution and Institutional Changes of China's Regional Economic Policy*, Master's Thesis of Chongqing Technology and Business University, 2006.

transfer, we should implement the performance evaluation of prioritizing industrialization and urbanization level, comprehensively assess contents such as economic growth, attracted population, quality effectiveness, industrial structure, resource consumption and environmental protection and weaken the assessment of indexes such as the investment growth rate.

4.2 *Clearly Divide Financial Rights and Administrative Powers*

The main reason of excessive competition among local governments lies in the unequal division of financial rights and administrative powers, especially in local governments below the provincial level. They have more duties of expenditure but lack the corresponding financial resources, making many city and county-level governments to have too many financial problems to solve while failing to make ends meet. Under great financial pressure, local governments tend to take short-term behaviors and get temporary finance at the expense of environment and resources. It is hard to implement coordinated regional development strategy, which is closely related to the finance pressure and interests driving of local governments. In accordance with the deployment of the Third Plenary Session of the 18th CPC Central Committee, and the requirements of the public finance framework and the equalization of basic public services, the powers of government at all levels should be clearly defined in terms of reality and the corresponding financial powers should be in place.

First, we should distinguish the financial rights relationship between the central and the local governments, establish a main tax fund system of local governments and define a main tax category of local taxes. Combining tax system reform, we should improve central and local tax structure, relax restrictions on local tax setting and cultivate local main tax category. We may consider developing consumption tax, property tax and resource tax as important local tax items, straightening out the division of central and local incomes and increasing local tax income. Under the premise of unified tax, for the general local tax, provincial governments should be given the right to adjust the interest rate of tax items, so local governments, especially those in Western and Central China, can be more independent to arrange tax income and have more enthusiasm to strengthen tax management. Therefore, governments at all levels will pay more attention to the effective supply of basic public services and create a better development environment. The basic systems of finance and taxation relationship and division of responsibility and authority among governments at all levels should be regulated by law, so as to limit the discretionary power of central government departments, eradicate the problem of "going to the upper departments for money" and reduce local governments' reliance on "selling the land-use right for fiscal need".

Second, according to public finance framework and the equalization requirement of basic public services, we should clearly define the powers of the central and local governments and build a fiscal system that matches the powers and expenditure responsibilities. We should strengthen the central government's powers and expenditure responsibilities in national defense, diplomacy and national security. Fields such as basic education, environmental protection, public health and food safety should be the common powers of the central and local governments. The power relationship between the central and local governments should be straightened out and they should take and share expenditure responsibilities in line with the division of powers.

Third, we should build a national safeguard mechanism for basic public services fund and narrow the gap of public services and infrastructure among regions. In terms of basic public services, for a long time, China has adopted the practice of central government making a principled framework and the local government formulating operative standards based on its financial power. This practice should be changed now. Practices over the years have proved that although the practice may have big flexibility, it's unavoidable that areas with more developed economy tend to have higher level of basic public services. Nationwide, the disparity of basic public services is enlarging rather than narrowing. We should learn from developed countries and shift the powers and expenditure responsibilities of basic public services undertaken by our basic-level government to governments above provincial level, so as to enhance the powers and expenditure responsibilities of the central government and provincial governments in public services. Firstly, we should shift the powers of compulsory education and social security to the central government who should afford all the expenses of compulsory education and governments below the provincial level undertake specific management responsibilities. A higher level of social insurance overall planning should be set and a national social insurance system with smooth connection should be established, so as to promote the unification of labor market and the orderly flow of labor force.

Fourth, we should solve the problem of the inconsistency of tax revenue and tax sources. We should formulate the distribution methods of horizontal tax among regional governments, promote the fiscal system construction of tax distribution system under provincial level and form an applicable model. A system should be established for governments at lower levels to report to the central government, so as to ensure that the distribution of horizontal tax revenue among regions is legal, reasonable, standard and easy to implement and solve the related system problem of tax allocation and reallocation among provinces, cities and districts. For the value-added tax, corporate income tax and business tax paid by enterprise groups, on the basis of not increasing the overall tax burden of enterprises, the tax payment should be allocated in some related areas according to the distribution of tax sources. People's income tax should belong to the local government of where they live, no matter where the location of withhold and remit tax unit is. According to the market demand for resources, the paid utilization mechanism and pricing mechanism of natural resources should be improved. We should accelerate the reform of resource price and form a pricing mechanism of resource products that can reflect the scarcity of resources, relation of market supply and demand, environmental governance and ecological restoration cost. Financial accounting of the cost of resource products should be formulated scientifically and some expenses should be listed into the cost structure of resource products. Such expenses include obtainment of the mining right, resource exploitation, environmental governance, ecological restoration, safety facilities investment, infrastructure construction, enterprise withdrawing and change of business, among others.

Fifth, we should improve transfer payment, enhance general transfer payment and reduce special transfer payment to build a finance transfer payment system that can balance local financial resources and support local construction and development. We should innovate general transfer payment, and on the basis of the current "Radix Method" of tax returns, calculate the tax revenue capacity of each region and establish general transfer payment based on equalization requirements of basic public service among regions.[15] We should explore to establish a standardized and institutionalized horizontal transfer payment system, on the basis of summarizing counterpart support system, and encourage developed areas to support the

[15]Xu Shanda: "Reform Suggestion on Special Financial Transfer Payment", *Inside Information on Economic Reform*, No. 1078.

development of underdeveloped areas. We should strengthen the legal system, financial supervision and management and information disclosure to build an open, transparent, fair and efficient fiscal transfer payment system.

4.3 Strictly Control the Number of National Regional Plans and Regional Preferential Policies

Regional planning and policies are indispensable means for the central government to guide and standardize regional development. In recent years, the state has issued many regional planning and policy documents, according to which, many specialized planning for regional development have been formulated by local governments. We should, according to the deployment of spatial planning system and planning system reform raised in the Third Plenary Session of the 18th CPC Central Committee, optimize regional planning formulation and strengthen the implementation of regional plans.

First, we should sort out and clean up over 100 national regional planning and regional policy documents issued in recent years. We should strengthen the implementation of the planning and its subsequent evaluation, entrust a third party when necessary and evaluate the implementation of national regional planning and policy documents issued in recent years. The emphasis of regional plans should be shifted from quantity to quality, from planning formulation to planning implementation and from general and regular planning to fundamental planning with overall importance. On that basis, the state should highlight the implementation of the strategy of coordinated development of the Beijing-Tianjin-Hebei Region, "Belt and Road Initiative" and Yangtze River Economic Zone. Trans-provincial regional planning should be promoted by each province and regional planning within a province should be coordinated on its own.

Second, we should strictly regulate the approval and examination of national regional plans, and no longer formulate large-scale regional plans at the national level. Before the issue of law in national territorial space planning, we should formulate the management method of national regional planning, define the scope and field of national regional plans and strictly control the formulation of national level regional plans. National regional strategy should focus on improving multilevel regional policy system, guiding regions to strengthen their cooperation on development strategies, infrastructure construction, industry development and ecological environment construction, avoiding repeated construction, cut-throat competition and the waste of resources, and stepping up forming a win-win development environment. At the same time, we should supervise the implementation as well as strengthen the evaluation and implementation of planning and policies, ensuring that it is put into practice and has a real effect. A number of development planning in key cross-regional urban agglomeration should be worked out appropriately.

Third, local governments should also reduce the number of regional plans. We should strengthen the implementation of the national regional strategy deployment, overall coordination of local economic and social affairs and enhance the construction of regional coordination and cooperation mechanism. Local governments should put the emphasis of coordinated regional development on creating a better environment for economic and social development, providing basic public service and safeguarding market justice, fair competition order and social stability, and ensuring the effective implementation of national policies, guidelines, laws and regulations of regional development. Meanwhile, we should explore the mechanisms of interregional cooperation and joint planning, carry out "three plans in one place", make pilot experiment and exploration of multiple planning integrations, and avoid vicious competition of industries and repeated infrastructure construction, thereby promoting the coordinated development of adjacent areas.

CHAPTER 5

Experiences of the Major Powers in Promoting Coordinated Regional Development

Unbalanced regional development is a common problem faced by the world's major powers. In order to narrow the development gap between regions, governments usually develop and implement a series of targeted regional policies. This is not only an important aspect for the government of market economy countries to regulate the economy, but also an important support for countries to build a unified domestic market and ensure people's livelihood.

For a long time, the major world governments of the United States, the European Union, Canada, Russia, Japan, Germany, Australia and other countries have formed distinctive regional policy systems under specific circumstances and specific historical conditions. By learning their regional policy experiences, it could be seen that their fiscal policy, taxation policy, industrial policy and financial policy have played an important role, and different stages have different focuses. Like an old Chinese saying goes, "the stone of other mountains can be used to polish jade", it is of great reference value for us to improve regional policies in the current and future period by carefully summarizing the practices of these countries in promoting coordinated regional development.

X. Song et al., *The Great Change in the Regional Economy of China under the New Normal*, The Great Transformation of China,
https://doi.org/10.1007/978-981-32-9475-2_5

1 Experiences of the United States in Promoting Coordinated Regional Development

The United States is a federal state. Governments at all levels have different priorities. The federal government's responsibilities are concentrated in the fields of diplomacy, national defense and security. The responsibility for economic development mainly lies in local governments. Even so, the US Federation has given important support to the development of recession areas and areas lacking public services.

Since the 1960s, the United States has adopted a series of practical and feasible strategic measures using market mechanisms and government intervention, gradually narrowing regional gaps. Their policy objectives targeting less developed areas were clear, mainly including the following aspects.

1.1 Paying Attention to Legislation and Promoting Management According to the Law

The U.S. government has placed aid to regional economic development in a rigorous legislative, law enforcement and judicial process. For example, in 1993, President Clinton signed and approved the *Federal Empowerment Zone and Enterprise Community Program* passed by Congress. It was a bill introduced by the United States to systematically solve development problems in underdeveloped areas. The federal government made plans according to relevant laws, reviewed application reports for aid projects, allocated a certain proportion of funds to state governments, and regularly audited the implementation of funds. The state government should formulate regulations and accounting systems on how to use aid funds, and give specific guidance to the implementation of aid plans. If backward areas want to get help, they must apply for it. After being approved, the assisted areas have the right to request relevant departments to provide guidance and help in the use of aid funds. At the same time, they must accept the supervision and audit of the federal government in accordance with legal procedures. Once violations were found, the aid would be stopped at any time, and the parties concerned would bear the responsibility. Strict laws and regulations were adopted to ensure the implementation of assistance projects. The bill also provided for the allocation of $2.5 billion in free tax incentives to enterprises in the empowerment zones, with specific incentives related to employment positions offered by enterprises. The Federation has identified 38 empowerment zones in three batches throughout the United States, of which 28 were urban and 10 were rural. The applicant areas should meet some conditions: first, the unemployment rate must be higher than 1% of the national average; second, the income level should be lower than 80% of the national average wage; and third, they were subject to special circumstances (such as disasters, etc.).

1.2 Formulating Comprehensive Development Plans for Key Regions and Supporting Policies with High-Quality Content

In 1961, the United States enacted the *Area Redevelopment Act* and established the Area Redevelopment Administration. In 1965, laws and regulations such as the *Appalachian Regional Development Act* and the *Tennessee Valley Development Act* were promulgated. The development and planning principles of the Appalachian Mountains were to treat poverty-stricken areas as a whole, starting with improving infrastructure conditions, giving play to mountainous advantages, and adjusting industrial structure for comprehensive development and governance. The US federal government has focused on the construction of transportation in this area, and used 75% of aid investment to build and develop national roads and local roads, striving to improve traffic conditions. Other public investments were mainly used to strengthen the construction of economic growth centers, regional energy and industrial development, as well as medical treatment, health, environmental protection, early childhood education, vocational training, etc. They were planned first and earmarked for special purpose, changing the "blood transfusion" relief to the development-based funding to enhance the "hematopoietic" function in poor areas. By improving the investment environment and adjusting the industrial structure, the employment and per capita income of the Appalachian region have increased considerably, and the policy effect was obvious. The Tennessee Valley Development Plan was a comprehensive plan which combined engineering measures related to the comprehensive development of water resources with economic development. Starting with flood control, the plan took into account shipping and hydroelectric generation, comprehensively developing and utilizing water resources while building flood control facilities. On this basis, they vigorously developed agriculture, animal husbandry, fishery, the high-power consumption industry and tourism, striving to provide a large number of employment opportunities for local residents. After more than 50 years of comprehensive development and management, the Tennessee Valley has undergone tremendous changes. It has not only become an important production base of electricity, aluminum metallurgy, military industry and chemical fertilizer in the United States, but also flourished in agriculture, forestry, animal husbandry and fishery, as well as the tourism industry. Since 1980, the per capita income has begun to approach the national average.

1.3 Strengthening Financial Support

In order to promote the economic development of backward areas, the federal government of the United States allocated about 10% of its fiscal revenue to subsidize states and localities by means of transfer payments, most of which were allocated to backward areas, mainly for enhancing the ability of state and local governments to provide public services and balancing the level of public services in different regions. This was also an important tool for the federal government to regulate the state and local economies and achieve its macroeconomic policy objectives. To further strengthen economic assistance to difficult areas, the Federal Government of the United States has established the Economic Development Administration (EDA). From 1966 to 1991, EDA provided funds of $4.33 billion only through financial assistance to public facilities projects in difficult areas. State and local governments were more concerned about regional development issues. They promoted regional transformation and reconstruction by means such as formulating loan, tax and land preferential policies, retraining workers, improving transportation infrastructure, managing urban environment, and attracting investment. In particular, state governments have supported the establishment of Enterprise Zones and Opportunity Zones, which have played an important role in helping the rapid reconstruction of declining areas. Enterprise Zones and Opportunity Zones are similar to development zones, whose concepts and practices originated from the United Kingdom. The government and other intermediary organizations provided all-round support to enterprises entering the region to attract foreign investment. Opportunity Zones have more preferential policies. Enterprises entering the zones could enjoy a 15-year tax exemption policy (i.e. exemption from individual income tax and corporate income tax in the state and local sectors). The main criteria for establishing an

Opportunity Zone in a region include three situations: a large loss of employment opportunities in the region; a low economic activity; and a lower income level than statewide average.

1.4 Strengthening Investment in Infrastructure and Public Projects in Backward Areas to Create a Favorable Development Environment for Regional Development

Under the condition of market economy, market is the basic means to allocate resources. Only by improving the investment and business environment in the region can more enterprises and investors be attracted to invest in the backward areas and provide more development opportunities, so that their self-development ability can be fundamentally improved. Since the 1930s, the U.S. government has focused on the following four areas in promoting the coordinated development of regional economy: (1) National highway network construction. At present, the United States has formed a crisscrossing interstate highway trunk network connecting more than 70,000 kilometers, accounting for two-thirds of the world's highway mileage and more than 600,000 kilometers of branch roads. (2) National information network construction. Over the past 20 years, the United States Government has attached great importance to the construction of information superhighway, which can be enjoyed by all regions of the country and even the whole world in terms of economy, science and technology. It has created conditions for some backward regions and old industrial bases to grasp market, science and technology information in time and catch up with other areas in high-tech industries. (3) Environmental protection. The federal government has formulated relatively complete environmental protection laws and policies, and environmental impact assessments were required for all regional economic development projects. (4) Basic education. In the United States, compulsory education has been basically realized from primary and secondary schools to state universities. The state government spends 85% of its financial expenditure on education each year. The federal government's education expenditure is mainly used in backward areas.

1.5 Close Cooperation Between the Public Sector, the Private Sector and Non-profit Organizations to Form a Joint Force

The United States has fully applied the new concept of Public Private Partnership (PPP) to practice, and has evolved a set of governance models that effectively promote regional transformation and development. It attracted a large number of non-profit organizations to participate actively, and was implemented by semi-official organizations, which were responsible for government funding arrangements and implementation of specific transformation projects. For example, the Southwestern Pennsylvania Commission was specifically responsible for the arrangement of federal and state funds and projects in Pittsburgh and the surrounding 10 counties. Similarly, there was a semi-official Detroit Economic Growth Corporation (SEGC) in Detroit, whose leader was directly appointed by the mayor. It undertook six important functions including brownfield land redevelopment and central urban development. These companies established partnerships with the government through public-private partnerships, obtained government support, and participated in the organization and implementation of public projects.

2 Experiences of the European Union in Promoting Coordinated Regional Development

The EU is one of the most developed regions in the world in terms of economic and social development, but the problem of uneven regional development within the EU also exists. The EU currently consists of 28 members, and the economic and social gaps between members are more obvious. Among them, one quarter of the region's per capita GDP is lower than 75% of the average of 28 EU members. In order to solve the problem of unbalanced regional development, the EU and EU members promoted the development of backward regions and achieved balanced regional and urban-rural development by setting up regional development institutions, formulating cohesive policies and arranging development funds.

2.1 Establishment of Specialized Agencies

The unbalanced development within the EU existed not only among its members, but also among the regions within its members. The differences between member regions were greater than those among its members. The EU has thus established a multi-level, network-like regional development coordination system. In the three most important institutions of the EU, the European Commission, the European Council and the European Parliament, special functions and advisory bodies have been set up for regional development. First, the European Commission has a Directorate-General for Regional and Urban Policy, which is responsible for formulating and implementing regional economic policies; second, the Council of the European Union has a committee on Regional Development, which is responsible for the communication and coordination of regional development affairs among countries; third, the European Parliament had 20 standing committees, including the Regional Policy Committee, the Transport and Tourism Committee, the Environment and Public Health and Consumer Protection Committee. These three committees were closely related to regional policy issues. Membership governments are at the second level. They generally have their own regional policies and accept the EU's unified regional policy coordination and integration. Their main powers are vested in national governments, especially parliaments, which deal with all laws related to regional policies, namely, approval or veto of aid measures, incentives, regional design and degree of decentralization. Parliaments can also approve the establishment or cancellation of a specific regulatory body. Local governments also participate in the decision-making of EU regional issues through the following channels: first, the establishment of regional policy institutions at the local level; second, most member local governments have some form of offices and representatives in the EU headquarters in Brussels; third, countries such as Belgium and Germany stipulate that if the issues discussed by the Council of Ministers fall within the jurisdiction of their local governments, the relevant heads of local governments will also attend the meetings of the Council.

2.2 Set Regional Policies

The EU regional policy is an investment policy, commonly known as the cohesion policy, which is under the overall responsibility of the Directorate-General for Regional and Urban Policy. It has three main purposes: to create employment opportunities; to enhance competitiveness and promote economic growth; and to improve the quality of life and maintain sustainable development. The EU cohesion policy is the general strategy of regional development and an important part of the whole EU strategy. It must be approved by the European Parliament and has legal effect. The EU has successively implemented the *EU Cohesion Policy for 1988–1993*, the *EU Cohesion Policy for 1994–1999* and the *EU Cohesion Policy for 2000–2006*. Not long ago, the *EU Cohesion Policy for 2007–2013* was under implementation.[1] At present, the European Commission has adopted the *EU Cohesion Policy for 2014–2020 (Draft)*. The *EU Cohesion Policy for 2007–2013* aimed at promoting regional economic growth and expanding employment opportunities through the concerted efforts of EU members. The core of the policy was to build and create regions that are competitive, attractive and creative, and to achieve the three major goals of convergence, regional competition and employment, and regional cooperation. The *EU Cohesion Policy for 2007–2013* stated that while continuing to assist the backward areas, efforts will be made to improve the regional competitiveness of other areas and strengthen regional cooperation. The European Commission gives each member a guiding annual EU Cohesion and Regional Development Fund based on criteria such as demographics, national wealth, regional wealth and unemployment, and each member decides the specific allocation of the fund between regions. According to the result, the *EU Cohesion Policy* has greatly improved public management, increased policy transparency and formed a good governance model. On the basis of ensuring that EU aid funds are fully utilized, member governments and local governments have established economic and social partnerships and promoted the effective use of these economic and employment assistance funds by the private sector, institutions of higher education and scientific research institutions.

2.3 Accurately Define the Scope of Regional Policy Assistance

In 1973, committee of the European Union's predecessor, the European Community, submitted a report on regional development to the Council of Ministers, proposing provision of financial assistance to "problematic areas" which include poor areas, declining industrial areas and areas affected by Community policies as well as multi-national border areas. The report was approved in March 1975, and the European Community formally established the European Development Fund (the structural funds), which was included in the unified management of the EU budget and was dedicated to regional policy financial allocations. At present, regional policy expenditure is the second largest expenditure after

[1] Wang Feng: *On the Evolution of EU Regional Policy and Its Enlightenment to China*[D]. Shandong University, 2009.

rural agricultural policy expenditure in the EU budget. From 2007 to 2013, the EU's cohesive policy support investment in regional development amounted to 347 billion euros, accounting for 35.7% of the EU budget. It was mainly used to subsidize areas with special problems (75% of them were used in poor areas and 15% in structural areas).[2] Funds were mainly invested in transportation, environment, research and development innovation, urban-rural coordination and support for the development of border areas. At the same time, the EU required a certain proportion of funds to bear the risks in each region. Generally, the matching funds were required to be 10–50%, and Germany and the United Kingdom can actually achieve 100% matching. All regions had great autonomy in the use of funds, but they should abide by the principle of common voluntary and the preconditions of environmental protection and freedom of the media in order to make effective use of funds. Specifically, in order to clarify the scope of benefits of regional aid policy, Eurostat has established a three-level Nomenclature of Territorial Units (NUTS) for Statistics in accordance with a series of indicators, such as economic development level, industrial structure and employment rate. The European Regional Development Fund used the NUTS system to strictly define the target of assistance (for NUTS-2, 213 in 2004 and 271 in 2013, basically equivalent to prefecture-level cities in China; 1091 in NUTS-3, basically equivalent to counties in China).

First, the economically backward regions, i.e., regions where the NUTS-2 per capita GDP was below 75% of the EU average. The EU provided financial support for economic development and structural adjustment, economic transformation, enhanced competition and EU territorial cooperation in these regions, and promoted economic development and structural transformation in regions whose per capita GDP was less than 75% of the EU average.

Second, regions with serious unemployment problems. According to the definition of the Directorate-General for Regional and Urban Policy, serious unemployment refers to a region where the unemployment rate in the industrial sector has been higher than the EU average in the past three years, and where the industrial sector is in a deteriorating state and

[2] Dai Bin: The Economic Development of the Underdeveloped Regions of EEC and Its Related Policies. *Journal of Southwest University for Nationalities (Philosophy and Social Sciences Edition)*, 2000(6).

the total employment rate is still declining.[3] The EU funds were mainly used to support structural adjustment and industrial diversification in regions with single economic structure, and to improve the education and training system and promote employment.

Third, cross-border areas and environmentally sensitive areas. The EU provided financial assistance or related technical assistance for environmental and cross-border projects in these regions.

In addition to the above-mentioned funds, the European Investment Bank also actively provided medium- and long-term credit. In recent years, the European Investment Bank has provided 70% of the total loans to the less developed regions of the EU. Two-thirds of the funds have been invested in areas eligible for application for structural funds and condensation funds, mainly in transport and communications infrastructure, industry and services, urban infrastructure, health and education infrastructure.

2.4 New Trends of EU Regional Policy for 2014–2020

In recent years, the European Union has begun to focus on promoting transnational cooperation, of which the Danube Region is the most typical. The Danube river is the second largest river in Europe (2857 km in length) and an important economic, environmental and shipping channel in Europe. It flows through nine EU members including Austria, Bulgaria, Czech Republic, Croatia, Germany, Hungary, Romania, Slovakia and Slovenia, as well as five non-EU countries, including Bosnia and Herzegovina, Montenegro, Moldova, Serbia and Ukraine. The basin covers an area of 800,000 square kilometers. International cooperation in the Danube Region has gone through many stages of development, from shipping to exploitation and utilization of hydropower resources, to water resources protection and then the full implementation of the *EU Water Framework Directive*. In 2014, the EU decided to invest 95 billion euros to promote the implementation of the Danube Region Strategy. It formulated an overall strategic report, divided 20 sub-areas of cooperation and drafted specific implementation plans in various fields, and identified 11 priority areas, including energy, science and technology,

[3] Research Group of the Revitalization Division of the National Development and Reform Commission, *Research on Financial Support Policies of Western Developed Countries for Declining Old Industrial Bases*, 2011.

public security, environmental protection, water power, human resources training, etc. The European Commission acts as a coordinator. Each field is led by two countries while other countries send representatives to participate. On this basis, a high-level decision-making committee is composed of state representatives. It meets twice a year to guide the basin countries to carry out cooperation and comprehensive development in various fields of economic and social development, including pollution reduction, flood control, water resources utilization and protection, shipping and so on, with the intention of helping the rapid integration process of EU member states in the Danube region and narrowing the gap between them.

Generally speaking, the EU's policy of promoting coordinated regional development has achieved remarkable results in narrowing the differences among its members and regions. It can be said that the continuous increase of new EU members and the development of integration of economic and monetary union are closely related to their regional policies.

3 Experiences of Canada in Promoting Coordinated Regional Development

Due to the differences in resources, geographical location and historical conditions among provinces and regions, Canada has formed a regional economic development pattern in which the southern region is economically developed while the eastern and northwestern peripheries are relatively backward. In view of this, Canada has formulated and implemented a series of policies and measures aimed at eliminating regional imbalances in economic development.

3.1 There Are Obvious Differences in Regional Economic Development

Due to the influence of geography, climate, history, ethnicity and other factors, there are great differences in the development of Canada between north and south, east and west, which has obvious regional characteristics. Canada's population and economy are mainly concentrated within 100 kilometers of the north-south border of the US-Canada border, and are mainly concentrated in Ontario and

Quebec. According to statistics, the economic sum of the two provinces accounts for nearly 70% of Canada's total national economy. Among them, Ontario has the most developed economy. Due to natural conditions, historical traditions and industrial structure, some provinces and regions in the west and east are relatively backward in economic development. The four western provinces of Alberta, Saskatchewan, Manitoba and British Columbia used to be dominated by agricultural, forestry and energy production sectors, with simple industrial structure and fewer categories, accounting for a small proportion of total economic output in the overall Canadian economy. Relatively less developed areas are New Brunswick, Newfoundland, Nova Scotia and Prince Edward Island along the eastern Atlantic coast of Canada. These four provinces are the least developed areas of Canadian economy, with slow development and difficult industrial restructuring. They mainly focus on fisheries, forestry and a small number of mining industries, with a high unemployment rate. Their total economic output also accounts for a small share of Canada's national economy.

Quebec, located in eastern Canada, is the largest province in the country. 80% of the population is of French descent and its official language is French. Quebec's social and economic development has two sides: on the one hand, it is the second largest province in Canada in terms of total population and comprehensive economic strength; on the other hand, its economic development is unbalanced. Quebec's long-term economic structure as a Canadian energy raw material and traditional industrial base needs to be adjusted, and the influence of political factors also largely restricts Quebec's economic development. As a result, Quebec has a high unemployment rate, a slow improvement in living standards and a widening gap between the rich and the poor.

3.2 Evolution of Canadian Regional Policy

Canada did not have a clear regional development policy for a long time after the establishment of federalism. Its economic development relies mainly on domestic resource distribution and production, and exports to countries such as the United States and Europe, forming an early division of labor. The initial focus of economic policy was mainly on the development of resource-intensive areas, but this pattern of over-exploitation and primary resource provision also led to the gradual depletion of resources in some areas and the economic recession brought about by the economic cycle, especially the changes in forest-rich areas. Since the 1980s, the government and academia has begun to pay attention to the unbalanced development in Canada, and proposed that regional policies and measures should be adopted to narrow the regional development gap, rather than allowing the natural flow of production factors and simple division of labor. It was suggested that in the context of international economic division of labor, the government should formulate a clear plan for regional revitalization and development and set up regional development institutions to ensure the implementation of the plan. In 1983, after Canada obtained full powers of legislation and constitutional amendment, the federal government began to implement an independent strategic approach to economic development, focusing on the overall promotion of regional economic development. In recent years, Canadian governments at all levels have set up special agencies to develop the economy of underdeveloped regions. They formulated and implemented incentive policies and measures, carried out various encouraging project plans, and achieved remarkable results.

3.3 Implementing Regional Overall Planning

Implementing overall regional development is Canada's long-term task and important measure to promote regional economic development. The Canadian government has taken a series of policies and measures to promote the development of underdeveloped areas and achieved remarkable results. The first was to implement classified guidance. Canada's economic territory was divided into five economic development regions. The government had different emphasis on the development planning, development goals and development priorities of the five regions. For example, the western region should focus on improving infrastructure conditions; the eastern developed areas such as Quebec and Toronto should focus on developing high-tech industries. The second was to set up corresponding service organizations. For example, in order to speed up the development of the backward areas in the west, the Canadian Federal Government established the Western Economic Diversification Canada (WD) in 1987; to promote the economic development of the four Canadian provinces, Atlantic Canada Opportunities Agency (ACOA) was established under the Industry Canada (IC) in 1988; and in the same year, the Federal Government upgraded the Regional Economic Development Office (Quebec Branch) to Canada Economic

Development (CED) for Quebec Regions. Recently, the Canadian Government announced the establishment of the Canadian Northern Economic Development Agency, which is specially responsible for the development of the northern region near the Arctic Circle. In order to coordinate the development needs of several municipal units, special agencies have been set up in some places, such as seven cities in southern Ontario. In order to promote coordinated development, the Regional Municipality of Waterloo has been set up to coordinate the overall planning, public facilities and public services in the region.

3.4 *Implementing Policy Guidance*

Policy guidance and government services were the basic methods to promote regional economic development in Canada. The first was to implement differentiated tax policy. In terms of intellectual support, in order to avoid the injustice caused by preferential policies, the government's focus on corporate support has gradually shifted from financial support to intellectual support. If small and medium-sized enterprises (SMEs) hired undergraduates who graduated from science, the government would provide 50% of their wages within three years. The gap between the income of college students in the western region and the income level in the eastern region has been greatly reduced, which has greatly attracted foreign immigrants and professionals to serve in the west. As for taxation, some provinces exempted from provincial sales tax and did not levy general property tax (GPT) and payroll tax (PT) on enterprises and individuals to reduce the tax burden of residents. Statistics show that Alberta's households with an annual income of $55,000 paid a tax of $2200 and $4600 less than their counterparts in Ontario and Quebec respectively. Second, the implementation of financial project support. The federal government of Canada supports regional economic development agencies and intermediary organizations with certain financial projects every year. For example, the Western Development Agency and the Northern Development Agency can receive relatively fixed funding projects from the government every year. Third, the implementation of preferential financial policies. For example, the federal government has a supplier development program, which mainly helps western enterprises to participate in the bidding of government procurement plans; promotes western enterprises and companies to other parts of Canada at the federal level; and collaborates with governments at all levels to continuously simplify and optimize policies and regulations for the development of Western enterprises. In addition, the federal government has also established the Western Industry Coalition to promote the formation of various forms of production alliances, technical cooperation alliances and marketing alliances among Western enterprises, so that local enterprises can gain cost advantages.

3.5 *Attach Great Importance to the Main Role of Fiscal Policy in Regional Development*

Canada's federal system is relatively decentralized, but Canada's Constitution clearly defines equalization payment, which enables provinces to receive a common level of financial resources. Equalization payment is an unconditional transfer payment project designed by the Federation to solve the imbalance of inter-provincial financial capacity and narrow the gap between provinces. Its ultimate goal is to achieve the equalization of public services throughout the country. It originated from the *Equalization and Tax Rental Agreement* signed between the federal and provincial governments in the 1940s. In the agreement, provinces lease the tax power to the federal government, and the federal collects the relevant taxes of the provinces on behalf of the federal government. At the same time, the federal pays the provinces a certain amount of compensation each year to compensate for the losses of the provinces.[4] From the practical point of view, the transfer payment amount of the equalization project is calculated based on a formula, and it is completely transparent and open to the society. Equalization fiscal transfer payment plays an important role in Canada's economic and political development. In 2013, Canada's equalization project transfer payment scale reached 20 billion US dollars, accounting for 25% of federal fiscal expenditure.[5] The mode of fiscal transfer payment has also changed from conditional transfer payment in the 1950s to unconditional transfer payment at present, but a mechanism of After-Action Review and public accountability has been established.

[4]Zhang Qichun: Fiscal Balance Mechanism of Equalization of Regional Basic Public Services: From the Perspective of Canadian Experience. *Journal of Central China Normal University (Humanities and Social Sciences)*, 2016(6).

[5]Lin Kaiwen: *Fiscal Transfer Payments in Large and Complex Economies: A Canadian Perspective*. Provided by the Canadian Embassy in Beijing, 2014.

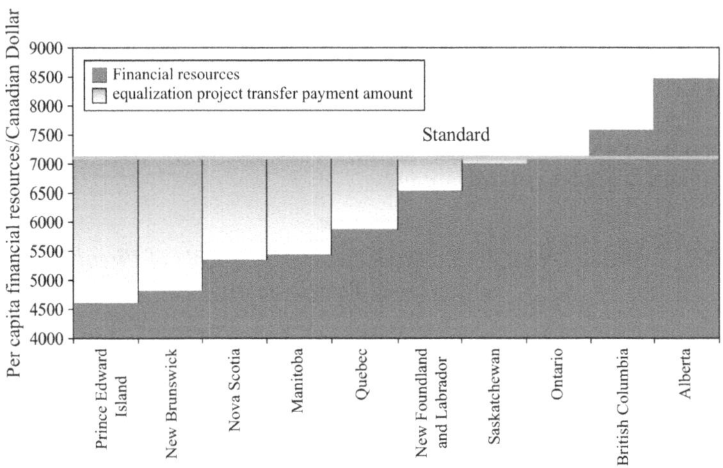

Fig. 1 未平衡前和经转移支付平衡后加拿大各省人均财力 (2013年) (Per capita financial resources of Canadian provinces before and after balancing transfer payments [2013])

- 人均财力/加元: Per capita financial resources/Canadian Dollar
- 财力: Financial resources
- 均等化项目转移支付的金额: equalization project transfer payment amount
- 标准: Standard
- 爱德华王子岛省: Prince Edward Island
- 新布伦瑞克省: New Brunswick
- 新斯科舍省: Nova Scotia
- 曼尼托巴省: Manitoba
- 魁北克省: Quebec
- 纽芬兰与拉布拉多省: New Foundland and Labrador
- 萨斯喀彻温省: Saskatchewan
- 安大略省: Ontario
- 大不列颠哥伦比亚省: British Columbia
- 阿尔伯塔省: Alberta
- 资料来源: 林凯文: 《大型复杂经济体内的财政转移支付: 加拿大视角》, 加拿大驻华使馆提供, 2014 年 (*Source* Lin Kaiwen: *Financial Transfer Payments in Large and Complex Economies: A Canadian Perspective*. Provided by the Canadian Embassy in Beijing, 2014)

By unconditionally transferring federal revenue, Canada provides a basically unified national public service at a basically uniform level of taxation. In 2013, the per capita financial resources of Canadian provinces before and after balancing transfer payments are shown in Fig. 1.

4 Experiences of Russia in Promoting Coordinated Regional Development

Russia's territory spans more than 10,000 kilometers from east to west, and there are huge differences in regional development. The economy is concentrated in the European part, of which Moscow and St. Petersburg account for 27% of Russia's GDP, while the Far Eastern Federal District of 6.17 million square kilometers (36.4% of Russia's total) accounts for only 4% of Russia's GDP. Of the 1100 existing large and medium-sized cities, 310 are located in the Central Federal District, 198 in the Volga Federal District, 145 in the Northwestern Federal District, while each less than 100 in the Southern Federal District of the South, the North Caucasian Federal District and the Far Eastern Federal District, of which the Far Eastern Federal District and the North Caucasian Federal District do not have a city with a population of more than one million. The average distance between some European cities in Russia is 45–75 km, while that between Siberia and the Far East is more than 200 km. In order to support coordinated regional development, especially in Asia, Russia has taken a series of measures in recent years.

4.1 Establishing the Main Objectives and Tasks of National Regional Policies

"Seeking unity in the diversification of regional development, maintaining and consolidating the economic and national integrity is the most important purpose of Russia's regional development strategy". In November 2008, the Russian Federal Government approved *Concept of Long-Term Social and Economic Development of Russian Federation Until 2020.*[6] The *Concept* defined Russia's economic and social development goals by 2020, made a choice of the country's future development model, and pointed out the development path. Among them, the part relevant to regional development clarified the national regional

[6]Website of Ministry of Regional Development of the Russian Federation: http://minregion.ru/.

policy objectives, stipulated the main tasks of national regional policy, established the main principles of regional policies and planned the development of regions with advanced economic growth and major economic zones. Subsequently, Russia established the Ministry of Regional Development, which is responsible for formulating the long-term economic and social development strategies of the eight major federal districts, and provided an interactive platform for the main federal authorities in the Federal District to formulate their respective regional development strategies. By the end of 2011, the long-term economic and social development strategies of the eight major Federal Districts have been promulgated and approved by the Russian President and the State Duma: the *Economic and Social Development Strategy for the Far East and the Baikal Region Before 2025* (approved by the Russian Federation Government Decree No. 553 in December 2009), and the *Economic and Social Development Strategy for the Siberian Federal District Before 2020* (Government Decree No. 1120 of July 5, 2010), the *Economic and Social Development Strategy for the North Caucasian Federal District of Before 2025* (Government Decree No. 1485 of September 6, 2010), the *Economic and Social Development Strategy for the Volga Federal District Before 2020* (Government Decree No. 165 of February 7, 2011), the *Economic and Social Development Strategy for the Southern Federal District Before 2020* (Government Decree No. 1538 of September 5, 2011), and the *Economic and Social Development Strategy of the Central Federal District Before 2020* (Government Decree No. 1540 of September 6, 2011), the *Economic and Social Development Strategy of the Ural Federal District Before 2020* (Government Decree No. 1757 of October 6, 2011), and the *Economic and Social Development Strategy of the Northwestern Federal District Before 2020* (Government Decree No. 2074 of November 18, 2011).[7] The long-term economic and social development strategies of the eight major federal districts analyzed the current economic and social development situation, existing problems and development conditions of each federal district; determined the development goals and tasks according to the priority direction and realistic development characteristics of Russian development, combined with the competitive potential of each region in

[7] Relevant contents of the plan are quoted from *Russian Regional Planning* compiled by the Revitalization Department of the Northeast Old Industrial Base of the National Development and Reform Commission, 2014.

the federal district. The strategies also established the pre-2020 (2025) development plan and forecasted the economic and social development situation; identified the development tasks, priority directions, indicator systems, development mechanisms in various economic sectors and social fields, and analyzed the resource guarantees ability. So far, the long-term economic and social development strategy system of the whole country and the federal district has been released, and the long-term development strategy system of the Russian region has gradually formed. The regional policy goal established by the strategy is to try to strike a balance between the following two aspects: first, support policies for regions with competitive advantages, and thus regional development; second, narrow regional differences, that is, implement regional balance policies.

4.2 *Promoting Regional Multi-polarization Development*

To achieve domestic regional multi-polarization development, form regional and cross-regional growth centers, and realize spatial diversification, Russia should utilize the strong economic growth, strong population and investment attraction of large-scale urban agglomeration areas; diversified urban functions, strong support for economic growth in service industries and industrial production in regional central cities; financial strength in oil and gas industry and metallurgical industry concentrated areas; the geographical advantages of some port areas in Europe; the unique natural resources, attractive natural landscape and rich historical and cultural traditions in the southern region and other regions. Give full play to the potential of science and technology and education in large urban agglomeration areas with high quality of human settlements, great potential of human capital development, better innovation and educational infrastructure, build regional production clusters in areas with high urbanization level, and specialize in the production of products in high-tech fields, such as aviation, shipbuilding, atomic energy industry, new material production, and information and telecommunications industry. Establishment and development of production clusters using modern technology specialty to engage in deep processing of raw materials and energy production in less developed areas; establishment and development of tourism and leisure areas in areas with unique natural climatic conditions to provide high-quality tourism and leisure services; relying on the 2014 Winter Olympic Games, establishment and development of tourism and leisure areas in the Black Sea coast; regional use of special economic zones mechanism to establish and develop similar tourism and leisure zones in the northern areas such as Altai, Baikal, Kamchatka Peninsula, etc.; develop large-scale transportation logistics and production centers on national transportation trunk lines, especially those with large traffic capacity, linking major economic growth centers and integrating into the world transportation system; maintain cultural diversity and retain the traditional way of life and work of the original inhabitants of ethnic minorities in the northern, Siberian and Far Eastern regions.

4.3 Give Full Play to the Comparative Advantages of the Federal Districts in Industrial Distribution

Russia's European Center is partly oriented to the European market; the North Caucasus is adjacent to the outer Caucasus and the Near East countries, and the ethnic and political situation is complex; the northern part of Europe is one of Russia's resource areas and major shipping bases; Ural and Siberia are the resource base of Russian economy and the technological backbone of economic cooperation with Central Asia and Southeast Asian countries; East Siberia and the Far East are Russia's resource bases, emerging development zones of major resources and outposts for cooperation with the Asia-Pacific region. As a result, the industrial layout outline of the Federal District has basically formed.

1. Central Federal District. First, the Moscow region will be built into a world-class modern metropolitan area; second, the Central Federal District will consolidate its leading position in Russian industrial and post-industrial development, and maintain its position as an intellectual service provider, a technology-intensive product producer and a high-quality maintenance service center.
2. Northwestern Federal District. The unique geopolitical and economic advantages of the Northwestern Federal District determine that its main function is to develop economic relations between Russia and the EU and its neighboring countries. It needs to develop transport infrastructure, cross-border cooperation and make some enterprises serve for foreign economic relations. It will play an important role in the exploitation of natural resources in the future, especially the resources in the Arctic region. Cities and urban agglomeration areas with relatively complete industrial structure in the southern region will focus on the development of imported alternative processing industries, while cities and towns

with single industrial distribution in the northern region will mainly develop mining and raw material processing industries.

3. Southern Federal District. The strategic objectives of the development of the Southern Federal District are: to build large-scale agro-industrial complex clusters and turn the Southern Federal District into a national food base; to develop the transport potential of the Federal District through the development of international transport corridors; to develop multi-functional leisure complex at the international level; to realize modernization by innovation, and to build new industrial zones and industrial clusters.
4. North Caucasian Federal District. The North Caucasus has the best ecological environment in Russia. The state's support policy to the North Caucasian Federal District is to enhance the self-sufficiency of the main federal bodies through investment, and to promote the integration of the region into the overall Russian economic system and even the world economic system. The priority industries are agro-industrial complex and tourism.
5. Volga Federal District. Relying on the modernization of large-scale industries and the development of modern service industry in urban agglomeration areas, innovative development can be achieved. The way of management will be improved, foreign investment will be attracted to develop technology, and new technologies will be applied to produce competitive industrial products. The competitiveness of the machinery manufacturing industry will be improved, including aerospace, automobile manufacturing, chemical and petrochemical industries. Division of labor among regions will be strengthened and joint development among regions on the basis of world innovative technology and relying on scientific research bases of regional industrial centers will be realized.
6. Ural Federal District. It was planned to establish two innovation centers: the Yekaterinburg Innovation complex and Innovation Center in Chelyabinsk on the basis of the South Ural State University. Innovative development of basic industries, especially in transportation, heavy machinery manufacturing, chemical industry, agriculture, energy machinery and instrumentation, medical equipment, metallurgy and other sectors will be achieved, and regional production clusters will be established. In addition,

five development zones including Siberia region, Ural Industrial Zone, Yamal Peninsula, Eastern Slope Area of Ural and South Ural Agricultural Zone will be built.

7. Siberian Federal District. Three development zones are planned: the Arctic Development Zone, the Northern Development Zone and the Southern Development Zone. In addition, relying on the Russian Academy of Sciences, the Russian Academy of Medical Sciences (RAMS) and the Siberian Branch of the Russian Academy of Agricultural Sciences, a national research-oriented university was established on the basis of Irkutsk, Kemorovo, Krasnoyarsk, New Siberia, Omsk and Tomsk institutions of higher learning to develop new technologies at the world level, to carry out industrial applications and to realize the integration of production, learning and research, thus innovation can become the dominant factor of economic growth and a new economic sector can be gradually formed, and the traditional economic and social service sectors can be modernized, so that competitiveness of the region can be enhanced.
8. Far Eastern Federal District. The entire Russian and even the world transport system will be integrated through solving the problem of natural gas, forming a unified energy distribution system, optimizing transportation and electricity costs, building a new seaport and modernizing the original port, developing container transportation, and establishing a unified transportation information system connecting major central cities in the Far East. Through the development of vocational education, research and development of marine development and natural resource extraction technologies, including biotechnology, nanotechnology and underwater robots, the innovative potential of urban agglomeration areas in Vladivostok and Habarovsk can be realized. In the urban agglomeration areas and island areas of the Far East, including the Sakhalin Island, Kamchatka Peninsula and Kuril Islands, as well as the harbor area in the Pacific region, a cluster of biological resources will be built, mainly engaging in the exploitation, processing of aquatic biological resources and mariculture. Technological transformation of the machinery manufacturing industry will be carried out to enhance the competitiveness of the aircraft manufacturing, ship manufacturing and ship repair industries.

4.4 *Attaching Importance to Solving the Problem of Cities with Single Industrial Structure*

According to the survey report of the Government Expert Council, there are two criteria for determining a town with a single industrial structure: one is that a single enterprise or an enterprise in the same industry creates 50% of the city's (town's) industrial output value or service industry output value; the other is that the same enterprise centralizes 25% of the city's (town's) employed persons. A large number of towns with single industrial structure are typical characteristics of urbanization in the Soviet Union. The establishment of new cities in the Soviet Union goes through four stages: establishment of enterprises—project commissioning—project completion—City formation. It can be seen that most of the small cities developed on the basis of large industrial and mining enterprises have the characteristics of single industrial structure, so they are called towns with single industrial structure. Typical cities and towns with single industrial structure are concentrated in the fields of coal mining, power generation, metallurgy, chemical industry, wood processing, machinery manufacturing, food and light industry. For example, a large number of textile towns have been formed in the Northwest Industrial Zone, Ivanovo Oblast and its adjacent areas, a large number of wood processing and pulp manufacturing towns have been formed in the north, northwest and even the north of the Central District, and coal towns have been formed in the Donbass and other areas. There are also cities and towns with single industrial structure in developed countries, but in terms of scale, the problems in Russia are much more serious. According to the data released by the Ministry of Regional Development of the Russian Federation in 2009, the number of cities with single industry in Russia was 335, accounting for about 40% of the total urban area. There were 16 million people in cities and towns with single industrial structure in Russia.[8] Among the cities with single industrial structure, 5% (with

[8]Russia's cities and towns with single industrial structure has become a new problem in recent years. The statistical data are incomplete and the data of all parties are quite different. In the report from the Ministry of Regional Development of the Russian Federation, *Cities in Russia with single industrial structure: how to overcome the crisis?* in 2008, data of the Government Expert Council from 2000 were cited, pointing out that there were 460 single industry towns, which centralized 1/4 of the population of Russia. However, according to the estimates of the Independent Institute for Social Policy,

1.4 million people) are in a serious crisis situation, which requires the federal government to take measures; 15% (5.4 million people) are in a high-risk state of crisis and need to be solved by the main federal government; 80% need to regularly monitor their economic and social development and formulate medium-term and long-term development plans. When the financial crisis broke out in 2008, the vulnerability of cities with single industrial structure was evident, especially those specialized in smelting black and nonferrous metals and manufacturing machinery. Since 2009, the Ministry of Regional Development of the Russian Federation has formulated special plans to support these cities. In 2010 and 2011, the Ministry of Economic Development of the Russian Federation formulated and implemented pilot projects of state assistance, which alleviated the labor market situation in these cities and created 60,000 jobs. The federal government has set up a special responsible agency to coordinate the stable development of single-structured cities with a federal budget allocation of 24 billion roubles. The main tasks were: first, to formulate a list of single industry cities, establish a risk assessment and development prediction system for urban development, and evaluate the efficiency of national support measures; second, to formulate a list of investment projects for single-structure cities, determine the implementation mechanism and raise funds; and third, to report to the government in time with local governments on the possibility of deterioration of the socio-economic situation of single-structure cities in order to take necessary measures.[9]

In a word, the central government of the Russian Federation is trying to gradually strengthen its intervention in local economic and social development, realize the unity and integrity of regional economic layout, realize the coordination of regional development, optimize people's living environment, strengthen infrastructure construction, cultivate new regional economic development centers and economic development zones, form interregional linkage and diffusion effects, and realize common development and innovation.

there are not fewer than 150 single-industry towns in Russia (excluding closed cities with military and nuclear industries). The resident population accounts for 8% of the total population of Russia and 11% of the urban population of Russia.

[9] Gao Jixiang: Urbanization and Urban Development in Russia. *Russian, East European & Central Asian Studies*, 2014(1).

5 Experiences of Japan in Promoting Coordinated Regional Development

In promoting coordinated regional development, Japan has gradually formed a set of comprehensive regional planning legislations and policy system to effectively narrow the economic development gap between regions.

5.1 Formulating Systems and Regulations

Japan's regional economic policy is centered on the legal system of regional development. It consists of a series of regional legislations, both national and local; there are industrial revitalization laws and region-specific laws. As early as 1950, Japan had promulgated the *Comprehensive National Land Development Law* which was the fundamental law for regional development. The *Law* made explicit stipulations on the formulation and implementation of the deliberative council for land and regional development, and the comprehensive development plans for the whole country, localities and designated regions. The *Law*, together with other legislations, have constituted a relatively complete regional development legal system and ensured that development in various regions is backed by rules and regulations. These legislations include: laws on the revitalization of designated backward regions, such as the *Remote Islands Development Act*, *Mountain Villages Development Act* and *Hokkaido Development Act*; guiding laws on the spatial layout of industries, such as the *New Industrial City Construction Promotion Law* and *Law on the Promotion of Industry Development in Underdeveloped Regions*; laws governing the industrial layout of metropolitan areas, such as the *Law on Controlling the Establishment of Factories in the Capital Region* and *Factory Location Act*. Japan has gone through four stages in the development of its legislation system.

First, the Post-War Recovery Stage (1945–1955). The main legislations and policies implemented during this stage included the *Comprehensive National Land Development Law*, *Hokkaido Development Act* and *Regional Development Act*. Comprehensive National Development Plan, Comprehensive Regional Development Plan, Comprehensive Prefectural Development Plan and Comprehensive Development Plan for Designated Regions have also been drawn up and implemented.

Second, the Early Stage of High Economic Growth (1955–1965). The main legislations and policies implemented during this stage included:

(1) the *Capital Construction Act*, which aimed to prevent the population and industry from being excessively concentrated in the capital region;
(2) the *Comprehensive National Development Plan*, which focused on preventing large cities from becoming too large, narrowing regional gaps and dividing Japan into over-concentrated areas, construction areas and development areas according to basic development methods. Among these, over-concentrated areas were areas that should control and guide industries (Keihin Region, Osaka-Kobe Region, Nagoya, Kitakyushu); construction areas were areas aiming to guide industrial decentralization by carrying out infrastructure construction and setting up large-scale industrial development areas and medium-sized development cities (areas other than the high-intensity areas, such as the Kanto Region, Tokai Region, Kinki Region and Hokuriku Region); development areas were areas that aimed to actively promote development carrying out infrastructure construction and setting up large-scale local development cities, large-scale industrial development areas and medium-sized local development cities (other regions).
(3) the *New Industrial City Construction Promotion Law* and *Law on the Promotion of the Development for Special Regions for Industrial Development*, which promoted development in and provided certain subsidies to designated areas.

Third, the Late Stage of High Economic Growth (1965–1973). The main policy introduced during this stage was the new *Comprehensive National Development Plan* implemented in 1965. The new *Plan* focused on building a new network of transportation and communications, industrial development and environmental protection projects and sought to promote "large-scale development projects". The *Plan* also proposed the concept of "wide-area living circle" to build core local cities and establish a transportation system that connects these cities to various areas within the circle.

Fourth, the End Stage of High Speed Growth (1974–1986). The third *Comprehensive National Development Plan* was formulated during this stage and the concept of "settlement circle" was introduced. The Plan emphasized on building a new living circle by creating a vibrant and affluent environment based on regional characteristics.

5.2 *Specifying the Financial Powers and Authority of the Central and Local Governments*

Japan's legislations, such as the *Constitution of Japan*, *Local Autonomy Act*, *Public Finance Act*, and *Local Public Finance Act*, have made clear stipulations on the authority and responsibilities of the central and local governments. Among these, the *Local Autonomy Act* has clearly defined the status, authority, and income and expenditure of local governments, and made clear stipulations on the relationship between local governments and the central government and their dispute resolution. The division pf central and local powers were mainly based on the scope of benefits, while taking consideration of improving efficiency and ease of supervision. Matters that could be addressed by a lower level of government were generally not referred to the higher levels. In 1997, the Japanese government passed *Relevant Decisions on the Promotion of Decentralization* and began the reform on decentralizing the powers of governments, which would later continue for almost 20 years. In 1999, *Law on the Preparation of Legislations for Promoting Decentralization* was enacted, which further specified the relevant authorities of local governments and the division of local and central administrative affairs. In 2006, the *Decentralization Promotion Law* was enacted and the Decentralization Promotion Committee was founded. In 2009, the "Strategic Conference on Local Autonomy" was held with the main purpose of discussing, implementing and promoting policies and measures on "local autonomy", thus consolidating the concept of "local matters shall be decided by local residents". The conference was convened by the Prime Minister and there were 19 attendees in total, including the Deputy Prime Minister, Chief Cabinet Secretary, Minister of Internal Affairs and Communications, Minister of Finance, some governors, mayors and local members of parliament, as well as experts from research institutions. The *Decentralization Reform Promotion Plan* was introduced at the conference, which specified that moderate adjustments would be made to the division of powers. A detailed account list was also announced. The aim of decentralization reform was to adjust the division of powers among the central and local powers, loosen the policy restraints placed on local areas, enrich local finance and strengthen land utilization, etc.; while the principle was to appropriately decentralize some powers under the premise of ensuring the stability of major powers. For example, the powers that were transferred from the central government to the prefectural governments at the 2013 conference mainly included: registration and regulation of passenger transport for self-use vehicles, management of some state-owned roads and waterways, free introduction of employment, and the approval and administration of some agricultural land transfers.

The division of specific functions. The central government would be responsible for national defense and foreign relations; social security, medicine and healthcare, public welfare, and other public goods and services featured by income redistribution or require national uniform standards would be the responsibilities of the central and higher-level local governments; educational functions would be split between the various levels of government; local governments at all levels would be responsible for functions that have a direct impact on people's production livelihood, such as fire protection, urban planning, public health and housing. The basic framework of various functions is shown in Table 1.

The expenditures of the central and local governments were determined in accordance to specific functions. After implementing the increase in consumption tax in 2014, the budget expenditure of the central government was 9.59 billion yen (including various transfer payments to local governments), while that for local governments was 8.34 billion yen. For details on the specific functions and their expenditures after the division of powers in 2012, see Table 2.

Japan adopts the full-covered statutory budget system, which is a tax-sharing system with centralized fiscal legislative power, decentralized executive power and no shared taxes or taxes with the same origin. Differences between national and local taxes are mainly specified in legislations such as the *Public Finance Act* and *Local Public Finance Act*. Although some items of taxation share the same origin, national tax and local taxes are clearly defined and separately levied. For example, *Consumption Tax Law* distinguishes consumption tax (national tax) from local consumption tax (prefectural tax); *Corporation Tax Act*

Table 1 Division of powers among the central and local governments

	State	*Prefectures*	*Municipalities (cities/towns/ villages)*
National defense, public security	Foreign relations, national defense, judiciary	Police	Fire protection, household registration, basic household accounts
Basic infrastructure construction	Motorways, state-controlled national highways, level-one waterways	Non-state-controlled national and prefectural highways, level-two and non-state-controlled level-one waterways, ports, public housing, regional planning	City planning, roads below city-level, irrigation channels, public housing, sewers
Education	National public and private universities	Prefectural-level universities, teachers' salaries and human resources of secondary and primary schools, private schools, special education schools	City-level universities, junior secondary schools, primary schools and pre-schools
Social security, medical services and healthcare	Social security, licensing of medical practitioners, licensing of medicines and drugs, standards	Relief for towns and villages, welfare and healthcare for children and the elderly, environmental supervision	Relief for cities and wards, children's welfare, healthcare for the elderly, healthcare insurance, tap water, waste and sewage treatment
Industries, economy	Tariffs, currency, postal services, communications, etc.	Regional economic revitalization, vocational training, guidance for small and medium enterprises	Regional economic revitalization, agricultural land use

Source Ministry of Internal Affairs and Communications, Japan: http://www.soumu.go.jp/

Table 2 A comparison of expenditures of the central and local governments

Type of authority (including: local authorities)	*Proportion of local expenditures (%)*	*Proportion of central expenditures (%)*	*Proportion in the total budget expenditure (%)*
Total expenditures	58.3	41.7	
Health expenses (healthcare, waste disposal)	98	2	3.8
School education expenses (secondary and primary schools, pre-schools, etc.)	87	13	9.2
Judiciary, police, fire protection, etc.	79	21	
Social education expenses (libraries, museums, etc.)	74	26	4.0
Welfare expenses (child welfare, elderly care and welfare, living welfare, etc., excluding annuities)	72	27	2.7
National land development expenses (planning, roads, bridges, public housing, etc.)	76	24	8.1
National land conservation expenses (rivers, coasts)	74	26	1.3
Business and labor costs	61	39	6.2
Post-disaster reconstruction expenses	77	23	0.8
Public debt	38	62	20.9
Expenses of the agriculture, forestry and fisheries industries	37	63	2.0
Residential expenses	38	62	1.7
Entitlement expenses	4	96	0.4
Annuity-related fees in the welfare expenses	100	0	6.3
Defense expenses	0	100	2.9
General administrative expenses (household registration, basic residential accounts, etc.)	82	18	6.7
Others	0	100	2.1

Source Ministry of Internal Affairs and Communications, Japan: http://www.soumu.go.jp/

distinguishes corporation tax (national tax) from the two prefectural corporation taxes (corporate residence tax and corporate enterprise tax) and the municipal corporation tax. In terms of the allocation of tax sources and number of taxable items, the central government has an absolute advantage to ensure that it can exercise macroscopic regulation and control on the economy and plays a guiding role to the local economy. For a list of national and local taxable items, see Table 3.

In the composition of national taxes and local taxes, the proportion of direct tax in local taxes is greater than the proportion of direct tax in national taxes. In 2014, the ratio of direct tax in local taxes was 84.3:15.7, and after adding the special local corporation transfer tax, 85.2:14.8; the ratio of direct tax in national taxes was 54.6:45.4, and after adjustment, 52.6:47.4. As an indirect tax, consumption tax has the characteristics of a wide tax base. Consumption tax covers all areas other than land transfer and leasing, financial insurance, medical care, education, social security and rent. Since April 1, 2015, the Japanese government has increased the consumption tax rate from 5 to 8%. In 2014, the proportion of consumption-type taxation in national taxation increased to 28.6%, becoming the largest source of national tax; the proportion of local consumption tax in prefectural tax was 20.5%, ranking behind direct taxes such as the individual municipal residence tax and the two prefectural corporation taxes.

Japan's local governments are generally responsible for the taxation of assets. In 2014, fixed assets tax accounted for the highest proportion in municipal taxes with 42.2%, while municipal residence tax came in second with 34.6%. Maintaining a high proportion of asset-related taxes provided a driving force for local governments to increase their income and property levels. Japan's fixed assets tax played an important role in stabilizing asset prices. It mainly covered land, housing and demolition, with a standard rate of 1.4%, plus the standard tax rate of 4% for real estate.

Japan conducts necessary adjustments to the taxation system every year, but major changes such as changes in taxation items and adjustments of tax rates will only be introduced during the annual taxation reform. The procedures for tax reform are more stringent and transparent than adjustments in the taxation system. These procedures must be based on the legislation of relevant bills and be included in the relevant annual tax adjustment program.

Table 3 A list of national and local taxable items

	Tax on income	*Tax on assets*	*Tax on consumption*
National taxes	Income tax, corporation tax, special local corporation tax, special reconstruction income tax, special reconstruction corporation tax, local corporation tax	Inheritance tax, registration exemption fee, stamp duty	Consumption tax, alcohol tax, tobacco tax, special tobacco tax, automobile tax, local petrol tax, oil and gas tax, automobile weight tax, aviation fuel tax, petrol and coal tax, electricity development and promotion tax, tariffs, etc.
Local taxes	Residents tax, personal business tax, corporate residents tax, corporate enterprise tax, partial interest of municipal residence tax, partial dividend of municipal residence tax, shares of municipal residence tax, partial tax on real estate acquisition from transferals	Fixed assets tax, urban planning tax, business tax, special land holding tax, non-statutory general tax, non-statutory purpose tax	Local consumption tax, local tobacco tax, light oil purchase tax, automobile purchase tax, gold course utilization tax, bath tax, automobile tax, light vehicle tax, mineral tax, hunting tax, mining area tax

Source Ministry of Finance, Japan: https://www.mof.go.jp/

5.3 *Formulating Standard Transfer Payment Policies*

On the basis of specifying financial powers and authority, Japan has established a sound fiscal transfer payment system. Fiscal transfer payment plays a critical role in regulating and controlling regional economics, standardizing the fiscal relationship between the central and local governments, and balancing local financial resources. It mainly includes three forms: local allocation tax, treasury disbursements and local transfer tax.

5.3.1 Local Allocation Tax System

The local allocation tax is a financial grant given by the central government to local governments for the purpose of balancing local financial resources and achieving fiscal balance. According to Article 6 of the *Local Allocation Tax Act*, in the national taxation revenue, the total sum of local allocation tax is calculated by 32% of personal income tax and alcohol tax, 34% of corporation tax, 22.3% of consumption tax, and 25% of tobacco tax. This grant is given by the central government to the prefectural and municipal governments with no preconditions. In the 2014 budgetary expenditure of the central government, "local allocation tax grant" was 161,000 yen, accounting for 16.8% of the total expenditures and the third largest expenditure after social security and national debt. In 2014, the ratio of national tax to local tax was 60.1:39.9. After adjustment of the "local allocation tax grant", the ratio changed to 43.7:56.3, and after adjustment of the local transfer tax, the ratio changed to 39:61—transfer payments from the central government to local governments exceeded local fiscal revenues. The total amount of local allocation tax is determined by the statutory sharing ratio of central and local shared taxes. Typically, 94% of the allocation tax are general allocation tax, while the remaining 6% are special allocation tax. The special allocation tax is a special grant given by the central government to local governments when the standard fiscal revenue calculated by the local governments in accordance to the standard formula is evidently higher, or when special financial needs that cannot be reflected by standard financial needs arise (such as the occurrence of natural disasters in local areas). The general allocation tax is a grant given by the central government to local governments in accordance to the difference between standard local fiscal revenue and expenditure needs. Total amount of

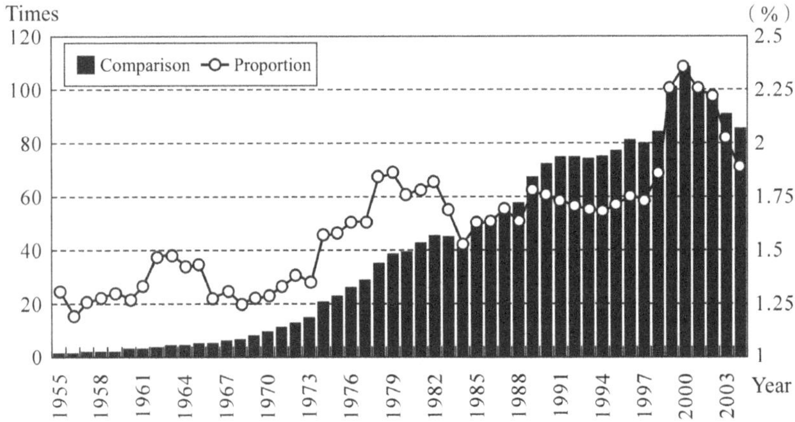

Fig. 2 1955—2004 年日本地方交付税总额及占 GDP 的比重 (Japan's total amount of local allocation tax and its proportion in the GDP from 1955 to 2004)

- 倍: Times
- 对比: Comparison
- 比例: Proportion
- 年份: Year
- 资料来源: 日本 GDP 数据来源于矢野恒太纪念会《从数字看日本的100年》(第5版), 2006 年。日本地方交付税交付额数据来源于 http://www.econ.keio.ac.jp/staff/tdoi/index-J.html: (*Source* Japan's GDP data from Yano Tsuneta Kinenkai (2006). *Japan Through Numerical Figures* (5th ed.). Japan's local allocation tax grant data from http://web.econ.keio.ac.jp/staff/tdoi/index-J.html)

allocation tax given to a certain area = the standard financial needs of the area—standard fiscal revenue of the area. Japan's total amount of local allocation tax and its proportion in the GDP from 1955 to 2004 is shown in Fig. 2.

Japan's fiscal transfer payments, which were mainly based on the local allocation tax, had a significant effect on narrowing the regional financial gap during the stage of high economic growth. In 1955 and 1965, Japan's regional financial gap improved by 68.2 and 62.1% respectively thanks to fiscal transfer payments; the variable coefficient before and after transfer payment decreased from 0.6624 to 0.2103 and from 0.5391 to 0.2044 respectively.[10]

5.3.2 Treasury Disbursement System

The treasury disbursement system is a form of transfer payment that combines the specified use and additional conditions, which is equivalent to China's special transfer payment. There are three categories of treasury disbursements. First, government-subsidized fund, a financial subsidy given by the central government to local governments for macroscopic regulation and balanced development; it is mainly used as rewards for specific local undertakings. Second, state liability fund, a subsidy given to local governments when they develop projects that affect the interests of the whole country in accordance to the central government's share of liabilities; it is mainly used to support important public undertakings with shared responsibilities between the central and local governments. Third, state delegation fund, a subsidy given to local governments when the central government delegates its responsibilities to local governments; it is mainly used to pay the expenses of central delegations. In 2012, the final accounts of treasury disbursements were 15.53 trillion yen, accounting for 14.3% of local revenue. The treasury disbursements are funded by the central government at the same level and are allocated to local governments on the condition of the designated use. The central government has the supervisory responsibility for the use of this fund. Specifically, it is supervised by the Ministry of Finance and audited by the Board of Audit.

5.3.3 Local Transfer Tax

The local transfer tax is a special type of tax levied by the central government to supplement the construction of local finance; all proceeds will be returned to local areas.

In 2012, the final accounts of local transfer tax were 2.27 trillion yen, accounting for 2.1% of local revenue. Among this, the special local corporation transfer tax accounted for the highest proportion with 73.6%, automobile weight tax with 12.4%, local petrol transfer tax with 12.4%, while the remainder was taken up by the local gas and oil, aviation fuel and special tonnage of ships transfer taxes. As the quota of local transfer tax is small, it does not have the effect of balancing local finance.

[10]Yamaguchi Nobiharu: *A Comparative Study of Economic Policies in China and Japan on Regional Economic Disparities*, Master's Thesis, Xiamen University, 2008.

5.4 *Formulating a Sound Comprehensive National Land Development Policy*

Japan's regional economic policies not only take into consideration the development issues of specific regions, but also enables economic development strategies to be formulated from a national perspective. These policies address important strategic issues such as the development of infrastructure in all regions and particularly in backward regions, construction of living and cultural facilities, as well as protection and conservation of the natural environment. In 1998, Japan formulated a new strategy titled *Grand Design for the 21st Century—Promotion of Regional Independence and Creation of Beautiful National Land*, with restoring the natural ecological environment, improving the urban living environment, and improving the economy and quality of national land as the strategic objectives. The strategy emphasized on balancing development in the country, enriching life, beautifying the environment, opening to the world, especially to Asia, building the main axis of land development, and striving to promote the development of economically underdeveloped regions or regions with a scattered industrial layout such as the Southwest, Northeast, Okinawa and Hokkaido. The strategy has laid the foundation for balanced development within Japan's territory. The proportion of Japan's central finance in the total fiscal revenue is 70%, most of which is allocated to local governments, and adjustments are made in a timely manner. In the period of encouraging the development of key areas, funds are mainly allocated to key development; in the period of resolving unbalanced regional development, funds are mainly allocated to backward areas. Japan also actively develops regional development financial enterprises which are seen as an important component of policy-based finance. To promote the development of industries in specific areas, objects for loans are limited to enterprises or corporate persons in specific regions. For example, Hokkaido-Tohoku Development Finance Public Corporation is Japan's first state financial institution to guide regional development. The institution promotes industrial development in Hokkaido and Tohoku with low-interest loans and stimulus policies. In 1999, Hokkaido-Tohoku Development Finance Public Corporation was merged into the Development Bank of Japan, with regional development of finance as one of its main functions. The Banks's main task is to promote the revitalization and development of designated areas by supplementing or rewarding private investment and the financial activities of general financial institutions. This includes investing in the research and development of factories and equipment related to industrial development, energy, environment and urban engineering with low-interest and long-term loans. Meanwhile, the state-controlled Japan Highway Public Corporation focuses on investing in and building cross-regional highway networks. As Japan's highways continue to extend to remote and backward areas, the economic ties between these areas and the metropolitan areas have strengthened, which has thus played a significant role in promoting the economic development of backward areas.

6 Experiences of Germany in Promoting Coordinated Regional Development

Germany is a highly developed industrialized country, yet imbalance between regional economic development still exists. In the long history of Germany, a number of regional economic centers have gradually formed, such as Berlin, Hamburg, Munich, Frankfurt and Stuttgart. This decentralized pattern has made the imbalance between regional development minor compared to other countries. After the end of World War Two (WWII), the imbalance between regional economic development became increasingly prominent. Due to the confrontation between the occupied areas of the Soviet Union and the occupied areas of the United States, Great Britain and France at the time, the population loss in the border areas was serious and economic development was hindered. In the subsequent economic recovery of the western region, a large number of rural residents swarmed into cities to obtain stable jobs and a higher quality of life. Since the end of the 1950s, with the development of oil, natural gas and nuclear energy, the Ruhr region and Saarland, which rely on traditional industries such as coal and iron and steel, have suffered tremendously. A large number of people became unemployed and social problems surged. By 1997, the unemployment rate of the Ruhr region reached 14%, much higher than the national average of 10.3% and the 8.8% average of western states. As a result, a national regional economic policy is necessary in both the old states and new federal states of Germany. The main problem of the old states is dealing with structural changes in the regional economy due to rapid environmental changes, such as pressure from regional adjustments and high labor costs, pressure on some old industries from emerging countries and increasing global competition, as well as pressure from lags in rural development and population issues (aging and population decline). The main problem of the new states is that reconstruction processes and tasks are still incomplete even after 20 years of transition from a planned economy to a market economy. In addition, many issues still exist in terms of promoting the modernization of enterprises, creating new competitive jobs and achieving self-sustaining growth, as well as responding to population challenges in rural areas. The German government attaches great importance to narrowing the gap in regional development and has formulated a series of regional economic development policies such as fiscal transfer payment and solidarity tax. In particular, the *Joint Federal Government/Länder Task for the Improvement of Regional Economic Structures* (GRW) was developed and enacted, which aims to enhance the internal driving force for development of economically backward regions, improve their economic structures, and promote their overall economic development.

6.1 Developing Legislations to Ensure the Implementation of Regional Economic Policies and Tasks

Germany's regional economic policies are based on the *Basic Law for the Federal Republic of Germany*. The *Basic Law* stipulates the adoption of the social market economy system as well as the establishment of a society with equal civil rights and development opportunities, social reconciliation and shared prosperity on the basis of ensuring the values of individual freedom and efficiency of the market economy. Therefore, creating equal living conditions in different regions and narrowing the gap in regional development is not only the greatest goal of Germany's regional economic policies but also the common task for all levels of government. In 1953, the German government approved the DM100 million stimulus package to specially assist the economic development of border areas and other backward regions. The principles of targeted support were established and the foundation of regional promotion policies was initially established. For more than 60 years, the regional economic policies of Germany have continuously improved, with both medium- and long-term plans, which have become an important part of the national economic and social development policies. Among the regional economic policies, the *Joint Federal Government/Länder Task for the Improvement of Regional Economic Structures* (GRW) issued by the German government in 1969 is of great significance and is the cornerstone of Germany's regional economic policies. The GRW mainly has four characteristics. First, it divided economically backward regions into different classes of Assisted Area and enterprises that invest in these areas may enjoy preferential policies. Second, it set up a Coordination Committee with the then Federal Minister of Economics as chairman and the Federal Minister of Finance and the various state ministers for economic affairs as its members to develop an economic promotion framework for backward regions that included providing support on a regional scope, fund allocation and regulation. The federal government was involved in the development of the macro-coordination framework and, if necessary, provided financial subsidies and concessional loans for specific projects. As the administrator, the state government was responsible for formulating regional development strategies, establishing the future image of the region and conducting project approvals by determining the key focus of assistance, purpose of funding and proportion of funding. Third, it fully mobilized the initiative of regional economic entities and enterprises and stipulated that for enterprises that apply for subsidies, their own investment must not be lower than 25% of the total investment, while the federal and relevant state government will each bear 50% of the public finance subsidy. Fourth, to ensure fair competition and avoid adverse impacts on other regions, the implementation of the GRW was subject to the supervision of the federal government and the European Union (EU). Resolutions of the Coordination Committee must be approved by the federal government representatives and a majority of the state governments; each state must report their fund usage to the Federal Ministry of Economics and their project approvals to the Federal Office of Economic Affairs and Export Control on a monthly basis; the Ministry of Economics shall regularly report its status to the Bundestag (federal parliament) and the Bundestag shall approve the total amount of subsidy for the next fiscal year based on the status. Since 1969, the German government has continuously revised, supplemented and improved the GRW in accordance with the trends of economic development and new changes in regional economic development. The GRW has thus become one of the most important regional economic development policies.

6.2 Supporting Regional Areas with Policies that Adapt to Local Conditions

To ensure the maximization of capital efficiency and to support the development of backward regions to the greatest extent, the German government has dynamically adjusted the regions that require assistance and rationally allocated subsidy grants according to the situation and needs of each place. In 2006, the German government issued the *2007–2013 Map of Assisted Areas* in accordance with relevant requirements of the EU. The *Map* was based on four indicators, namely the 2002–2005 average unemployment rate (50% weighting), the annual gross income of persons who participated in the statutory social insurance (40% weighting), the 2004–2011 employment forecast (5% weighting), and infrastructure (5% weighting). The *Map* divided the country into 270 employment areas, with areas that ranked the lowest (structurally the weakest and in terms of economic performance) marked as Area A, B or C. Area A included most of East Germany other than Berlin and parts of West Germany, with a population of 14.045 million and accounting for 17.1% of the country's total population. Selected enterprises that invest in this area shall receive the highest rates of financial subsidy (including the EU and subsidies from the federal and state governments of Germany). Among the selected enterprises, small and medium enterprises (SMEs) received 50% subsidy, medium enterprises with 40%, while other enterprises receive 30% subsidy. Area B included most of Berlin, some rural areas in West Germany, old industrial bases and the contiguous area between eastern Bavaria and Czech Republic, with a population of 9.075 million and accounting for 11% of the country's total population; SMEs, medium enterprises and other enterprises may receive up to 35, 25 and 15% subsidy for their investment respectively. Area C had a population of 9.96 million and accounted for 12% of the country's total population; SMEs and medium enterprises may receive up to 20 and 10% subsidy respectively, while other enterprises will receive no more than 200,000 euros in three years. The total population of the above three areas was 33.18 million, accounting for 40.1% of the country's total population.

6.3 *Establishing a Vertical and Horizontal Transfer Payment System*

Article 72 of the *Basic Law for the Federal Republic of Germany* stipulates that the development of each federal region and the living standards of their residents should be consistent; Article 1 of the *Federal Spatial Planning Act* stipulates that development should be carried out across all federal territory; the GRW stipulates that the federal and state governments shall each provide 50% funding to be given to backward regions as subsidies. One of the core elements of Germany's regional economic policy is to narrow the per capita income gap between states by implementing horizontal and vertical fiscal equalization policies. In spite of this, the government also allows for a 10% gap in per capita income across states. The German government takes into account the 4 indicators of income levels, unemployment rate, level of infrastructure and potential for future development to determine whether the living standards of each state is consistent. States that have exceeded the national average have to allocate some of their revenue to low-income states; states that are below the national average have the opportunity to receive financial subsidies. Horizontal fiscal equalization is mainly based on the distribution of corporate tax, tax transfers and special federal grants in order to promote the equalization of tax revenue across states. Through the distribution of corporate tax, states with low fiscal income have been able to reach 92% of the average financial resources of all states; through tax transfers, states with weak financial resources have been able to reach 95% of the national average of per capital fiscal revenue; the remaining gaps have been filled by the federal government in the form of special federal grants. The main purpose of vertical fiscal equalization is to promote the fiscal balance between states and towns and its procedures are similar to that of horizontal fiscal equalization. Granting backward regions with financial subsidies and using subsidies as the basis to improve the regional economic structure is yet another important aspect of Germany's regional economic policy.

Germany has made great achievements in its 40 years of implementing regional economic development policies, promoting regional economic development and balancing regional development. In 1991, the per capita GDP of eastern states was only 43% of the western states. By 2009, this figure had increased to 71%, while the per capita disposable income increased from 60 to 80%.

7 Experiences of Australia in Promoting Coordinated Regional Development[11]

Australia is a federal state and its administrative system mainly follows the Anglo-American model. Australia has three levels of government: federal, state or territory (6 states and 2 territories) and local (approximately 863). Each state is a political entity with a high degree of autonomy and is responsible for administering local governments. Australia is sparsely populated and rich in natural resources, but its population and resource

[11]Training Team of the National Development and Reform Commission of China: *The Intergovernmental Fiscal Relations of Australia and References to China*, 2013.

endowments vary greatly from region to region. The socio-economic structure varies between states, with some relying on mineral resources and some on tourism or agriculture and animal husbandry to develop their economies; there are also differences in financial resources. On the other hand, due to differences in population, economic structure and geography, the amount of funding into public services also differs greatly. Through the division and separation of administrative powers and financial powers, the federal government has formulated a standardized and transparent fiscal transfer payment system to balance regional development and provide its citizens with equal access to public services. Fiscal policy plays a central role in Australia's regional policy.

7.1 Adopting the Division of Powers

The Australian federal government is responsible for matters involving the whole country, which mainly includes national defense, international trade, foreign affairs, financial system and monetary policy, immigration, national taxation, interstate infrastructure, social insurance and macroeconomic management. In line with the division of federal powers, the expenditures of the federal government are also mainly for administration and defense at the federal level, as well as transfer payments to states and territories. Transfer payments account for about 60% of the total federal expenditures. The state and territory governments are responsible for all other matters outside the federal authorities. As the third level of government, the powers and revenue of local governments are determined by state legislations. In general, state and territory governments are the providers and administrative bodies of public services, including education, public order, healthcare, transportation and state infrastructure. In the 2012–2013 financial year, medical expenditures accounted for the highest proportion of state expenditures with 27%, followed by education which accounted for 24%; expenditures in public order and security, transportation and communication facilities, social welfare, housing security and community welfare facilities, and culture and leisure accounted for 12, 7, 7, 7 and 3% respectively; other expenditures accounted for 13%. Local governments, which are below state and territory governments, are only responsible for some specific affairs of local regionalization. These affairs mainly include: community services, social security, environmental services (waste and sewage treatment), urban planning and maintenance of infrastructure. In recent years, the administrative reform of local governments has attached more importance to providing humanized public services to the public and community. In the 2012–2013 financial year, culture and entertainment accounted for the largest proportion in the expenditures of local governments with 27%; expenditures in local roads and bridges, family and community services, commercial services, services for the elderly, transportation and street management, waste collection and disposal, and other infrastructure services accounted for 14, 12, 11, 10, 10, 9 and 8% respectively; operation expenditures of local governments only accounted for 5%.

On average, expenditures in education, health and social security and welfare account for more than 15% in all levels of the Australian government. Together, these three categories account for 60% of the total expenditures and are the main expenditure items of the government. Social security and welfare is Australia's largest expenditure item and falls under the responsibility of the federal government. Within the social security and welfare expenditure, the federal government accounts for 90% while the state and territory governments account for 10%. Healthcare is Australia's second largest expenditure item and it mainly falls under the responsibility of the state and territory governments, although the federal government also bears some direct expenditures and supports the state and territory governments through transfer payments. Authorities in healthcare are divided such that: the federal government bears the expenditures in medical insurance subsidies, pharmaceutical and medical services and epidemic prevention; the state and territory governments are responsible for providing public hospital services, mental health services, hospice care, community healthcare and supervision of public health. Among the total healthcare expenditures, the federal government accounts for 42%; the state and territory governments account for 43%; the transfer payments from the federal government to state and territory governments account for 15%. Education is Australia's third largest expenditure item. Like healthcare, education mainly falls under the responsibility of the state and territory governments, although the federal government also bears some direct expenditures and supports the state and territory governments through transfer payments. Authorities in education are divided such that: the federal government is mainly responsible for higher education and provides the states and territories with public education funding; the state and territory governments are responsible for primary and secondary education, vocational education, etc. Among the education expenditures, the federal government accounts for 22%, transfers payments from the federal government to state and territory governments accounts for 23%, and the state and territory governments account for 55%.

7.2 *Standardizing Transfer Payments*

Australia's transfer payment system was developed mainly due to the imbalance of financial resources and power between the federal government and the state and territory governments. Australia has successively taken several measures to resolve the issue of such imbalance, including: delegating some taxation powers to the state and territory governments, such as the delegation of payroll tax from 1971 to 1972; transferring some expenditure responsibilities to the federal government, such as the transferal of compulsory education in 1974; allocating some specific tax revenues to the state and territory governments, such as the GST revenue which has been allocated to states and territories in the form of transfer payments. In 2008, the Council of Australian Governments (COAG) passed the *Intergovernmental Agreement on Federal Financial Relations* (IGAFER), specifying objectives for transfer payments between the federal and state and territory governments. Specifically, the objective was to enable citizens in different regions to enjoy equal public service levels and achieve horizontal fiscal equalization through transfer payments. The IGAFER also specified the main types of transfer payments and their distribution. Currently, transfer payments from the federal government to state and territory governments are divided into general revenue assistance and specific purpose payments. In the 2012–2013 financial year, the total amount of transfer payments was AUD90.37 billion, of which general revenue assistance was AUD49.38 billion, accounting for 54.6%, while specific purpose payments was AUD40.99 billion, accounting for 45.4%. Given the development trend in recent years, since 2009, the proportion of general revenue assistance has generally increased.

At present, transfer payments of the Australian federal government have become the main method to resolve the imbalance in financial resources between the federal and state and territory governments. Revenue from transfer payments has become the main source of revenue for state and territory governments. Specifically, the proportion of transfer payments in the revenue of state and territory governments has increased from 37% in the 1901–1902 financial year to 46% in the 1946–1947 financial year, and has gradually remained stable at 40–60%, with 50% in the 2010–2011 financial year.

The Goods and Services Tax (GST) was a new tax introduced in 2000 to clarify the fiscal relationship between the federal and state and territory governments; it accounted for the greatest proportion in transfer payments. All GST revenue is directed to state and territory governments according to the principle of fairness, with the aim of balancing differences in financial resources. The principle of the Standing Committee on Appropriations and Administration in allocating GST is to allow each state or territory government to have a relative level of financial resources to provide residents with standardized services (such as education, healthcare, housing, legal services and transportation). A series of complicated models has also been designed with primary consideration of the financial resources and cost of services of the state and territory governments.

The financial resources of state and territory governments include its taxation revenue and the special transfer payment from the federal government. Due to the different resource endowments and economic development levels of each state and territory, there is a wide gap in terms of tax revenues. For example, Western Australia is rich in mineral resources and its mineral tax revenue has increased rapidly in recent years. As a result, the annual GST revenue of Western Australia has progressively increased while the GST transfer payment revenue has decreased year by year. In addition, the special transfer payments of the federal government are also an important factor that affects the financial resources of states and territories.

The cost of service mainly includes the direct cost of providing standardized services and the cost of building infrastructure. The direct cost of standardized services refers to the cost incurred by the state or territory government for providing basic education, medical care, housing, law, transportation and other services. Due to differences in population, age structure of the population and the proportion of indigenous population, the cost of providing public services vary greatly. For example, the cost of providing standardized services to residents in the Northern Territory is much higher than the other states and territories due to its large area, sparse population and a relatively high proportion of indigenous people. The cost of building infrastructure refers to the costs incurred by the government for investing in infrastructure required for the provision of standardized services.

Based on the above two factors, the Standing Committee on Appropriations and Administration calculates the allocation ratio of GST transfer payments to each state and territory according to the annual forecasted amount of GST revenue, combined with the gap between the per capital financial resources and cost of service of each state ad territory. In states and territories with strong per capita financial resources and low cost of service, the GST allocation ration is relatively low; in states and territories with weak per capita financial resources and high cost of service, the GST allocation ratio is correspondingly higher.

The division of powers among Australian governments has played an important role in promoting coordinated regional development. In particular, the division of powers ensures that the income capacity of governments in backward regions reaches a basic level, thus providing better and more balanced public services to residents across the country.

Appendices

Appendix Figure 1: Basic Information of National-Level Regional Planning and Policy Documents in Recent Years (From 2003 to 2013, Incomplete Statistics)

X. Song et al., *The Great Change in the Regional Economy of China under the New Normal*, The Great Transformation of China,
https://doi.org/10.1007/978-981-32-9475-2

1. Regional Policy Documents Categorized by Province (District, City) (67 in total)

Province (District, City)	Names of regional documents
Tianjin Municipality	1. Opinions of the State Council on Promoting the Development and Opening-up of Tianjin Binhai New Area
	2. Reply of the State Council on the Overall Plan for the Comprehensive Reform Test of Tianjin Binhai New Area
	3. Reply of the State Council on the Construction Plan of the Core Function Zone of Tianjin North International Shipping Center
Hebei Province	4. Reply of the State Council on the Development Planning for Hebei Coastal Areas
Shanxi Province	5. Reply of the State Council on the Overall Plan for Comprehensive Reform of Shanxi's National Resource-based Economic Transition
Inner Mongolia Autonomous Region	6. Several Opinions of the State Council on Further Promoting the Sound and Fast Development of Inner Mongolia's Economy and Society
	7. Letter from the General Office of the State Council Concerning the Approval of the Construction and Implementation Plan for the Key Development and Opening Experimental Zones of Dongxing in Guangxi Province, Ruili in Yunnan Province and Manzhouli in Inner Mongolia
Liaoning Province	8. Reply of the State Council on Liaoning Coastal Economic Belt Development Plan
	9. Reply of the State Council on the Overall Plan for the Comprehensive Reform of New-type Industrialization in Shenyang Economic Zone
	10. Reply of the State Council on Approval of the Establishment of Dalian Jinpu New Area
Jilin Province	11. Reply of the State Council on the Outline of China's Tumen River Regional Cooperation and Development Plan
	12. Several Opinions of the General Office of the State Council on Supporting the Construction of the Tumen River (Hun Chun) Regional International Cooperation Demonstration Zone in China

Province (District, City)	Names of regional documents
Heilongjiang Province	13. Reply of the State Council on the Overall Plan for the Comprehensive Reform of Modern Agriculture in the Two Plains of Heilongjiang Province
	14. Reply of the State Council on the Economic Transition and Ecological Protection Plan for the Forest Areas of the Greater and Lesser Khingan Mountains
	15. Reply of the State Council on the Planning for the Development and Opening-up along the Heilongjiang Border and the Northeast Inner Mongolia Border
Shanghai Municipality	16. Opinions of the State Council on the National Comprehensive Reform Pilot Project in Pudong New Area of Shanghai (Decision of the Executive Meeting of the State Council)
	17. Opinions of the State Council on Promoting Shanghai to Accelerate the Development of Modern Service Industry and Advanced Manufacturing Industry and Construct International Financial Center and International Shipping Center
Jiangsu Province	18. Reply of the State Council on Jiangsu Coastal Area Development Planning
	19. Reply of the State Council on the Overall Plan for the Construction of the National East-West Regional Cooperation Demonstration Zones
Zhejiang Province	20. Reply of the State Council on the Planning for Zhejiang Marine Economic Development Demonstration Zone
	21. Reply of the State Council on the Overall Plan for the Pilot Project of Comprehensive International Trade Reform in Yiwu City, Zhejiang Province
	22. Reply of the State Council on Approval of the Establishment of Zhoushan Islands New Area in Zhejiang Province
	23. Reply of the State Council on Approval of the Establishment of China (Hangzhou) Cross-border E-Commerce Comprehensive Pilot Area
Anhui Province	24. Reply of the State Council on the Planning for Demonstration Zones for Undertaking Industrial Transfer in Wanjiang City Belt

(continued)

Province (District, City)	Names of regional documents
Fujian Province	25. Several Opinions of the State Council on Supporting Fujian Province to Speed up the Construction of the Western Taiwan Straits Economic Zone
	26. Reply of the State Council on the Development Planning for the Western Taiwan Straits Economic Zone
	27. Reply of the State Council on the Overall Development Plan of Pingtan Comprehensive Experimental Zone
	28. Reply of the State Council on the Overall Plan for the Comprehensive Reform of Deepening Cross-Strait Exchange and Cooperation in Xiamen
	29. Several Opinions of the State Council on Supporting Fujian Province to Deeply Implement the Strategy of Eco-province and Speed up the Construction of the Pioneer Demonstration Zone of Eco-civilization
Jiangxi Province	30. Reply of the State Council on the Planning for Poyang Lake Eco-economic Zone
	31. Several Opinions of the State Council on Supporting the Revitalization and Development of Former Central Soviet Areas Including Southern Jiangxi Province
Shandong Province	32. Reply of the State Council on the Development Planning for the Efficient Ecological Economic Zone of the Yellow River Delta
	33. Reply of the State Council on the Development Planning for Shandong Peninsula Blue Economic Zone
	34. Reply of the State Council on Approval of the Establishment of Qingdao West Coast New Area
Henan Province	35. Guiding Opinions of the State Council on Supporting Henan to Accelerate the Construction of Central Plains Economic Zone
Hubei Province	36. Reply of the State Council on the Overall Plan for the Comprehensive Reform of Resource-Conserving and Environment-Friendly Society Construction in Wuhan Metropolitan Area
Hunan Province	37. Reply of the State Council on the Overall Plan for the Comprehensive Reform of Resource-Conserving and Environment-Friendly Society Construction in Changsha-Zhuzhou-Xiangtan Metropolitan Region

Province (District, City)	Names of regional documents
Guangdong Province	38. Reply of the State Council on the Outline of the Pearl River Delta Regional Reform and Development Plan (2008–2020)
	39. Reply of the State Council on the Overall Plan of Comprehensive Reform in Shenzhen
	40. Reply of the State Council on the Overall Development Planning for Hengqin
	41. Reply of the State Council on the Overall Development Planning for Qianhai Shenzhen-Hong Kong Modern Service Industry Cooperation Zone
	42. Reply of the State Council on the Development Planning for Guangdong Marine Economic Comprehensive Pilot Zone
	43. Reply of the State Council on the Development Planning for Guangzhou Nansha New Area
Guangxi Zhuang Autonomous Region	44. Development Planning for Guangxi Beibu Gulf Economic Zone
	45. Several Opinions of the State Council on Further Promoting the Economic and Social Development of Guangxi
	46. Letter from the General Office of the State Council Concerning the Approval of the Construction and Implementation Plan for the Key Development and Opening Experimental Zones of Dongxing in Guangxi Province, Ruili in Yunnan Province and Manzhouli in Inner Mongolia
	47. Outline of Guilin International Tourism Resort Construction and Development Planning
Hainan Province	48. Several Opinions of the State Council on Promoting the Construction and Development of the Hainan International Tourism Island
Chongqing Municipality	49. Several Opinions of the State Council on Promoting the Reform and Development of Urban-Rural Coordination in Chongqing
	50. Reply of the State Council on Approval of the Establishment of Chongqing Liangjiang New Area
Sichuan Province	51. Reply of the State Council on the Overall Plan for the Comprehensive Reform of Urban-Rural Coordination in Chengdu
	52. Reply of the State Council on Approval of the Establishment of Sichuan Tianfu New Area
Guizhou Province	53. Several Opinions of the State Council on Further Promoting the Sound and Fast Development of Guizhou's Economy and Society
	54. Reply of the State Council on Approval of the Establishment of Guizhou Gui'an New Area

(continued)

Province (District, City)	Names of regional documents
Yunnan Province	55. Opinions of the State Council on Supporting Yunnan Province to Speed up the Construction of an Important Bridgehead Opening to the Southwest
	56. Letter from the General Office of the State Council Concerning the Approval of the Construction and Implementation Plan for the Key Development and Opening Experimental Zones of Dongxing in Guangxi Province, Ruili in Yunnan Province and Manzhouli in Inner Mongolia
	57. Reply of the State Council on the Overall Plan for Accelerating the Construction of Important Bridgeheads in Yunnan Province to Open to the Southwest
	58. Reply of the State Council on Regional Development and Poverty Alleviation Planning in the Western Yunnan Border Region (2011–2020)
Shaanxi Province	59. Reply of the State Council on Approval of the Establishment Shaanxi Xixian New Area
	60. Reply of the State Council on the Revitalization Plan of the Old Revolutionary Areas in Shaanxi, Gansu and Ningxia
Gansu Province	61. Several Opinions of the General Office of the State Council on Further Supporting the Economic and Social Development of Gansu Province
	62. Reply of the State Council on Approval of the Establishment of Lanzhou New Area
Qinghai Province	63. Overall Plans for the National Comprehensive Experimental Zone for Ecological Conservation at Sanjiangyuan, Qinghai
Ningxia Hui Autonomous Region	64. Several Opinions of the State Council on Further Promoting the Economic and Social Development of Ningxia Hui Autonomous Region
	65. Reply of the State Council on the Planning for Ningxia Inland Open Economic Pilot Zone
Xinjiang Uygur Autonomous Region	66. Several Opinions of the State Council on Supporting the Construction of Kashgar and Horgos Economic Development Zones
	67. Reply of the State Council on the Development Planning for the Economic Belt on the North Slope of Tianshan Mountains in Xinjiang

2. Regional Policy Documents across Provinces (District, City) (33 in total)

Regions	Names of regional documents
Shaanxi Province and Gansu Province	1. Reply of the State Council on the Development Planning for Guanzhong-Tianshui Economic Zone
Hubei Province and Hunan Province	2. Reply of the State Council on the Planning for Dongting Lake Eco-economic Zone
Shanxi Province, Shaanxi Province, and Henan Province	3. Reply of the State Council on the Planning for Regional Cooperation in the Golden Triangle Area of the Yellow River in Shanxi, Shaanxi and Henan
Hubei Province, Hunan Province, Chongqing Municipality, and Guizhou Province	4. Reply of the State Council on the Regional Development and Poverty Alleviation Planning for Wulingshan Area (2011–2020)
Sichuan Province, Guizhou Province, and Yunnan Province	5. Reply of the State Council on Regional Development and Poverty Alleviation Planning in Wumengshan Area (2011–2020)
Henan Province, Hubei Province, Chongqing Municipality, Sichuan Province, Shaanxi Province, and Gansu Province	6. Reply of the State Council on the Regional Development and Poverty Alleviation Planning for Qinba Mountains (2011–2020)
Henan Province, Hubei Province, and Shaanxi Province	7. Reply of the State Council on Economic and Social Development Planning for Danjiangkou Reservoir Area and Its Upper Reaches
Henan Province, Hubei Province, Shanxi Province, Anhui Province, and Shandong Province	8. Reply of the State Council on the Central Plains Economic Zone Planning (2012–2020)
Guangxi Zhuang Autonomous Region, Guizhou Province, and Yunnan Province	9. Reply of the State Council on Regional Development and Poverty Alleviation Planning for Rocky Desertification Areas in Yunnan, Guangxi and Guizhou (2011–2020)
Shaanxi Province, Gansu Province, Qinghai Province, and Ningxia Hui Autonomous Region	10. Reply of the State Council on the Regional Development and Poverty Alleviation Planning for Liupanshan Area (2011–2020)
Inner Mongolia Autonomous Region, Jilin Province and Heilongjiang Province	11. Reply of the State Council on the Regional Development and Poverty Alleviation Plan for the Southern Piedmont of the Greater Khingan Mountains (2011–2020)

(continued)

Regions	Names of regional documents
Hubei Province, Shanxi Province, and Inner Mongolia Autonomous Region	12. Reply of the State Council on Regional Development and Poverty Alleviation Planning for Yanshan-Taihang Mountain Area (2011–2020)
Sichuan Province and Chongqing Municipality	13. Reply of the State Council on Regional Planning for Chengdu-Chongqing Economic Zone
Inner Mongolia Autonomous Region, Ningxia Hui Autonomous Region, and Shaanxi Province	14. Reply of the State Council on the Development Planning for Hohhot-Baotou-Yinchuan-Yulin Economic Zone
Guangdong Province and Guangxi Province	15. Reply of the State Council on the Development Planning for the Pearl River-Xijiang Economic Belt
Shanghai Municipality, Jiangsu Province, and Zhejiang Province	16. Guiding Opinions of the State Council on Further Promoting Reform, Opening up and Socio-economic Development of the Yangtze River Delta 17. Reply of the State Council on Regional Planning for the Yangtze River Delta
Western region	18. Several Opinions of the Central Committee of the Communist Party of China and the State Council on Further Implementing the Western Development Strategy 19. Several Opinions of the State Council on Further Promoting the Development of the Western Region 20. Reply of The State Council on the Eleventh Five-Year Plan for Promoting the Development of the Western Region 21. Opinions of the General Office of the State Council on Responding to the International Financial Crisis and Maintaining a Stable and Rapid Economic Development in the Western Region 22. Reply of The State Council on the Twelfth Five-Year Plan for Promoting the Development of the Western Region

Regions	Names of regional documents
Northeastern region	23. Several Opinions of the Central Committee of the Communist Party of China and the State Council on the Implementation of Revitalization Strategy of the Old Industrial Bases Including Northeast China
	24. Opinions of the General Office of the State Council on Implementing the Promotion of Further Opening-up of the Old Industrial Bases in Northeast China
	25. Reply of the State Council on the Revitalization of Northeast China
	26. Several Opinions of the State Council on Further Implementing the Strategy of Revitalizing the Old Industrial Bases Including Northeast China
	27. Reply of the State Council on the 12th Five-Year Plan for the Revitalization of Northeast China
	28. Reply of the State Council on the Outline of Planning (2012–2020) for Northeast China's Regional Opening to Northeast Asia
	29. Opinions of the State Council on Major Policy Measures for Supporting the Revival of Northeast China in the Near Future
Central region	30. Several Opinions of the Central Committee of the Communist Party of China and the State Council on Promoting the Rise of the Central Region
	31. Reply of the State Council on the Planning for Promoting the Rise of the Central Region
	32. Several Opinions of the Central Committee of the Communist Party of China and State Council of the CPC on Promoting the Strategic Rise of the Central Region
Central and Western regions	33. Guiding Opinions of the State Council on the Central and Western Regions' Undertaking of Industrial Transfer

Source The data above are compiled from websites of the State Council of the People's Republic of China and the National Development and Reform Commission

Appendix Figure 2: Data on Major Economic Indicators of China's Provinces and Regions in 2014

Region	Gross regional product		Fixed-asset investment (100 million yuan)	Total retail sales of consumer goods (100 million yuan)	Growth rate of value-added of industry above designated size (%)	Per capita disposable income of urban residents (Yuan)	Per capita net income of rural residents (Yuan)
	Total current price (100 million yuan)	Growth rate (%)					
Nationwide	636463	7.4	502005	262394	8.3	28844	9892
Eastern region							
Beijing Municipality	21331	7.3	6873	9098	6.2	43910	20226
Tianjin Municipality	15722	10.0	10490	4739	10.1	31506	17014
Hebei Province	29421	6.5	26147	11690	5.1	24141	10186
Shanghai Province	23561	7.0	6013	8719	4.5	47710	21192
Jiangsu Province	65088	8.7	41553	23209	9.9	34346	14958
Zhejiang Province	40154	7.6	23555	16905	6.9	40393	19373
Fujian Province	24056	9.9	17912	9026	11.9	30722	12650
Shandong Province	59427	8.7	41599	24492	9.6	29222	11882
Guangdong Province	67792	7.8	25843	28471	8.4	32148	12246
Hainan Province	3501	8.5	3039	1091	12.0	24487	9913
Central region							
Shanxi Province	12759	4.9	11977	5550	3.0	24069	
Anhui Province	20849	9.2	21069	7321	11.2	24839	
Jiangxi Province	15709	9.7	14677	5129	11.8	24309	
Henan Province	34939	8.9	30012	13836	11.2	24391	
Hubei Province	27367	9.7	22492	11806	10.8	24852	
Hunan Province	27048	9.5	20575	10082	9.6	26570	
Western region							
Inner Mongolia Autonomous Region	17770	7.8	17431	5620	10.0	28350	9976
Guangxi Zhuang Autonomous Region	15673	8.5	13288	5717	10.7	24669	8683
Chongqing Municipality	14265	10.9	12137	5096	12.6	25133	9470

Region	Gross regional product		Fixed-asset investment (100 million yuan)	Total retail sales of consumer goods (100 million yuan)	Growth rate of value-added of industry above designated size (%)	Per capita disposable income of urban residents (Yuan)	Per capita net income of rural residents (Yuan)
	Total current price (100 million yuan)	Growth rate (%)					
Sichuan Province	28537	8.5	22662	11666	9.6	24381	8803
Guizhou Province	9251	10.8	8778	2580	11.3	22548	6671
Yunnan Province	12815	8.1	11074	4547	7.3	24299	7456
Tibet Autonomous Region	921	10.8	1069	324	6.0	22026	7471
Shaanxi Province	17690	9.7	16840	5573	11.3	24366	7932
Gansu Province	6835	8.9	7760	2410	8.4	20804	5736
Qinghai Province	2301	9.2	2789	615	9.1	22307	7283
Ningxia Hui Autonomous Region	2752	8.0	3094	673	8.3	23285	8410
Xinjiang Uyghur Autonomous Region	9264	10.0	9058	2280	10.0	22160	8296
Northeastern region							
Liaoning Province	28627	5.8	24427	11793	4.8	29082	11191
Heilongjiang Province	15039	5.6	9587	6964	2.9	22609	10453
Jilin Province	13804	6.5	11255	6081	6.6	23218	10780

Source The data above are compiled from China Economic Information Network Statistical Database, work reports and statistical bulletins of relevant provincial and municipal governments, and so on

Postscript

Under the auspices of Song Xiaowu, the title and conceptions, text structures and writing of this book were discussed and determined together with Wu Shiguo and Xu Xin. Xu Xin took on the data collection and collation work of most chapters. Wu Shiguo collected and compiled some information on the coordinated development of some foreign regions. Song Xiaotong wrote the introduction to this book and was responsible for the revision and finalization of the book.

All three authors have experience in administrative work in regional development coordination. This book can be considered as the refinement and sublimation of the authors' years of engagement in regional development coordination and deep thinking about its relevant problems today. On the basis of reviewing and summarizing the transformation of regional development strategies since the founding of New China, the authors put forward a regional development strategy oriented to the New Normal of the economy: with equalization of basic public services between regions as the main goal and the construction of a unified socialist market economy as basic norms, reasonably defining the administrative power and financial power between the central and local governments, and deepening reforms of relevant taxation systems that hinder coordinated regional development. On the basis of giving full play to the respective advantages of the "four major regions", we should combine

X. Song et al., *The Great Change in the Regional Economy of China under the New Normal*, The Great Transformation of China, https://doi.org/10.1007/978-981-32-9475-2

regions with axial belts, domestic regions with international regions and position the Belt and Road Initiative, the Yangtze River Economic Belt and the coordinated development of Beijing-Tianjin-Hebei as the three new support belts for coordinated regional development, which will greatly enrich China's regional development strategies and form a new pattern of coordinated regional development in China.

We would be more than satisfied if this book can provide certain references for the theoretical researchers who study regional economies, and offer some guidance for administrative personnel engaged in coordinated regional development. If you have any suggestions or criticism on this book, we would like to express our sincere gratitude!

September 15, 2015 Authors

References

Chen Dongsheng. *Regional Economics*. Zhengzhou: Henan People's Publishing House, 1993.

Chen Dongsheng. *Theory and Practice of Economic Layout*. Shenyang: Liaoning University Press, 1989.

Chen Fengying. Design of the G20 Mechanism Architecture and China's Strategic Countermeasure. *Economic Information Daily*, 2010 (6).

Chen Xiushan et al. *Regional Coordinated Development: Objectives, Paths, Evaluation*. Beijing: The Commercial Press, 2013.

Chen Xiushan. *Evaluation on the Regional Effect of West-to-East Power Transmission Project*. Beijing: China Electric Power Press.

Chen Xuanqing & Zhang Keyun. *Strategic Issues and Policy Research on Regional Development Coordination*. Beijing: China Market Press, 2007.

Cheng Biding, Chen Dongsheng, & Xiao Jincheng. *Regional Scientific Development Theories*. Beijing: Economic Science Press, 2009.

China Statistical Yearbook, China Statistics Press, 2003–2012.

Dai Bing. The Economic Development of the Underdeveloped Regions of EEC and Its Related Policies. *Journal of Southwest University for Nationalities* (Philosophy and Social Sciences), 2000 (6).

Development Research Center of the State Council of the People's Republic of China. *Strategic Priorities for Changing the Mode of Economic Development*. Beijing: China Development Press, 2010.

Division of Regional Economy, National Development and Reform Commission of the People's Republic of China. *Compilation of Documents, Planning and*

X. Song et al., *The Great Change in the Regional Economy of China under the New Normal*, The Great Transformation of China, https://doi.org/10.1007/978-981-32-9475-2

Programs for Promoting Regional Harmonious Development (2003–2009). 2010.

Dong Zhikai & Wu Jiang. *The Cornerstone of New China's Industries: Research on "156" Construction Projects*. Guangzhou: Guangdong Economic Publishing House, 2004.

Du Ying. China Regional Economic Development Yearbook (2013). Beijing: China Finance and Economics Press, 2013.

Feigin. *Capitalist and Socialist Production Distribution*. Beijing: SDX Joint Publishing, 1957.

Guo Tengyun, Lu Dadao, & Gan Guohui. China's Regional Development Policy and Its Sound Effects on the Economic Development of Coastal Zones and Central & Western Areas over the Past Two Decades. *Geographical Research*, 2002, 21 (4).

Information Office of the State Council of the People's Republic of China. *White Paper on New Progress in Poverty Alleviation and Development in Rural China*. 2011.

Information Office of the State Council of the People's Republic of China. *White Paper on China's Ethnic Policy and the Common Prosperity and Development of All Ethnic Groups*, 2009.

Jiang Xiaoping. Common Trends and Regional Differences in China's Basic Public Service System—Based on the Comparison of National and Local Basic Public Service Plans in the Twelfth Five-Year Plan. *Journal of Jishou University* (Social Science Edition), 2014 (2).

Li Ming. *EU Regional Policy and Its Enlightenment to the Rise of Central China*. Wuhan: Wuhan University Press, 2010.

Li Shantong. *Policy Research on Several Key Issues of China's Economic and Social Development during the Twelfth Five-Year Plan Period*. Beijing: Science Press, 2011.

Lin Zhaomu. Several Major Issues in Implementing the 12th Five-Year Plan. *China Securities News*, 2011 (6).

Liu Junlin. On Mao Zedong's Exploration of China's Industrialization Road. *Journal of the Graduates of Sun Yat-Sen University* (Social Sciences), 2000 (3).

Lu Dadao & Yao Shimou. *China Regional Development Report in 2006—Urbanization Process and Spatial Expansion*. Beijing: The Commercial Press, 2007.

Lu Dadao. *Theory and Practice of Regional Development in China*. Beijing: Science Press, 2003.

Lu Jiangyong. Regional Agglomeration of China's Manufacturing Industry and International Comparison. *Economic Research*, 2006 (3).

Mao Zedong. *Selected Works of Mao Zedong (Volume V)*. Beijing: People's Publishing House, 1977.

National Development and Reform Commission of the People's Republic of China. *Compilation of National Special Planning for the Twelfth Five-Year Plan*. Beijing: People's Publishing House, 2013.

National Development and Reform Commission of the People's Republic of China. *Main Statistical Indicators for Revitalization of Northeast China*. 2013.

Office of the National Natural Resources and Geospatial Basic Information Base Project of the People's Republic of China. *China Regional Planning and Sustainable Development Analysis Report*. 2013.

Outline of the Eleventh Five-Year Plan for the National Economic and Social Development of the People's Republic of China, 2006.

Outline of the Twelfth Five-Year Plan for the National Economic and Social Development of the People's Republic of China, 2011.

Party Literature Research Center of the CPC Central Committee. *Selected Works of the 30th Anniversary of Reform and Opening up* (I). Beijing: Central Party Literature Press, 2008.

Party Literature Research Center of the CPC Central Committee. *Selected Works Since the 18th National Congress(I)(II)*. Beijing: Central Party Literature Press.

Publicity Department of the Central Committee of the Communist Party of China. Reading of General Secretary Xi Jinping's Series of Important Speeches. Beijing: People's Publishing House, 2013.

Qin Wanjun. Preliminary Thoughts on the Deviation between Regional Taxation and Tax Sources. *Tax Research*, 2007 (1).

Research Center of China's Special Economic Zone of Shenzhen University. *Literature on China's Special Economic Zones*. Beijing: Social Sciences Academic Press, 2010.

Research Group of Hubei State Taxation Bureau. Study on the Deviation between Taxation and Tax Source of the Three Gorges Hydropower Station. *Tax Research*, 2007 (5).

Research Group of Shaanxi State Taxation Bureau. Probing into the Deviation between Taxation and Source of Taxation. *Tax Research*, 2007 (5).

Research Group of the Development Research Center of the State Council of the People's Republic of China. *Research on Regional Scientific Development in China*. Beijing: China Development Press, 2007.

Research Group on Taxation and Tax Sources. *Regional Tax Transfer Survey*. Beijing: China Taxation Publishing House, 2008.

Song Xiaowu. Vigorously Promoting the Sustainable Development of Resource-based Cities in China. *Northern Economy*, 2006 (18).

The First Five-Year Plan for the National Economic and Social Development of the People's Republic of China, 1953.

The Seventh Five-Year Plan for the National Economic and Social Development of the People's Republic of China, 1986.

The Ninth Five-Year Plan for the National Economic and Social Development of the People's Republic of China, 1996.

Wang Feng. On the Evolution of EU Regional Policy and Its Enlightenment to China. Master's Thesis of Shandong University, 2009.

Wang Haibo. *History of Industrial Economy of New China* (October 1949–1957). Beijing: Economic Management Press, 1994.

Wang Luolin & Wei Houkai. *Strategies and Countermeasures of Economic Revitalization in Northeast China.* Beijing: Social Sciences Academic Press, 2005.

Wei Houkai. *A New Pattern of Regional Economic Development.* Kunming: Yunnan People's Publishing House, 1995.

Wei Houkai. Changes of China's Regional Economy in the 30 Years of Reform and Opening-up. *Economic Dynamics*, 2008 (5).

Wei Houkai. China's Regional Economic Development Trend and Policy Orientation. *China Development Observation*, 2010 (5).

Wei Houkai. *China's Regional Policies—Evaluation and Prospect.* Beijing: Economy & Management Publishing House, 2011.

World Bank, Joint Research Group of Development Research Center of the State Council. *China in 2030: Building a Modern, Harmonious and Creative Society.* Beijing: China Finance and Economic Press, 2013.

Writing Group of Spiritual Learning Guidance Reading Books for the Central Conference on Ethnic Work. The Spiritual Learning Guidance Book of the Central Ethnic Work Conference. Beijing: The Ethnic Publishing House, 2005.

Wu Runsheng, et al. *Study on the Connotation and Condition Change of China's Important Strategic Opportunity Period.* Beijing: China Yan Shi Press, 2014.

Wu Xiaojun & Zhao Haidong. Industrial Transfer and Economic Development in Underdeveloped Areas. *Contemporary Finance & Economics*, 2004 (6).

Xie Fujian, Editor-in-Chief. Policy Research and Decision-Making Consultation: *Selection of Research Achievements from the Research Department of the State Council.* Beijing: China Yan Shi Press, 2009.

Xu Shanda. *National Taxation.* Beijing: China Taxation Publishing House, 2008.

Xu Xin. A Study on the Differences of Economic Growth Among the Four Major Regions (2000–2010). *China Economic and Trade Guide*, 2012 (33).

Yamaguchi Nobiharu. A Comparative Study of Economic Policies between China and Japan on Regional Economic Disparities. Master's Thesis of Xiamen University, 2008.

Zhang Jiliang. *Research on China's Regional Competitiveness.* Nanjing: Southeast University Press, 2008.

Zhang Junkuo, Hou Yongzhi. *China's Regional Policies and Development*. Beijing: China Development Press, 2010.

Zhang Keyun. *Regional Economic Policies*. Beijing: The Commercial Press, 2005.

Zhang Ping. *Guidance Reading of the Twelfth Five-Year Plan Outline for National Economic and Social Development of the People's Republic of China*. Beijing: People's Publishing House, 2011.

Zhang Qichun. Fiscal Balance Mechanism of Equalization of Regional Basic Public Services—From the Perspective of Canadian Experience. *Journal of Central China Normal University* (Humanities and Social Sciences), 2011 (6).

Zhang Zhiyong. Research on Tax Management of Large Enterprises' Collection and Merger. *Tax Research*, 2007 (5).

Zheng Zhiguo. The Historical Evolution and Institutional Changes of China's Regional Economic Policies. Master's Thesis of Chongqing Technology and Business University, 2006.

The manufacturer's authorised representative in the EU is Springer
Nature Customer Service Centre GmbH, Europaplatz 3, 69115 Heidelberg,
Germany. If you have any concerns regarding our products, please
contact ProductSafety@springernature.com

Printed and bound by CPI Group (UK) Ltd, Croydon, CR0 4YY
25/09/2026
02222897-0010